A New Generation Reckons with Motherhood

JUDITH D. SCHWARTZ

THE MOTHER PUZZLE

Simon & Schuster

New York London

Toronto Sydney

Tokyo Singapore

SIMON & SCHUSTER
Simon & Schuster Building
Rockefeller Center
1230 Avenue of the Americas
New York, New York 10020

Designed by Pei Loi Koay
Manufactured in the United States of America

1 3 5 7 9 10 8 6 4 2

Library of Congress Cataloging-in-Publication Data
Schwartz, Judith D.
The mother puzzle : a new generation reckons with motherhood /
Judith D. Schwartz.
p. cm.
Includes bibliographical references (p. 276) and index.
1. Motherhood—United States. I. Title.
HQ759.S2918 1993
306.874'3—dc20 92-37531 CIP

ISBN: 0-671-76768-2

To my parents,

Pauline and Alvin

ACKNOWLEDGMENTS

Because writing a book is more than anything else a solitary venture, the friends and colleagues who provide an oasis of companionship and support are greatly appreciated. I owe thanks to many people but want to mention Adele Scheele, Lisa Gossels, Susan Hertzberg, Judy Langer, Barb Takahashi, Tara Framer, Vicki Ritterband, Susan Williams, and Eleanor Davis, all of whom gave time and more. Then there are the seventy or so women and men I interviewed (whose names and identifying characteristics I've changed to protect privacy), whose willingness to share brought the subject to life.

Thanks are due to the Dorland Mountain Arts Colony and the Blue Mountain Center for providing space to think. The Hunter Library staff helped keep me in books at crucial times, as did the libraries at the University of California at San Diego and Wesleyan University. Daphne Anshel gave a careful, astute reading of the final draft when I could no longer see it with clear eyes. Elizabeth Grossman deserves note as an agent who encourages writers to explore, and Sheila Curry has been an especially thoughtful and attentive editor. Finally, I want to thank three special people: my uncle, James Weil, who taught me to love language; my brother, Frederic, who taught me to think; and, most of all, Tony Eprile, who has given me the courage to question.

CONTENTS

Introduction

THE MOTHER IN THE MIRROR

Summer 1990

I am twenty-nine years old. As such, I am pretty well entrenched in adulthood, long past the point of no return. I have been able to support myself for the last seven years, vote for the last twelve, and bear children for nearly sixteen. But in this society, I am also considered "young," which means that no one criticizes my self-contained, possibly selfish, life because it's understood that I'm still creating it. Had I lived in a different era, I might have had four or five children by now. Starting at an age when I was still in college, a time when having babies was the furthest thing from my mind, I would have continuously been getting pregnant, being pregnant, and recovering from pregnancy. I would have been ruled by my fertility, by the whims and rhythms of my reproductive tract. Now, this fertility—which, as one who's never been pregnant, remains a potentiality only vaguely connected to my life—is completely ruled by me.

From the time I first discussed sleeping with my college boyfriend (and, like the mature, responsible adults we played at being, we did discuss it), I've always accepted birth control as serious business. The consequence of not using contraception loomed so ominously that I couldn't even allow myself to acknowledge it. I thought not of a life taking form but of some grave "or else," a horrendous "accident," or a grim "you'll be sorry." For years, I waged a messy war against my own pregnancy potential: I used a diaphragm. It never felt quite right. It burdened the act of making love with too many moving parts. I often felt there were three of us in bed: me, my boyfriend, and the diaphragm. As a result of an improper fitting, I later realized, I got so many bladder infections that I used to plan my week around trips to the doctor, my day around bathroom stops. And I knew that even with the most dexterous technique, it was all too easy to slip up.

Now each morning I swallow a tasteless pill, a fraction of the size of an aspirin. The pills assure me I won't get pregnant, even as the hormones contained in them are tricking my body into thinking that I *am* pregnant. They relieve me of the state of potential motherhood, a state that in other times would have defined my role as a woman. But this seemingly perpetual prescription doesn't keep me aware of the fact I could get pregnant; it separates me from it.

Having recently gotten married, my husband and I sometimes talk about having children, circumspectly, speaking around the issue rather than to it. That's fine. I can deal with the question this way—in bits and pieces, staying on the periphery of it. I can talk about our respective careers, when would be a good time, the finances involved—the practicalities of the matter—but it's the actual physical prospect that overwhelms me. Childbirth is still an abstraction. How do I know my body could pull it off? I've spent the last dozen years telling it not to have babies. If I suddenly decide to change my mind, how do I know my body is going to listen to me?

I realize I've been living in a biological vacuum. Over the better part of three decades, I've gotten fairly used to this body of mine: I've exercised it, dieted it, exhausted it, rested it—exerted control over it in numerous ways. But to grant my body free rein, to let it expand and bring life into the world, that's too much to comprehend. I'm only five-foot-one and weigh ninety-eight pounds. How do I know there will be enough room—enough of me—to spare?

As a woman, I feel I'm expected to have a natural affinity for infants. I imagine I'm supposed to have something appropriately maternal to say to a baby, or some comment of solidarity to offer his mother. But rather than affirm my membership in the grand female club, the sight of a baby leaves me humbled. Infants are alien to me. I'm clueless as to what to do with them. When given a baby to hold, I don't quite know where to place my hands, what angle to set him at. My dealings with babies are tentative, shy. I don't know them, what they're about. When would I have had the chance to? I've been putting all my energy into emotional and financial survival among adults.

When I had a part-time job in college, the six-year-old daughter of a coworker was running around the office one day. She and I exchanged smiles as she emerged from her hiding place, under the boss's desk.

"Who are you?" she asked me, somewhat rhetorically. "Do you have any children?" Her question caught me short. At first I honestly thought it was a joke. Then I realized that I had identified with this little girl being dragged around all day by her mother, rather than with my adult colleague. It occurred to me that I was unquestionably closer in appearance, if not in spirit, to the mother than the child, and that at my age, twenty, I could well have a child myself. The little girl had picked up a possibility I had remained blind to. What an astute observation, I thought.

Even now, several reproductive years later, the notion of motherhood as something that could or would happen to me still seems remote. Some of my friends, mostly those a few years older, are beginning to have children. I've felt like the proverbial little sister with them, an asker of stupid questions that I should either know the answers to myself or have the sense not to bug them about. The smells and textures of baby powders, clothes, and skin that linger about their homes, though not unpleasant, seem foreign, almost exotic. I marvel at how comfortable my friends are in this soft, precious world, how easy and swift their mothering gestures. I find myself looking for changes in their very natures, expecting them to have developed certain qualities—patience, equanimity, wisdom—practically overnight.

To get from where I am to where they are seems to be a tremendous leap, an insurmountable one, perhaps. I simply can't imagine twisting my voice into a shrill, teasing coo, that cloyingly sweet baby-talk tone that hangs high in the upper register as if suspended; nor can I picture an invasion of pink, blue, and other pastel objects in our spartan, bookshelf-lined home. Even more difficult to conjure up is the very reason for the high-pitched babble, the purpose for the playthings: the child.

I do want to have children, although I could not explain why with any conviction. I expect that this desire, however murky right now, stems from a combination of factors: chronology, conformity, curiosity, with at least a little altruism, arrogance, and resignation, not to mention romanticism, devotion, and faith. It's not anything mystical; nor can I attribute it to mechanics (the ticking clock I keep hearing about notwithstanding).

But my feelings about it are never clear, never all one way or another. In the mountains where I'm living this summer, I see lots of families with small children. On my way to a nearby lake one day I passed a young, athletic-looking woman wheeling a stroller. She was leaning into the carriage as though it was an extension of herself, propelling it forward with firm, measured steps. Her shoulders, bent slightly, were tight with determination as she pushed her baby along. She seemed immersed in her task: the baby before her, the grip of her hands on the metal bar, the stretch of road that seemed interminable, absurd even, considering the pace at which she progressed.

Walking briskly, I glided ahead of her. With nothing to carry but a towel and a paperback book, I felt frivolous compared to her, bereft. The woman, the baby, and the stroller seemed one complete unit, sharing movement, momentum, purpose. By contrast I was unconnected, detached from any one or thing. It was an unnerving truth to acknowledge. I felt somewhat ashamed of my own ease of movement, a bit guilty; it seemed as I passed her that I was somehow cheating. Yet at the same time I felt so wonderfully light. I let my arms swing back and forth in time with my step as I headed toward the turnoff. I was suddenly conscious of how free my limbs were, how they were owed to no one. I had the urge to sprint the rest of the way to the water merely because I was physically free to do so. I felt empowered by my very singularity and reveled in my lack of encumbrance.

My sister-in-law, my husband's sister, has five bright, independent, positively thriving kids. To someone whose feelings about motherhood tend toward the uncertain, Irene can be somewhat formidable. An attractive woman who can wear a bikini and look glamourous in a simple black dress, she adores her kids with an awe-inspiring fierceness. She has loved every stage of mothering, from being pregnant to nursing to playing diplomat amidst children's quarrels. She says she grew a half an inch in height during each pregnancy.

One morning, while visiting her family at the seashore, we adults were having a late breakfast when three of the children burst into the house after some amusing but unavailing fishing. They, too, decided they wanted some toast. Several rounds of bread popped out of the oven before Irene was able to nab a piece for herself. As a child-free adult and a guest, I had been the first one served. There seemed to be two sets of protocol operating here—in one, whoever sits down first gets the first piece; in the other, the kids are always served before anyone else. I was being treated according to the politeness of adult society, while Irene's actions were governed by family. The day had hardly begun and already Irene was reminded that others' needs came first.

When I think of the daily demands of being a mother, I fear I'm too selfish to cope with them. I wish I saw the world through selfless, endlessly giving eyes, but I don't. I've had only myself to care for all these years, and only myself to care for me. The odd piece of toast wouldn't bother me, but when it came to every piece of toast, every free hour, every unpleasant chore, I don't know how I'd handle it. I doubt I could ever rise above my own appetite, my need to be alone, my threshold of frustration. I've spent half my life learning to stand up for myself and my needs. I don't know how I'll feel about stepping down. Irene's philosophy of mothering is, "They only have one childhood." Lurking in the back of my mind would be the awareness that I only have one *life*. As far as I can see, we'd both be right.

When I try to imagine myself as a mother, it's as though, like Alice, I'm standing in front of a looking glass. Staring back at me is the me I know, the me who travels among adults. The me who is a mother is a woman other than the existing me, my counterpart. She is on the other side of the glass, living a life other than mine, a parallel one. To know her world I have to pass through the glass, but that means leaving life as I know it behind. Beyond the glass is a world of altered perceptions. Once across, my perspective on everything—time, body, mortality, sound, sleep—will turn backward and flip upside down. I will be plagued by new fears (what if something happens to the child?); I will have new dreams (a larger cast of characters to draw from). The scene from my side of the mirror is clear to me now, the lines and shapes distinct. The sight is pleasing to me, if mainly for its familiarity. I am comfortable with the self I see, its quirks, its economies, its symmetry. The scene on the other side is blurry.

The world through the mirror runs according to different rules, rules that are, in fact, the antithesis of those I've learned to live by. I've strived to attain a degree of control over my life and have come to expect a certain predictability. In dealing with others there's a logic I rely on, with any angers or misunderstandings expressed with verbal precision. My primary obligations are to my own personal development and professional success. My gifts are reciprocated, my work recompensed.

Life on my side of the mirror makes sense to me. I've worked to sharpen the skills that propel one forward in this realm. I can function here. The alternate, looking-glass world calls for a different set of faculties, a composite of expertise and experience that I can't yet claim. Unprepared and underschooled, I fear that I would certainly falter. But my present routine is hardly grooming me for passage. It's as if I've been saving and earning money only to move to a new country that won't accept my currency.

The spectacle at the mirror is complicated by other, competing, images, fantasies and figures that inform the way I view motherhood. For me, when I try to peer through the mirror, squinting and shifting my head around to catch a glimpse, a picture of my mother keeps reflecting back. I'm looking at myself, looking *for* myself, maybe, but my mother is what I see. It seems that no matter how I try, I can't separate the idea of being a mother from that of being *my* mother. When I try to imagine myself as a mother, the memory of her mothering intrudes. It's as though she were standing right behind me, looking over me, breathing, fogging up the glass.

There's a photograph of my mother, taken a year or so before I was born, that appeared in an ad in *Reader's Digest.* "Mrs. Schwartz uses Brillo Soap Pads," the copy announced. And there she is, apron across her breast and steel wool in her hand, with an ironic, mischievous smile, just shy of a wink. She looks beautiful, with her broad, knowing grin, yet she seems somehow to be mocking the role she had been cast in, amused by it, perhaps. She was both the perfect image of motherhood in the early sixties and completely ill suited for it. An intelligent, competent woman, housewifery left her overwrought. Around every corner lurked some unseen disaster. She followed recipes religiously, carefully counting aloud the number of cups or teaspoons so as not to lose track. She'd ask my brother and me not to disturb her concentration, but sometimes we did. She'd beg us not to muss up the rooms she had just finished straightening, but we couldn't always resist. She lived in dread of our upsetting the order of the house, a fear that was realized more often than not. She gave us too much power.

My mother and father had left New York City to move to a growing suburban town three hours away with unlimited promise for education, security, and discount shopping. It was North. It was cold. In memory, my entire childhood was set amid subzero temperatures. We all got heavy, as though our bodies had expanded to meet the dimensions of our large, sprawling house, all that undefined space. Our meals were prepared from boxes and cans and magazine recipes that promised to be simple. My mother and I got into the habit of licking out the bowls together. It passed the time. I wore chubbies, or "half-sizes" as they were called; my mother wore shifts, clothes that defied sizing. My mother, brother, and I shared a combination of restlessness and tedium, a mood as constant as the whir of heating, cooling, and cleaning machines in the house. Only my father, engrossed in the urgent matters of his medical practice, was spared.

For me, growing up meant growing away. It proved difficult to wean myself from the anxious air I had breathed. I went to school, started a career, and ultimately created a life of my own. On the surface, at least, my mother and I are as dissimilar as two women could be. I've struggled with that. I've wished she were different. I've wanted her to be someone *I'd* want to be. I've wanted her strengths to make sense in *my* world so that I would have someone to follow. We find it hard to meet. Always beneath the surface there's her need to defend her choice of life; my need to defend mine. I have trouble accepting the fact that she's content with life within the margins she has drawn for it; she shows little interest in what's important to me and why. Because of this, we're anything but a well-oiled mother/daughter machine, the close, loving pairing I think a mother and daughter are supposed to be. Our conversations are awkward, the rhythm off.

So when it's her image that flickers back at me from the glass—engaged in her endless pantomime of domesticity, redeeming coupons, driving the car, assigning us chores, then taking them over herself when she didn't approve of the results—I'm thrown a bit. I'm completely different from my mother. How, then, could I become what she is—a mother? And would I *want* to?

As the light shifts and I again see my own reflection with a reassuring clarity, I make a note of one comforting aspect: my relatively slender shape. Maybe it's not the most perfect of physical specimens, but I've worked on that body, chiseled it down to tolerable size. Evolving as an independent person meant taking control of my physical self—losing the weight, overcoming shyness by becoming active in team sports—so how could I give over that control to nature's whim? Pregnancy will put on weight, make me fat. Motherhood will tie me to the kitchen, a dangerous place. For me, this is less a matter of vanity than of terror. Will I be thrust back to my old chubby self, with all the pain and insecurity that went with it? Will I have a choice? Slimness, control, independence, and self-worth are too tightly interwoven for me to pretend to any rationality about it.

Still more images reflect in the glass, catching the light and then fading. Of my father, for instance. In important ways, I've modeled my life on his as opposed to my mother's. He was the parent with the career, the one who relied on intellect. When I want to talk about professional or financial matters, it's my father I turn to. If my mother's in the room, she'll leave to do the dishes or go to bed, carefully staying within the boundaries she has set for herself, those of the woman's world. I'm living in the world of men, she's telling me with her indifference, playing men's games. That has never bothered me. I've learned to thrive there.

My father has always been proud of my journalistic adventures. He gets a kick out of the ingenuity and sheer nerve involved. I bask in that pride, save up stories for him. But there's a price to his esteem. I've come to let his expectations guide me. I've willfully assumed the same drive that catapulted him out of a poor neighborhood in the Bronx, and with it the principle of "what next?" (You've written a story; how about a novel? You've sold to this magazine; how about *that* one?) I'm afraid of disappointing him, especially when the line between failing him and failing myself is so unclear. I hold on to the pressure, for I believe that's what keeps me going. Because of this, I'm reluctant to slow down. But once I make the magic crossing into the mother-world, I might have to ease up. Maybe I'll even want to, a disconcerting notion in itself. Time filters through the day differently over there; my grip on it will be loosened. So, I fear, will my grip on who I am, for my life has been so centered on my work that it's hard not to let it define me. Can I still be the scrappy reporter when I no longer feel like scrapping?

Then there's my husband. Here's where things really start to get fuzzy. If I set my gaze at a certain angle, I can just make out the faint contours of an exquisite little tableau. I can see my husband, myself, and an infant, barely touching one another, the way God touches Adam in Michelangelo's mosaic ceiling, as though giving one another life. If the mirror had sound effects, there would be a soft flute or violin concerto fluttering in the background. This is probably some residual from a Hollywood portrayal of domestic bliss that's still lingering around my psyche somewhere. Just before the credits roll, the still, final frame shows that love has again triumphed, and the newborn child confirms it. But wait—something's missing in this idyllic, if hazy, portrait. Where are the diapers, the messes, the *money?* Floating in paradise would be fine for a while, but at some point we would have to find some ground for ourselves.

Aha, the side of myself fueled by fantasy butts in. My husband is no *ordinary* guy. He's not, after all, terribly invested in the macho. He's someone who would prefer spending an afternoon in the library to going to a football game, even if tempted by the beer. He cooks, he listens, he's concerned that we each do our share. That's the thing about us. We're not caught up in "traditional" roles. So, here's how we could do it: I'll work in the mornings, he'll work in the afternoons, we'll each spend time with the baby, and we'll each enjoy the privacy we've had before, and get to cook all sorts of exotic things, oh yeah, and exercise . . . If this sounds too perfect that's probably because it is, and I should probably enjoy the daydream before reality shakes me out of it. The truth is, over the past several months I have noticed that our duties have started to divide themselves along gender-specific lines. I wash the dishes; he works the grill. I write the thank-you notes; he changes the oil. Equal roles in parenthood? Him get out of bed to soothe a crying infant before his delicate circadian rhythm gives him the cue? Who am I kidding?

When I first started pondering the questions of the looking glass—when I could first stand within reflective range without turning my head away—I thought I was the only one who approached motherhood with such ambivalence. I assumed that, aside from the tangible concerns of money, scheduling, and child care, for most women becoming a mother was as smooth a transition as that of, say, moving from freshman to sophomore, assistant to associate. But it wasn't long before I realized I wasn't alone in my fears. I found that other women, too, are plagued by a mistrust of their own bodies, a dread of repeating their childhoods, doubts about their independence. But no one was talking about it, at least not directly.

That fact in itself was interesting to me. It occurred to me that I had very little idea of what my close friends felt about becoming mothers—I mean, *really* felt about it. While I might have heard all the minute details of their romantic pasts or the petty feuds among their office mates, I was completely in the dark as to their views on this major life issue, an issue that cuts to the core of who they are. When the topic was raised with the women I knew, married or single, it would be dismissed with a remark like, "Maybe in a few years," or "I wouldn't want to bring up children in the city." I found it odd that women who could wax lyrical about a chance encounter on a train, whose passions could be aroused by the change in ownership of a favorite restaurant, could talk only in clichés about motherhood.

Until, of course, it happened to them. Then we get into the looking-glass problem, with me struggling to look through it, to see where they're coming from and where I may someday be, and them peering back from the other side, trying to relate to my world and, in the process, reflecting back on their former selves. Their trip across the mirror, like so many of ours today, was taken without guidance or true preparation. In part that's because we've all been silent about the questions hovering about the looking glass, the images that lurk there, twinkle, and dissolve. It can be difficult to communicate with a glass barrier—especially one so crowded with pictures and imaged scenes— between us.

Why was this so? Why are our feelings about motherhood so secret they're often a secret to ourselves? As I probed my own feelings and began broaching the topic with friends, one reason suggested itself to me: not knowing how our concerns about motherhood can be resolved, we are afraid to confront them. And so we go on, marrying or not marrying, having children or not having children, working or not working, bearing the weight of our ambivalence because we accept that that's the way it has to be.

Why is there such ambivalence about motherhood among educated women today? After all, we were the very women blessed with new freedoms, the liberation of the sixties and seventies having dropped a basketful of goodies in our laps. And, with our snazzy careers and confidence in our skills, we *seemed* to have it all under control. When I found myself confronted with an intriguing question, I did what every journalist is trained to do: I went out and searched for any clues that would tell the story. I interviewed doctors, psychologists, and women, including those with and without children and those on the verge of becoming mothers. The transition to motherhood was starting to seem more interesting and certainly more complex than today's popular books and magazines would lead us to believe.

Then I headed for the library. I read works of social history, medical history, women's history, and the history of everything from fashion to sex to eating disorders. These included many of the feminist classics of our era (*The Second Sex, The Feminine Mystique, Of Woman Born,* and many others), books that, I have to confess, I had never read before. I was living in an enlightened age when women had "choices." I didn't have to read any of that stuff, did I? Fool that I was.

At this point the issue of grappling with motherhood ceased to be merely intriguing: I saw that it was essential. We're in a time when our reproductive rights are under siege, when every legislative gain for women's welfare is answered by a defeat, when women are terrorized by reactionary rhetoric that calls into question our autonomy, our integrity, our worth. (Two recent books, *Backlash* by Susan Faludi and *The Beauty Myth* by Naomi Wolf, offer fine examples of the one-step-forward, two-steps-back pattern of contemporary women's history.) If we're not defining what motherhood means to women today, who is? If we're uncertain about what our roles should be, how are we going to withstand any assaults on our rights? If we remain silent, who's going to speak for us?

As the female members of our generation—those of us born at the end of the baby boom and just after, a generation that's hard to define elegantly—we're understandably a confused bunch. Society is sending us so many signals (be successful, have babies, be independent, look like a fashion model) that none of us knows where to begin—or when to take a break. We're the first generation of women who have grown up with the expectation of educational and professional achievement. While we've been raised to identify with our mothers domestically, it's our *fathers* whom we identify with professionally. So when motherhood threatens to transfer our focus from the workplace to the home, our sense of identity gets thrown out of whack. Who are we? Who have we *been?* When our view of our mate shifts from partner in life to partner in parenthood, what happens to the bond? Compared to cohorts of women before us, we have different expectations of our relationships, our doctors, our careers, our capacity to control our bodies and our lives.

We're not necessarily in a *bad* place, merely a disorienting one. There's no question that we've benefited from many developments of the last few decades, among them advances in the women's movement and in medicine. But we're also living in a society that both wants women in the job market and demands that they be home with their kids. At one time or another in our reproductive lives we may worry about getting pregnant or about not being able to get pregnant; about work interfering with motherhood or about motherhood interfering with work. The individual's experience of motherhood has changed while society's image of it hasn't. Yet aside from piecemeal explorations of specific topics—child care, maternity leave, single mothers, stay-at-home dads—we have not really delved into the overall experience of becoming a mother today.

Today's new mothers or would-be mothers are facing new dilemmas: How does a woman feel about pregnancy when she has come to view herself as the breadwinner? How do years of using birth control affect a woman's sense of her fertility, and how, in turn, might this affect her feelings of femininity? If a woman has modeled her life on her father, might she have trouble envisioning herself as a mother?

Much of this confusion stems from cultural attitudes, from what our society expects from women. In the course of our own lifetimes, motherhood has changed from being a hallowed profession (in the fifties and sixties), to a dubious avocation (in the seventies), to an essential part of a woman's personal résumé, an extracurricular activity to be pursued in addition to her career. In our wish to avoid being coerced into it, we may fear choosing motherhood for ourselves—or put off the decision long enough so that the decision is effectively made for us. We also may be reacting to pressure to *have* children (or to rush having them) that we're not even aware of.

Currents of thought come from all directions, leaving us caught between conflicting visions of womanhood. Feminist theory, psychoanalytic theory, and developmental theory, coupled with changes in the economic, social, and political climates, keep women's accepted roles shifting. By examining where these ideas come from, we can sharpen our understanding of how motherhood, or the potential for motherhood, figures into our own lives—and why.

A glance backward through history reveals patterns of attitudes toward motherhood, cycles that emerge again and again through American life, depending on the conditions of the time. For example, we in the 1990s did not create the conflict between working mothers and homemakers. In this era of the Mommy Track versus the Mommy-less track, as we debate whether a mother's working is bad for her children, or if her staying home is bad for her career, we forget that these very questions have haunted us for centuries. Since the Industrial Revolution, when economic opportunity first became centered outside the home, "experts" have wondered whether women who worked or studied were "overdrawing" their energy reserves, only to leave their offspring languishing from neglect.

At different points in our nation's history, children have been viewed as miniature adults who could basically be left on their own; helpless creatures who needed to be "socialized" and instilled with moral purpose by their mothers; or the embodiment of pure, natural instincts that should not be tampered with by interfering adults. In the same way, at various times women's sexuality has been regarded as a distraction from the true calling of motherhood (in the mid-1800s, frequent intercourse was thought to make women infertile); experienced through pregnancy and breast-feeding (psychological theorists in the 1940s believed that each satisfied women's sexual needs); or essential to a woman's proper functioning (frigidity was deemed a major health problem in the 1950s and was blamed for everything from menstrual pain to barrenness).

These views form the backdrop for the view from the mirror on both sides. You can try to move them out of your range of vision, shift your stance to either side, but they're still there, coloring the images and shaping the forms before you. Even though we may not consciously be aware of it, attitudes lugged around from decade to decade contribute to our own pressures and confusion. Discovering the roots of these ideas can ease and clarify our own experience.

This book is an exploration. It began with the personal—as any such exploration must—and it spiraled out to include voices of other women contending with the role of motherhood in their lives, and the social and historical sources of our ambivalence. As the exploration fanned out into separate topics, the discussions of those topics became chapters. I may not cover in depth every topic that would interest a given reader (it would be ridiculous even to try, as each of us carries her own map of ambivalence), but I do try to present a broad picture of the issues. My hope is that these points of inquiry will serve as a springboard for others.

This is not a how-to book. Nor am I taking a stand for or against childbearing. The emphasis rather is on *process,* on our recognizing points of tension and working through them. The exploratory route can lead to some surprises. As for myself, I've always looked at everything psychologically. I believed we were all these Freudian units and that most conflicts could be resolved with a little psychic rewiring. The assumption was that what went on outside was by definition normal; if there was "confusion" about motherhood or any other issue, the problem was on the level of the self. In retrospect I see I was too stubborn and too naive to question the social reality that was handed me. While I still have a great respect for psychoanalytic inquiry, I see that our responses are also informed by our social surroundings, as well as by history.

My quest took me to another place I hadn't expected to go, or at least to dwell in so long: the women's movement. The writings of feminists past and present are, I've found, startlingly relevant to the issues we face, regardless of affiliation. These works have been a tremendous source of strength, inspiration, and perspective to me. The process of researching and writing brought me from complacent "postfeminism" (a phrase often used to describe our generation, although I avoid the term because it implies that the women's movement is over) to active feminism.

I'm not sure where your exploration will take you, although I suspect it will be, like mine, circuitous (dipping into the past, moving across the mirror and back) and full of unexpected detours.

We may be ambivalent, but we're not without vision. We have reached adulthood in a time of flux and are still coming to grips with the implications of many recent changes. The lives we aspire to reflect both our independence and our nurturing. As mothers or nonmothers, we want to build on the strengths our autonomy has afforded, not negate them. But we need to be clear about our own feelings, which necessarily means understanding the *sources* of those feelings, in order to get there.

Chapter 1

SCRAMBLED SIGNALS

"Many of my friends and I are opting to start baby making now, before we turn 30 . . . I think I can fuse my family and work life more successfully than the women before me and I believe it is my birthright to follow a more biologically sound reproductive schedule."

Kim Flodin, twenty-seven, *The New York Times,* 1989

"It's a good deal easier to be liberated if you're not also a parent."

Nancy and Chip McGrath, *The New York Times Magazine,* 1975

Motherhood, which secured a woman's sense of identity in generations past, now threatens it on many levels. "I'm scared to death about becoming a mother," Cindy, thirty-four, a newspaper reporter on the West Coast confesses. "If I have a kid, I'm going to lose the independence I've struggled my whole life for, lose the career I've worked so hard to create, and I'm not going to do the creative work I love so much." "I felt I wasn't a person anymore," Jane, a twenty-eight-year-old new mother laments. "I had been this confident woman, then it all disappeared." From our post–baby boom, post-Freudian, dual-career perspective, motherhood brings with it a whole new set of meanings, forcing us to make new bargains with ourselves.

"I see a lot of women torturing themselves about motherhood," says Judith Langer, whose market research firm specializes in focus groups and has conducted large studies for women's magazines. Whether or not they're contemplating having children or have already done so, "very few women escape the inner turmoil. It's not a situation where you simply make a decision and stick to it. There's constant reevaluation, asking yourself whether you're doing the right thing."

One reason we keep worrying about doing right is that no one knows what the right thing is. First we come to believe that developing ourselves is the right thing. Then we hear that motherhood is the right thing after all. But how are we supposed to integrate the two? The only role model presented to us that attempted the mix has been the "having-it-all" woman who has a slick career and perfect children, and collapses from exhaustion each night after the last dinner plate is cleared. All we can conclude is that motherhood and career are two distinct paths and that the values, rules, and rewards of one are completely untenable in the other. We get the idea that our careers have somehow lowered our qualifications for motherhood, while having a child will similarly compromise our ability on the job.

Where do we get such notions? Certainly not because economically productive women are worse mothers, or because mothers are incompetent at work. But over the last few years—as the birth rate has gone up, as babies have become "in," as "family issues" are debated everywhere from talk-show circuits to political platforms—tensions about motherhood have come to the fore. At the same time, we're trying to make sense of our own lives in terms of the values and expectations we grew up with.

In the realm of popular culture, "motherhood" has always been a malleable theme, to be played up or played down, infused with various meanings and associations. Some may have thought that the women's movement left us immune to peer pressure regarding maternal roles, but the confusion many of us feel belies our vulnerability. So many conflicting messages have been hurled at us—some well meaning, some manipulative, some merely sensational—that it can be hard to make sense of them. It's tempting to assume that after the pro- and anti-motherhood extremes of recent decades, the messages have gotten healthier, that some important balance has been attained. A closer look at contemporary images of motherhood reveals that this is not necessarily the case.

First we need to take a look at the attitudes our own mothers confronted. They came of age in the decade and a half after the Second World War, an era when raising children was seen as the female equivalent of winning a Purple Heart in battle. The economy was flourishing, the national mood was optimistic, and newly formed or recently reunited couples were encouraged to fill up the newly created suburban towns, towns whose aesthetic virtually demanded the presence of children in the streets and yards.

A nation that had been concerned that sluggish fertility rates during the depression would erode its position in the world cheered on its citizens to reproduce themselves in ever-escalating numbers. The Great American Family, the nation gloated, is what fueled the wartime triumph and what made it all worth fighting for. Perhaps even more important for the revved-up economy, enhanced baby production helped generate larger, insatiable consumer markets. In the words of *Life* magazine, children represented a "built-in recession cure."[1] To keep those families growing and fed, the contribution and cooperation of American wives were essential. Women were lauded for their lavish devotion to home and children. Any woman who felt otherwise was not just different, but unpatriotic.

After the social, familial, and political chaos that we've experienced since, it's alluring to look at the fifties as a long evening by the fire, sipping homemade hot chocolate and watching cheery sit-coms. We forget that the country was shaken by the social and economic changes brought by the war, fearful that a depression could return, and horrified by the advent of the bomb. In fact, the era's domestic ideology may well have formed in direct *response* to the threats of the atomic age, the family serving as a physical and psychological refuge from the dangers that lurked beyond the home.

Historian Elaine Tyler May suggests that the cold-war ideology of containment of communism had a parallel domestic version: "contained" within the home, potentially disordering forces (including women's sexuality and power) could be held in check. The ideal nuclear family of the nuclear age was epitomized by the well-planned bomb shelter: self-sufficient, secure, and with rigidly stratified gender roles. In the context of the cold war, procreation was a civic duty. One writer called children a "defense—an impregnable bulwark" against the uncertainties of the age.[2]

The story of how full-time homemaking—along with the consumer durables that accompanied the role—was aggressively sold to women has been told many times, notably by Betty Friedan in *The Feminine Mystique.* This phase of heady prosperity and domesticity was but a brief moment in historical time, and an atypical one at that, with women marrying and starting families at a younger age than either their predecessors or successors. Yet society clings to the memory. Although nowadays most mothers work outside the home (and have been doing so in increasing numbers since before the turn of the century), society has yet to come up with an accurate depiction of women's lives, one that addresses all of the complexities. It's as though we've been looking through a slide projector and there's one picture of proper motherhood, circa 1959, stuck in the machine, impossible to dislodge.

We were brought up with one idea of what motherhood is—one that was confirmed by every television show we watched, not to mention every product advertisement in between—but given the course of our lives, we see that our experience must take another form. But *what* form? The old pattern may not have been perfect, but at least it was something of a known quantity. Today we live with the risk that our way may not turn out to be any better, that we might, in fact, take actions we'll later regret. Part of our pain stems from our sense that in making our decisions—opting not to quit our jobs when our infants are young, choosing to have an abortion because we feel we're not ready to care for a baby—we're rejecting everything that has come before us. Yet unlike many of our older sisters, who reached adulthood amidst the upheaval of the sixties, it's not our intention to rebel.

The fact that the prototypical suburban, 2.8-child family was less than idyllic is well known to us. We may still see that picture contained in the slide as "normal," but we know there are scratches in it, as well as sinister shadows—the hypocrisy, the isolation, the thwarted dreams—cut out of the frame. Whether or not we read books like *The Feminine Mystique,* the frustrations they disclosed have forever altered the plastic portrait's cast. We've seen the consequences that a glorification of motherhood can have on a woman's life, often in our own homes. Housewives of that era felt imprisoned in the house, experienced panic when they left it, and felt guilty that they were floundering in lives that battalions of psychologists, physicians, and marketing experts had assured them were ideally suited to their natures. It took the women's movement to reveal that any degree of autonomy was missing.

Women of our generation have made that autonomy central to our lives. It is absolutely nonnegotiable with us. And our mothers told us it should be so. "For the first time, the message women get from their mothers is, 'Don't do as I did; do as I wish I did,' " says Judith Langer. It's a message young women have taken to heart. "My mother was eleven credits from a teaching degree when she got married," recalls Laura, a twenty-nine-year-old mother and stockbroker currently struggling with the question of whether or not to leave her job. "At that time, they wouldn't allow pregnant women in school, so she quit soon afterward and didn't go back to complete her degree until all seven of us kids were grown. All along she would say to me, 'Don't postpone your work.' "

An awareness that the marital bond is tenuous at best only strengthens our commitment to autonomy. Any marriage forged in the 1970s or 1980s had a one in two chance of ending in divorce.[3] We were children when the number of divorces skyrocketed in the sixties and early seventies, sending tremors through our assumptions of family stability. "My mother survived her divorce, but a lot of her friends didn't fare so well," Molly, a thirty-year-old medical researcher reflects.

> *They may have thought they had a good deal at the time, but after their marriages broke up, they had nothing. They were basically stranded in life, lost because they had no sense of self, had developed no skills to work from. I would not give up my career for anyone. I couldn't imagine leaving a job and then being in a situation where the man brings home the money. During short periods when I was involved with wealthier men, I felt incredibly uncomfortable, especially when we would go out to places that were beyond my means. During those times I would ask myself, "How could women have lived like this? Where did they get their sense of personal power?"*

The lessons that came billowing down from our mothers, feminists, our fathers, from all those who knew more about the world than we did, were these: "Take care of yourself." "Get married, but don't mortgage your existence to a man and his job; the terms will always be against you." "Self-sacrifice is just this side of masochism." "Full-time motherhood is yet another effort to enslave women." Even if our mothers denied that these realities reflected their own lives—perhaps in a last-ditch attempt to assert the validity of their lifestyles, even as they were rapidly becoming obsolete—we came to regard the full-time homemaker route as a personal, professional, and psychic dead end.

The warnings have been heeded. Women today plan to build their career arsenal before moving on to motherhood. To do otherwise, we fear, is to offer ourselves up to exploitation and to be anchored in dependency. Aside from being a trap, choosing to place the role of "wife" or "mother" before "self" is perceived as a form of selling out, of selling *women* out. In both the individual and the global sense, it is to fail.

Certainly as we were growing up in the late sixties and seventies, having babies was not the fashionable thing to do. For one thing, a population explosion developed as the nation's fertility rate topped out, detonating a minor eruption of its own in the form of alarmist books and articles on the subject. In the years that followed, progressive, conservation-minded people came to regard childbearing as ecologically unsound. Buttons and bumper stickers appeared with slogans like "Stop at Two"; "None is Fun"; and "Pollution Is Your Baby."[4] Young people whose concern for the environment and the state of the world led them to despair often expressed the view that they couldn't justify bringing a child into a world already so crowded.

In 1969 the graduation-class speaker at all-women Mills College had this to say to her fellow students: "[W]e are breeding ourselves out of existence. . . . *I am terribly saddened by the fact that the most humane thing for me to do is to have no children at all.*"[5] Suddenly, childlessness, a state that previously would have started neighbors and relatives whispering, took on an air of moral superiority.

Such attacks on the mandate to have children encouraged women to question the mother role, but it also left a void in terms of sources of women's self-esteem and status. Women's influx into the workplace helped fill that gap. The tenets of the 1970s human potential movement presented another alternative: rather than becoming parents, women and men could concentrate on themselves.

With new pop psychology and quasi-religious movements appearing in places like New York, Berkeley, and avant-garde hot spots in-between, the self-improvement marketplace was bustling. Being a fully integrated, fully realized human being took a lot of work, it appeared. Books like *How to Be Your Own Best Friend* and *Looking Out for Number One* perched on top of the best-seller list for months at a stretch. Because it was assumed that you couldn't be grown up until you knew yourself, men and women in their twenties and thirties took a detour back into adolescence. Or beyond. As Barbara Ehrenreich and Deirdre English observe in *For Her Own Good: 150 Years of the Experts' Advice to Women,* all were encouraged to seek that perfect "child within us."[6] By the time people got around to the issue of having children, many were undoubtedly too wearied by the task of raising themselves to think about raising anyone else.

Another prevalent belief was that every person was entitled to emotional, personal, and sexual fulfillment, and whatever interfered with that was expendable—including marriage and children. In *The Joy of Sex,* a 1972 book touted as "A Gourmet Guide to Lovemaking," author

Alex Comfort, a British physician, put it bluntly: "The best modern sex is unreproductive . . . The development of a recreational erotic life needs privacy. Sexual freedom just isn't compatible with a childbearing life-style."[7] A study at the Princeton Office of Population Research found a 14 percent increase in marital lovemaking from 1965 to 1974. Political scientist Andrew Hacker gave his assessment to *New York* magazine: "There is no aphrodisiac in the world as powerful as the absence of babies."[8] Now that sexual fulfillment had become obligatory—as one other aspect of selfhood to be pursued and perfected—this was no mere frivolity. Having a family became just another of many possible lifestyles, and one regarded by many as decidedly passé.

Adults-only developments arose to house those who felt strongly that children should be neither seen nor heard. Any couple who changed their mind on the matter would have to forfeit their lease. The National Organization for Non-Parents selected a "Non-Father of the Year" in 1973 and designated August 1 as Non-Parents Day.[9] A husband-and-wife effort in the *New York Times Magazine* entitled "Why Have a Baby?" (quoted above) sums up what seemed to be the prevailing view of the seventies: "Sometimes . . . we get the impression that babies figure in the new scheme of things roughly the way ocelots and coatimundis did a few years ago—as rare domestic pets."[10]

At the peak of the postwar baby boom, American women were having 3.5 babies apiece. The 1960s saw a gradual descent in fertility, which then picked up speed in the early 1970s. By 1976 women's baby output averaged 1.8, close to half of what it had been two decades earlier. Schools across the country were shutting their doors. Economists predicted severe labor shortages. Hospital authorities were recommending that obstetrical units close down too, "not merely to save money but because the people working [there] are on the verge of becoming dangerously out of practice."[11]

Whereas men and women used to marry in order to have children, couples were now foregoing children for the sake of their marriages. A 1986 article in *Newsweek* on childlessness called "Three's a Crowd" cites a UCLA study finding that couples who opted not to have children rated higher on a "marital-happiness scale" than those who became parents. Among the reasons childless couples cited for foregoing parenthood were prestigious condos and fragile, easily stained furniture. "If we had [children], we certainly couldn't live here," one Houston man said of his well-appointed home.[12]

With all this antichildren chanting still ringing in our ears, there were other voices, just audible at the periphery. These were from women five, ten, fifteen years older than us, those who had chosen a one-bedroom condo over a four-bedroom ranch, those who enthusiastically partook of the freedoms of adults-only life and had most emphatically said "Children are not for me." Now, it seemed, some weren't so sure. With their launch into adulthood they came to believe that succeeding in the male world would be the path to fulfillment. Equality for women, said the feminists of the sixties and early seventies who were prominent when this group was finishing school, would derive from minimizing the differences between women and men. To acknowledge a desire for motherhood would have undermined women's claims of equality. It would also, from an individual career standpoint, have been incredibly inconvenient.

But as they were beginning to hit their professional stride, many of these women were also hitting the outer limits of their reproductive years. The cartoon that showed up on T-shirts and postcards a few years back, "I Can't Believe I Forgot to Have Children!" was hyperbole, but the point was that many women had come to feel that becoming a mother was not important to them, or that it shouldn't be.[13] Women went along, working and enjoying opportunities that had been denied their mothers, putting off the decision to have children one year, then two, and sometimes shrugging off the whole matter entirely. Which was okay because children had been unofficially removed from the checklist of life's essentials. According to Elaine Heffner, a psychotherapist and author of *Mothering: The Emotional Experience of Motherhood After Freud and Feminism,* "If women had been trapped by theories of biologically determined behavior, they would be freed by theories of culturally determined behavior. It was not enough to say that women wanted or needed a fulfillment beyond mothering. It was necessary to prove that there was never any reason for them to be mothers in the first place."[14]

Years later, many women looked at their lives and came to the conclusion that something was missing. It seemed their triumph earned them the right to spend interminable days in the office, fret about the next promotion, and get heart attacks. Like men. Perhaps, hidden among all the stereotypes and restraints, there was something inherently valuable in the experience of being a woman—in that disputed *difference*—that was worth preserving. Over the din of Xerox machines and the strobelike blinking of telephone hold buttons, women were asking themselves: "Is this *all?*" The very question home-bound women before them had asked of their manicured lawns and fruited Jell-O molds, working women were now asking of their hard-won careers.

After the initial exhilaration of being invited into the work club, women started wondering whether their membership was real or just honorary. Even though they had earnestly pledged and paid their full share of dues, many still felt like outsiders, not yet privy to the secret games and codes. There was talk of the "glass ceiling," that invisible barrier beyond which it was nearly impossible for women to ascend.

Why keep fighting, some women asked? What were they really getting for their loyalty? Throughout the 1980s, companies were merging, contracting, and casting off excess personnel like factory seconds. Even if you had a job today, you could find yourself without one soon enough. The work world was, ultimately, a cruel, cold place. Home and family were warm (at least in our nostalgia-fogged memory). Professional rewards were determined by what someone else chose to give, and all the bonuses, titles, and perks could vanish with one capricious corporate gesture. With parenting, the rewards are tangible, more intense, more *personal.* From this standpoint, having children now seemed to some women less their demise than their salvation.

A few women did actually pack up their files and head for home. Some decided that enough was enough, the job wasn't worth it. When this happened it usually reflected the business world's inability to accommodate mothers rather than an individual woman's inability to accommodate a job. But traditionalists, who had seen no reason for women to be working in the first place, were ecstatic. While the retreat to the home was really just a trickle, the media pronounced this a "trend" and published numerous accounts of high-powered businesswomen who fled the boardroom for the haven of the hearth.[15] The public was given the impression that anyone walking down Madison Avenue would be run over by a stampede of briefcase-bearing women, escaping their jobs—and that perhaps they would clear out for good. As one observer told *Fortune,* "If these [women MBAs] decided their careers are not worth the struggle, their example may deter younger women coming along behind them."[16]

Baby or no baby? Job or no job? The collective angst filtered down to those of us now in our twenties and early thirties. Maybe work wouldn't be enough for us either: Were we getting back what we gave on the job? On clear days, when our work load afforded us time to think, the next level or two up didn't always seem worth striving for. And in some ways, our very devotion to work had us trapped. "I've realized I'm discriminated against as a single woman," Leslie, twenty-nine, an advertising supervisor, says. "If upper management says I have to fly to Chicago the next morning, I have to do it. I have to do it because I've always done it, and because they know I'm 'available.' If I had a family, they couldn't just send me off like that. It's an unspoken understanding. But if I'm always on call, how am I supposed to *have* a life anyway?"

We knew we wanted to work—that part of the message had come through loud and clear. Largely because women before us had done the original bushwhacking, we were able to explore satisfying careers. And perhaps we started to get a little smug about it. After interviewing several women college graduates in 1982, journalist Susan Bolotin was startled by their grand career expectations (half expected to earn at a level achieved by only 2 percent of women). "[T]oday's young women seem extraordinarily sure they can have it all without even speaking up about unfairness at work," she wrote. ". . . Indeed, it would be sad if the majority of 20-year-olds were pessimists; my generation . . . certainly thought we could have it all. The difference is one of tone. This group's naiveté strikes me . . . as unidealistic; our expectations were ridiculous, but we spoke up for what we believed in."[17] We identified with the importance of professional equality but not with the struggle to attain it. Most of the ambitious young women Bolotin spoke to did not call themselves feminists because they viewed the movement as too "extreme."

The apathy of younger women, the questioning of some "liberated" women, and a general conservative trend all helped set the stage for the antifeminist backlash of the mid-1980s. (This has been documented elsewhere, most extensively in Susan Faludi's *Backlash,* published in 1991.) Now the word was that feminism was finished. Every time a dress with a shapely silhouette made the fashion pages, commentators announced a return to "femininity" and traditional roles. Every time a prominent female celebrity expressed an interest in motherhood or love for her child, it was presumed that maternity superseded the work she had done (and generally continued to do).

The forget-the-movement view was greatly hyped by the media. Headlines like "The Feminist Mistake" and "The Awful Truth About Women's Liberation" made great copy.[18] The real story, that feminism had greatly improved women's lives, was barely touched. Interestingly, it was in the last month of the decade that *Time* reported 94 percent of women polled thought the movement had helped women become more independent and 86 percent believed it had given women more control over their lives. One would never have guessed this conclusion from the cover line, however, which read: "In the 80s [women] tried to have it all. Now they've just plain had it. Is there a future for feminism?"[19]

It was in this context that babies came back into the picture. After reaching its low point in the late 1970s, the birth rate slowly crept up, especially first births of women over thirty. This was in part a function of demographics; baby boomers who had delayed having children (and thus had appeared to be "antichildren") were now ready to start their families. Another factor was economic; people tend to have more children in times of financial promise, and, with two incomes, many couples were feeling more prosperous.

But coming during a conservative-leaning period, the "boomlet" was interpreted ideologically: as a sign that women had finally realized they should be home birthing babies instead of in the office brokering deals. If traditionalists were to be believed, we should take back not just the baby but all the bathwater we had thrown out with it. This muddled the message for us still further: Had women moved far enough ahead that we could choose to have families without forfeiting our rights? Or were our "careers" to be those of wife and mother after all?

Adding to our confusion were crossed wires in the women's movement. In the late sixties and early seventies, the impetus had been to free women from motherhood, which was seen in the context of our patriarchal society. Then some feminist writers began to explore the experience of motherhood. Such writers started questioning the movement's previous stance that any acknowledgment of difference between the sexes was bad for women. More publicly, in *The Second Stage*, published in 1981, Betty Friedan asserted that for the feminist revolution to truly succeed, it must address issues of family. Some feminists expressed concern that the movement itself had taken a pronatalist bent. Flora Davis, author of *Moving the Mountain: The Women's Movement in America Since 1960*, recalls attending one major women's conference where some women said they felt uncomfortable in the movement because they had children, while others said they felt left out because they *didn't* have children. Clearly, motherhood was a problem.

With no coherent counter from the women's movement, the antifeminist rhetoric and the romanticism of motherhood only played into women's anxieties. Did any of us really know where our lives were going? Our own lack of clarity left us vulnerable to any statement or report that called our lifestyles into question. And these started coming at us with a vengeance.

One square hit was the now-notorious Harvard-Yale study of 1986, which placed a woman's likelihood of getting married in the same category of probability as her being struck by a terrorist (if she had the misfortune to be over forty and educated; if she were a single, educated woman of twenty-five, she still had a one-in-two shot). The study was found to be based on faulty assumptions and completely off base, but it still managed to spawn a mini-industry. The authors were paraded from talk show to talk show, the media rounded up young single women to comment on the findings, and reaction grew so heated that several women's magazines ran a second round of articles intended to calm readers down.

Women who had simply assumed they could get married when (and if) they wanted to were unnerved to learn that the pool of potential husbands was drying up. Maybe that man won't materialize when I'm ready to settle down, some started to think. Maybe my standards are too high. Maybe I've got my priorities wrong. Carolyn, a public relations executive who was then in her late twenties, recalls: "A bunch of us freaked out. I freaked out. We thought there was an urgency about getting married soon. It was panic, real panic, and we all tried to act on that panic somehow. Some of us ended up getting married, some of us didn't."

Even though studies suggested that nonmarried women perceived their lives to be full and satisfying,[20] singleness was portrayed as a devastating affliction. (Female singleness, that is. Male singleness was nothing a little growing up, or overcoming a "fear of commitment," couldn't cure.) The implication, often unstated, was that by insisting on liberation in the first place, women had done this to themselves: The soulless, manless existence of the single woman was the flip side of autonomy. In an essay arguing that feminism's critique of relations between the sexes had left everybody miserable (she used the example of her friends), a law student wrote: "If the single life were less glamorized, Sonia would very likely be married and fruitful by now. She might not be happy, but somehow I know my fingers wouldn't tremble as I dialed her phone number."[21]

The slew of books and articles on how to catch a man that appeared in the mid-eighties implied that having a man was more important than accomplishment, personal growth, or inner peace. Many women feared that while they were busy developing themselves, men were hankering for a less-developed model. In Wendy Wasserstein's 1988 play *The Heidi Chronicles,* a male romantic "hero" rejects the independent, intellectual heroine for a doting and demure young wife. This articulated a lurking fear: right under our noses, less-intelligent, less-confident, less-evolved women were stealing our men. The alternative, of course, was to steal someone *else's* man. The "other woman" came out of her gilded closet, and some writers conceded that dating married men was not so much a moral dilemma as making the best of a bad situation. (In *The New Other Woman,* for example, Laurel Richardson calls it "the married man solution.")[22]

The abortion question grew heated throughout the eighties, putting many women on the defensive. The right wing seized control of key elements of the debate, including rhetorical labels ("life"), basic definitions (using the words "baby" or "child" to mean "fetus"), and visuals (propagandist films like *The Silent Scream* and the displaying of fetal images in public places). Despite the fact that the vast majority of American women are prochoice, the subject of abortion became more fraught with discomfort than ever. The government came close to *institutionalizing* abortion guilt in 1987 when millions of dollars were allocated to study "postabortion syndrome," which allegedly posed a threat to women's health. (Professionals in psychology and public health, including then Surgeon General C. Everett Koop, maintained there was no evidence that such a syndrome existed.) The suggestion was that women would suffer if they resisted their own "maternal instincts."[23]

Recently, there has been a preoccupation with infertility. Magazines and newspapers have teemed with articles on new high-tech developments and testimonials of long, tortuous, and often unsuccessful attempts at parenthood. Terms like *postcoital test* and *endometrial scar tissue* have become common fare in broadcast and popular-magazine accounts. Today's readers seem genuinely more interested in a celebrity's fertility status than in her past or present romances. Emblazoned on the cover of *People* magazine in August 1990 were a picture of Connie Chung and the words *I Want a Child.* In the accompanying article, "Waking Up Late to the Biological Clock," every detail of the newswoman's quest to "brave the waning odds of late motherhood" was scrupulously reported. Chung, then forty-three, had announced her intention to cut back on her arduous schedule at CBS to facilitate her attempts to conceive. Although she allegedly suffered from no medical problems that would preclude pregnancy, Chung said, "Unfortunately time is running out for me . . . Just last week, after consulting with my doctor, I became convinced that to make this effort, I now need to take a very aggressive approach to having a baby." That same week, *Newsday* reported that Chung canceled a lecture to a Japanese group because it coincided with her time of ovulation.

With the fear of infertility looming in the air, many younger women don't want to wait around to test their own reproductive longevity. "I see a lot of women in their thirties having problems, so I don't want to wait too long," says Nancy, a twenty-nine-year-old doctor, articulating a common concern. In an op-ed piece in the *New York Times* (quoted above), one twenty-seven-year-old woman said she and her peers were making sure to have children now rather than putting it off until it was too late as they had seen so many women older than them do. This prompted a barrage of letters in response, many from women in their thirties and forties who resented the writer's apparent indifference to the challenges they had faced. But she was only echoing the message we were getting everywhere else: don't lose out on family like the women before us did.

The link between delayed childbearing and infertility seems fairly well established in people's minds. Yet according to demographers quoted in Linda Gordon's *Woman's Body, Woman's Right,* fertility among women over thirty has actually been growing steadily.[24] One reason it's assumed that delayed childbearing (meaning also, by association, the use of birth control and increased opportunities for women) is the culprit is that college-educated career women who have consciously postponed families are those most likely to seek medical attention for fertility problems. The high rates of infertility among black women, an estimated 18 percent, Gordon argued, "suggest that economic and general health factors have more to do with the problem than delayed childbearing."[25] As for an "epidemic" of infertility implied by all the recent coverage, the numbers fail to confirm it. Research from the National Center for Health Statistics suggests that the incidence of infertility at any given age has remained fairly stable over the last twenty-five years (excepting a slight increase among women in their early twenties, the result of a rise in sexually transmitted diseases).

And if the specter of infertility itself isn't enough to make women feel the heat, a new threat has come on the scene: premature menopause.

There have always been women who go through menopause before or after others (the average age is about fifty-one), but for some reason *Self* magazine saw fit to present early menopause as a trend. "We're seeing a virtual epidemic of early menopause," asserted one "clinician" who refused to state this on record. The case study offered was a "successful New York City marketing executive who is childless" and whose mother hit menopause at thirty-six (the tendency appears to be hereditary). Sounding like she's speaking not only for herself but for many women caught between pressures, she says, "I feel as if I'm backed into a corner. I figure I've got maybe four years left to have kids."[26]

As concerns that liberated women were losing the ability to get married and make babies continued to circulate, motherhood began to take center stage. According to a *Ladies' Home Journal* trade ad in the late 1980s, "Reproductive health will be the status symbol of the 1990s." An executive with TBWA, the ad agency that developed the campaign, explained that it grew out of a seminar/symposium on "What's Next for Women in the Nineties." "A BMW is no longer the status symbol. Now it's to see a woman pregnant," he said. "Women, themselves, their work—it's a complete reversal from what we saw a few years ago."

There certainly has been a reversal in *interest* in mothering in the media. Robin Young, a documentary filmmaker and former NBC correspondent, recalled: "When I signed my first contract for a major broadcasting company in 1975, it stated I could be fired if I became 'pregnant or otherwise disfigured.' " More recently, Faith Daniels, then of CBS News, was told by her executive producer that her pregnancy "would be great for ratings." Young, childless at this writing, was disqualified from hosting a new daytime talk show because "the marketing guys wanted a mother type."[27]

This turnabout seems to be taking us back several decades. As the domestic consensus was forming in the 1940s, celebrity profiles began to focus less on stars' successes and exploits and more on the joys of family life. Former sex symbols were featured as wives and mothers and former he-men as fathers.[28] Actresses like Joan Crawford, Claudette Colbert, and Ann Sothern were presented as the ideal models for women of the age—not for their independence but their domesticity.[29]

We're seeing something similar now. *Redbook* profiled actress Melanie Griffith, stressing that "motherhood is her most satisfying role yet."[30] "Mom's the Word" *Ladies' Home Journal* announced in "The New Romance of Being a Mom," another paean to celebrity mothers.[31] A recent

McCall's article claims that "sushi may be chi-chi, and voguing in vogue, but there's a new, even hipper trend on the rise in Tinsel Town these days: babies," adding that "[e]ven Madonna has said the one thing she really wants is a baby."[32]

Articles like "Hollywood's Late-Blooming Moms" in *McCall's* are but a modern echo of a 1940 feature in *Photoplay* headlined "Hollywood Birth Rate—Going Up! A Bumper Crop of Babies Brings a Message of Renewed Faith and Courage." In both pieces, glamourous photo spreads of models and actresses with their babies showed that rather than being a hindrance, motherhood could make beautiful women *more* beautiful.[33] The recent *McCall's* article informs us: "Once upon a time, not so long ago, movie stardom and maternity . . . were antithetical ideas. The studios . . . implored [leading ladies] not to have babies, please. Motherhood would taint their 'goddess' images. . . . But nowadays: Behold, enlightenment! Major movie studios agree: Motherhood makes an attractive actress only more attractive." The only new part is the age factor: "And if she's around 40, well, so much the better."[34]

A similar point was made in the summer of 1991 when, in the baring all style of the contemporary media, pregnant actress Demi Moore was pictured nude on the cover of *Vanity Fair*. While many commentators applauded the message that pregnancy was beautiful, some wondered whether the picture had been airbrushed, contending that no expectant mother looked quite that good.[35]

The film industry rapidly joined in the sentimentalization of parenthood. Some critics observed a little airbrushing on the big screen, or at least some heavy cosmetic touches. Molly Haskell points to popular movies like *Baby Boom, Raising Arizona, She's Having a Baby, For Keeps,* and *Three Men and a Baby,* in which "gurgling, picture-perfect newborns arrive to rescue selfish, work-oriented men and women from the evils of feminism and the me-decade." Never have infants been so irresistible, she writes, "nor their arrival into the world so painless. They are chosen for optimum cuteness: past the wrinkled peach stage and before the terrible twos."[36]

In Haskell's view, there are positive aspects to the current crop of baby films: chiefly, that mothers aren't forced to give up their ambition, power, or sexuality upon the baby's arrival. But as columnist Ellen Goodman notes, not only do such movies downplay the less-cute aspects of motherhood, they reduce the plot to a formula in which having a child is the key to maturity and success.[37] Interestingly, in three of the movies—*Raising Arizona, Baby Boom,* and *Three Men and a Baby*—the babies arrived fully made. In the latter two they arrive uninvited, possibly projecting the fantasies of a generation ambivalent about parenthood.

Some fifteen years ago cars wore bumper stickers that read: "Zero Population Growth." Now they're more like to boast: "Baby On Board." T-shirts designed for maternity wear have bold arrows across the front with messages like "Under Construction" and"Baby!" as if observers had any question as to what was going on. With the kind of pride and enthusiasm today's new parents have, ordinary birth announcements aren't enough. According to *The New York Times,* some professional couples in their thirties are sending out attention-getting birth notices in the form of baseball cards, comic strips, three-dimensional dolls, and diapers, costing anywhere from seventy cents to twenty-five dollars apiece.[38]

The market for baby items has soared, despite the sluggish economy. In 1990 sales of products for children up to the age of two reached $2.45 billion, nearly twice what it was ten years earlier.[39] Brand-name baby products like Aprica strollers and Graco swings have come to dominate adult conversation the way Rolexes and BMWs did a decade ago. Three basic factors have fuelled the boom: the upturn in the birth rate; the fact that parents who delayed childbearing are more likely to have saved up for it; and the high percentage of firstborn children—close to 43 percent in 1986. First-time parents need to go out and buy all the essential baby products for homes that have never seen so much as a crib.

Critics began to describe babies themselves as the "ultimate accessory."[40] Women started confessing "baby lust"[41] or, as one writer in *Glamour* termed it: "SIBCS (Sudden Inexplicable Baby-Craving Syndrome), a virus that sporadically affects young women. The symptoms range from . . . a sudden interest in miniature furniture [to] an urge to dress the dog in dog clothes."[42] As novelist Ann Hood wrote in *The Washington Post,* "All of society is like a giant voice whispering, 'Babies, babies, babies.' "[43]

Propelled by the demographic and economic shifts, the change in attitude toward children seems to have been quite abrupt. About 60 percent of the "clock watchers," career women hoping to have children, interviewed in the mid-eighties for *The Biological Clock: Balancing Marriage, Motherhood, and Career,* said that they had had nearly a complete turnaround on the question of having children within just the last few years.[44] These women had postponed having children, believing that they needed to take care of themselves before bringing anyone else into the world. By this time many felt secure in their independence and were now in a position to take on the responsibilities of having a child.

Despite their ambivalence, women today feel freer to express an interest in having children now that they're back in style. "I used to say that I don't need a man and I don't need to have a child to be happy," says Jenny, thirty-six, who recently had her second baby. "I knew I didn't mean it, but that was just the thing to say in the seventies and early eighties." In *New York* magazine, a mother confessed: "My daughter was the single most important, most wonderful thing in my life, but for years I was ashamed to mention anything to friends because enjoying motherhood was the deepest, darkest secret of the seventies."[45]

So now the popular media's version of the typical woman was not only husband-crazy (in the wake of the marriage study) but *baby*-crazy. Men were put on the alert. This has created additional tensions between men and women. "Men say, 'Uh-oh, she's thirty-five. She'll want a baby. Stay away,' " says Ellie, a film editor. "One man told me he usually tried to date younger women because he didn't want to be rushed into a decision to have children. Now to some extent I can understand not wanting to be pushed into parenthood because of someone else's biological needs, but it does hurt. My so-called handicap—my age—is seen before my assets. It's a pretty shallow way of approaching a relationship."

A growing number of women are bypassing this scenario completely by having children on their own. Hollywood stars like Farrah Fawcett, Amy Irving, and Jessica Lange brought glamour to single motherhood.[46] Of course, most go-it-alone mothers do not have the vast funding celebrity mothers enjoy, but many do it anyway. Two in five single women told *Working Woman* they were considering single parenthood. Of the mothers surveyed, 20 percent had their children without being married.[47] Many unmarried women say they've set their own deadlines, that if they haven't met or married a potential father by the time they reach thirty-five (or thirty-six, or thirty-eight), they'll ask a willing male friend to help out or visit a sperm bank. In an article in *GQ*, one man, clearly gloating over his sperm's high market value, described how several female acquaintances had requested that he father their child.[48]

In the 1990s variation on the standard fiction formula, romance novels now feature women who get pregnant and are set on having the babies on their own (although in this genre, the men beg them to get married anyway).[49] On popular television shows like "Murphy Brown," "Designing Women," and "Cheers," key single characters have gotten pregnant or have sought to. As *New York Times* critic Caryn James put it, "It is just four weeks into the new television season, and already you can't tell the pregnancies, the false alarms and the in vitro fertilizations without a score card." She concludes that today, the drama surrounding pregnancy offers the same ratings boost that weddings used to.[50]

In a clear statement of how pressures have shifted, while Diane English, Murphy Brown's creator and executive producer, was comfortable enough with the lead character becoming a single mother, she felt that an abortion would have prompted such protest "it would have been lights out." In the early seventies, the title character of the comedy "Maude" did make that choice. Maude was married, but, says Kathryn Montgomery, author of *Target: Prime Time: Advocacy Groups and the Struggle Over Entertainment Television,* "twenty years ago, having a baby out of wedlock would have been taboo."[51]

Advertising, too, has changed with the times. In the brief business-is-beautiful moment of the eighties, a growing number of ads featuring women took place in the boardroom.[52] Today, while many ad-land females are professionals, the emphasis is less on what they do than whom they serve. The upscale, high-priced, outdo-yourself pitch has gone the way of 1980s prosperity. The family, which, though unstable, is at least seen as more stable than the economy, has come center again. As an ad for the 1991 Geo Prizm, which shows a mother holding a baby next to a sleek new car, puts it: "In a Disposable World, Some Things Are Made To Last."

One company whose ad strategy documents this change in focus is Calvin Klein Cosmetics. In the mid-eighties the company brought out a perfume called Obsession and used ads startling in their level of sexual innuendo. A few years later a fragrance called Eternity was introduced. Eternity's ads feature warm, soft-focus shots of women and men with babies. Calvin Klein explained that his new product "reflects a less selfish world than that of 1985," the year of Obsession's promotion.[53] Another fragrance brand playing on the cozy, family feeling is Liz Claiborne's Realities. A 1991 print ad shows a couple smiling as their toddler is about to join his mother in the bath. The copy, set off on a full page, reads: "Reality Is the Best Fantasy of All." In ad parlance, "fantasy" usually implies erotic imagery, unattainable luxury, or exotic settings. The message here is that the nuclear family is better than all that.

Family life is now so appealing that even nonfamily types are joining in. In a trade ad for *Family Circle* that appeared in the *New York Times* in early 1992, a long-haired, tattooed man adorned with biker/hippie paraphernalia holds a small child, naked but for a strand of beads that matches Dad's. The copy says, "We were just driving along in the family bandwagon and SUDDENLY everyone else jumped on." The magazine's new logo is "Everything Comes Full Circle." The point seems to be that even those who appear nontraditional secretly crave family life and that we're "coming around" to the ideal of life with children embodied in the magazine.

But—as the bizarre outfits in this ad suggest, perhaps in spite of the intended message—we're not *really* going back to some golden age of the family. The economic and social changes of the last several decades are far too entrenched, too integral to how we see the world. Media images that attempt to restore a mythic vision of family reflect a culturewide anxiety about the family in light of those changes. But if anything, the recent trends—delayed marriage and childbearing, women seeking equality—are merely continuations of tendencies that have existed throughout the century. It was the fifties, with early childbearing and a retreat to domesticity, that represented the aberration.

The real American tradition appears not to be any particular domestic configuration but rather *worry* that the "family" is on the verge of collapse. (In *Embattled Paradise,* sociologist Arlene Skolnick shows how "the crisis of the family" has been a persistent theme throughout U.S. history.) The family, in its most basic sense as an intimate unit with strong emotional, and often genetic, ties, has actually proved quite resilient. In themselves, positive messages about childbearing and marriage are not problematic because this does reflect how many, if not most, people feel. It *is* troubling, however, when these positive images become attached to other issues—such as women's economic, sexual, and reproductive freedoms. There's still much reckoning to be done on the meaning of family in an unstable world, but the answer is not to blindly worship some seemingly more "simple" time.

Unfortunately, this is what appears to underscore some of these recent "back to the future" messages. As an example, there has been much talk recently about the "Victoriana" trend, marked by the success of *Victoria* magazine, Victoria's Secret lingerie, and hostessing virtuosi like Martha Stewart. While there's nothing terribly momentous about a liking for attractive desserts or pretty underwear (actually, about half of Victoria's Secret's sales are to men),[54] some have commented that this trend heralds a flight to domesticity. In Martha Stewart's words, "A lot of women are discovering that their jobs aren't so great. . . . They're wondering, 'Why do I have to go to work? I'd rather stay home and sew.' "[55]

Stewart, along with entertaining and decorating compatriots Alexandra Stoddard and Mary Emmerling, are typical among highly touted businesswomen: they're making lots of money, but on "feminine" terms. Think of other celebrated women entrepreneurs: Debbi Fields (cookies), Joan Barnes (started the Gymboree Corporation, which offers children's exercise classes and products), Ruth M. Wimmer (founder of Wimmer-Ferguson, Inc., maker of visually stimulating baby toys), and, from the movies, Diane Keaton's character in *Baby Boom,* who makes organic baby food.

Society still seems uncomfortable with women in traditional business roles. When Karen Valenstein, a first vice-president at E. F. Hutton, was profiled in *The New York Times Magazine* in 1985, readers were appalled by this seemingly "cutthroat" career woman who was a mother in her "spare time." The piece caused such a stir that negative references to Valenstein appeared in *Newsweek, The Wall Street Journal,* and the New York *Daily News.* Why the fuss? According to Ellen Hopkins, writing in *Working Woman,* "the reason seems tied to the central, anxiety-provoking question the article posed: What price success for a woman? Feminism and the eighties work ethic somehow came to be linked in this article and personified by Karen Valenstein." So devastating was the response that Valenstein left the industry altogether. She now runs a clothing store in Jackson Hole, Wyoming. Whatever lesson she was supposed to learn, she apparently learned it.[56]

What price success indeed? No doubt because of such reports, some young women seem more haunted by "success" than by the inequities and prejudices of a system that puts added stress on women. In *Feminist Fatale,* Paula Kamen says that many young women considered older female colleagues to be "negative role models" because they make obvious the personal costs of success. "There are many women in this field in their late thirties who don't have a family, and their entire social life revolves around the job and people [on the job]. I think that's horrible," said one woman she interviewed.[57] This sounds suspiciously like the attitude Betty Friedan found among young women rushing to get married and have babies in the fifties. As one magazine editor then lamented to Friedan, "The girls we bring in now as college guest editors seem almost to pity us. Because we are career women, I suppose."[58]

The very term used to describe women who combine career and motherhood, "having it all," is in itself a confounding message (and an ironic one in that the woman who wrote the book *Having it All,* Helen Gurley Brown, is herself childless). It smacks of gluttony, something like wanting your cake and wanting another cake. And yet what man would be thought presumptuous for assuming he can work and be a father? The understanding is, of course, that he can. The implication is that women are demanding too much.

And with potentially dangerous results, women are constantly reminded. On the heels of the single-woman panic and the infertility panic, now comes the day-care panic. While media horror stories (with headlines like " 'Mommy Don't Leave Me Here!' The Day Care Parents Don't See"[59]) abounded in the eighties, the anxieties coalesced in the 1992 movie *The Hand That Rocks the Cradle,* in which a woman bent on revenge becomes a "nanny from hell."[60] The moral of the story: If you shirk your domestic duties, disaster will follow. Actually, most experts argue that serious abuse rarely occurs in child-care situations; the abusers are nearly always parents, relatives, and family friends.[61]

Even a magazine as astute as *New York Woman* ran a report on modern parents "raising their children by remote control. . . . It seems a terrible by-product of the gains so doggedly fought for through the seventies and eighties: that women's struggles for equality in the workplace, for recognition and success, have led to children—who, after all, were the other half of the 'having it all' equation—who are being deprived of both parents instead of the one they have traditionally learned to live without."[62]

Sure there are parents—and, yes, mothers—who don't give enough emotionally to their children, but linking this to women's liberation is not quite the point. What about wealthy mothers of other eras who turned their infants over to governesses? Or mothers who put their children second to tennis at the club? And what about men?

While we're trying to decipher the cultural dispatches, we're also getting strong signals from those in our personal lives. From our parents: "Before I got job encouragement. Now that I have a child I get the reverse—stay at home," says Laura. From our doctors: One woman's doctor told her, "You're over thirty, you're married, what are you waiting to have babies for?"

And certainly from our workplaces: "Every woman in my office who has become pregnant has left," observes Kelly, a twenty-eight-year-old product manager. "The men I work with all have families with wives who stay at home, but if you're a woman and you get pregnant, you have to leave. It's not said in so many words, but it's understood that there should be nothing important going on in your life outside of work. The secretaries can have children and a job, but not 'us'." Three months pregnant, Debbi, thirty, a medical resident, is afraid to tell anyone at work. "Someone else was just on leave, and the resentment was terrible," she explains. "We're all overworked enough. If I need to take time off, someone else will have to fill in. No one's going to be thrilled for me."

With a successful merger of home and career possible in theory but not always so simple in fact, we're understandably anxious about attempting the mix ourselves. As a result, we may feel a sense of urgency (hence the marriage and infertility scares), or we may deny the dilemmas until we can put them off no longer. One reason conflicts about motherhood hit women so hard is that they seem to have snuck up silently on us. We thought these issues had been worked out. Our launch into professional life had been, comparatively speaking, smooth; our relationships with men were based more on a peer model than ever before; we didn't have to fight for sexual freedom (at least not yet); why shouldn't our foray into motherhood proceed with similar ease?

"There's a common belief among young women that the problem is solved, that there have been provisions made for them, and that their plans are workable," says Carol Nadelson, M.D., professor of psychiatry at Tufts University. "All around them, in college, in the home, in their jobs, the idea has been reinforced that you can do what you want, that you can control your life. A lot of women have simply put off the decision to have children because they think that time will minimize the conflicts, but rather than eliminate them, it merely postpones them."

We need to come up with a definition appropriate to our lives, our expectations, our experience. Instead, we have let our roles be defined for us by happenstance. The messages aimed at women continue to shift back and forth, with each progressive statement matched by a regressive one. With our own ambivalence so entrenched, we may forget to read between the lines. Until we can articulate what motherhood means for our generation, and get that message out, we will continue to live with the disconcerting sense that our lives and our feelings are not fully our own.

Chapter 2

THE MATERNAL LEGACY

As long as people have been conscious of gender, the role of "mother" has been contested. One problem inherent in defining the role is that motherhood is something no one can be objective about. Every one of us has been mothered ourselves, so our vision of motherhood cannot help but be affected by our own experiences, disappointments, and fantasies. Consciously or otherwise, we each have a stake in seeing motherhood in a certain way.

In *The Second Sex,* Simone de Beauvoir contends that woman's place in the world derives from the fact that she is the Other: ". . . humanity is male and man defines woman not in herself but as relative to him."[1] As for the mother, this expression of duality—this separateness—that de Beauvoir describes, is taken one step further. The maternal figure is "other" not merely to men but to all human beings. Our awareness of self begins as we distinguish our body from hers. Our earliest rages, fears, and joys arise in response to her providing or withholding. Mother, what she was or what she was imagined to be, continues to be a reference point, even when the vision that endures bears little likeness to the actual woman who assumed the role. Just as the individual projects his needs and ideals on his own mother, society does the same thing on a massive scale: imbuing the *institution* of motherhood with a series of attributes that keeps the prevailing culture feeling safe, building an ideal that *nurtures* the status quo and those who sustain it—much like mothering itself.

Which leaves us with some rather odd definitions of motherhood, that, given human nature, are improbable if not nonsensical. The essential paradox is that while we accept the fallibility of the individual, we expect one half of the human race, by dint of its reproductive capacity, to be beyond reproach. But since mother is "other," we can make such a demand. Because so many ideas surrounding motherhood are born of fantasy and need, there are plenty of contradictions within the conventional view: Maternal behavior is assumed to be inborn, so that any woman is thought able to mother, yet "bad mothering" has been blamed for a host of societal ills (everything from homosexuality to delinquency to overeating); in her own life a woman may have limited power, but as a mother we assign her strength; on an individual level, mother is taken for granted or minimized, while in the popular rhetoric she is glorified.

In the same way that mother recalls to the individual a simpler, more perfect time—that period of being consummately cared for—to society she represents an ideal past. As counterpoint to all that ails civilization, she is its antidote. Images of perfect motherhood stick because that's what people need to see. In a society frightened by its own darkness, mother is light. (In movies the hardened criminal weeps at the mention of his dear mother.) In an era dizzied by the rapidity of its own changes, mother is stability, a constant. When all around us are driven by self-interest, mother is altruistic. In a period of numbing alienation, mother is familiarity, home.

These views of motherhood so pervade our culture that we absorb them without demur. Mother as "the perfect mother" has been indelibly cast on the American stage. We've grown up watching commercials in which mothers couldn't clean enough, bake enough, buy enough for their children. We've been treated to cloying depictions of maternal love and wisdom in sit-coms, books, and movies. What we're offered is caricature, yet, because it's so pervasive, we accept it as fact.

Even with such images piled high in our memory—like holiday snapshots, more emblematic than actual—those of us grappling with motherhood in the 1990s have no choice but to reject them. We can't believe that all roads lead to and end at maternity, that the richness of our present lives peters out into a sluggish, static contentment once a child lands in our arms. In the past, as literary depictions would have us believe, women may have moved fairly directly from girlhood to motherhood, with the phase in between mostly dominated by courtship. We've had active lives as women, challenging, full lives independent of the families we were raised in and the families we will form. We can't believe that those sides of ourselves that we've developed and enjoyed are simply going to be crushed by the juggernaut that is motherhood. We won't let that happen.

Despite a substantial and sustained questioning of the motherhood ideal, that ideal is rapidly being resurrected. Our ambivalence stems from the fact that we identify with both the ideal *and* with its critique. The question is: How can our vision of what we want for our lives be integrated with this long-lived, inviolable picture of motherhood? The two don't mesh very well, or at least not easily. At this point they can only coexist, run parallel to each other, leaving today's women scrambling to follow two separate paths: one is the reality we know, and the other is some blend of memory, fantasy, and propaganda. Women today are caught in a bind. We're sufficiently aware of our needs to know that we can't spend our lives in a house waiting for the next coo or cry. But because of the ideas we've been fed, we have to live with the idea that not doing so will make us bad mothers.

If we believe, as most of us do, that a total monopoly of a woman's time, energy, and thought is unduly demanding, what is an appropriate place for motherhood in a woman's life? Is motherhood a state of being that can exist contemporaneously with other aspects of ourselves, or does it by definition subsume everything else that we are? Is motherhood our liberation, allowing us to experience our power as women in what could be its most ascendant, elemental form? Or is it our oppression? To the extent that it does restrain us, is it physiology or culture that holds sway?

This latter question—of biological or cultural determinism—has been endlessly debated. In order to assess whether maternal behavior is intrinsic to femaleness, hormones have been assayed, animals have been observed, and various theories of human motivation have been analyzed and reanalyzed. I'm not going to go into such research except to say that, for the most part, the precise role of biology is still open to question. Nor do I think that it's an all-or-nothing matter, that at any suggestion of biologically induced conduct we can just go home and forget the cultural implications. Personally, I do believe there are essential differences between the sexes and that much of this difference relates to women's ability to mother. But I also think it's at least as important to examine the cultural factors, for the culture dictates how these differences (if you choose to view them as such) are interpreted. And neither biology nor psychology alone can situate motherhood within the complexities of modern societal and family life.

The common depiction of motherhood that we recognize as the ideal is grounded in three basic myths. Looking at the individual psyche, for a moment, this standard may well have evolved in response to what all who have been mothered want to believe; it seems that our collective childhood fantasy has been created in the form of the ideal mother. We all began our lives in a perfectly solipsistic state: the world revolved around us, it *existed* for us, particularly our mothers, who were the part of the world that we knew best. Therefore, we've needed to accept the three myths: the idea of maternal self-sacrifice (when young, we *expected* those sacrifices; later on, we've wanted to believe they were appropriate so we won't feel guilty for having forced them upon our mothers); the belief in an innate, unvarying maternal instinct (wasn't our mothers' purpose in life to give birth to and care for us?); and the notion of maternal fulfillment (isn't creating *us* enough for one mortal human to achieve in life?). Similarly, we've needed to see mother as all-good and all-knowing (if she's not, who is?) and asexual (any sexual needs would detract from *our* specialness in her life).

But these myths speak to more than the personal (which is itself informed by culture); they have political implications as well. The mothering themes crop up again and again, particularly in periods when society perceives a need to affirm woman's role as mother. The ideas may be perpetrated by religious sentiment (in the medieval era), by medical pronouncements (in the Victorian age), by political rhetoric (around the turn of the century), or by science (in the twentieth century).

In the late 1940s and '50s, maternal self-sacrifice was interpreted so broadly as to mean maternal *masochism.* Women were told that they needed to give up their pleasures and ambitions for the good of their children—*and* for themselves. It was woman's *appropriate state* to sacrifice, the argument ran, and this *desire* to sacrifice that compelled her toward motherhood. "Natural childbirth," as popularized by British obstetrician Dr. Grantly Dick-Read in *Childbirth Without Fear,* became a national passion around this time. A "real" woman, Read's interpreters concluded, would not shirk from pain during labor. Because the discomfort would be "deeply meaningful" to her, she would want to be sure not to miss out on it.[2]

By this point in time, sexuality was acknowledged to be an important aspect of a woman's self-expression, but what was apparently to be expressed was self-abasement: According to psychoanalyst Helene Deutsch, sexual intercourse involved "being masochistically subjugated by the penis." Her contemporary Marie Bonaparte noted that woman's compliant disposition "impels her to welcome and to value some measure of brutality on the man's part."[3]

If a midcentury woman insisted on pursuing goals other than motherhood, then she had revealed herself to be suffering from a "masculinity complex" and was thus "unwomanly," not fit to mother at all. In *Modern Woman: The Lost Sex,* a pseudopsychoanalytic book that created quite a stir in the late 1940s, Ferdinand Lundberg and Marynia Farnham, M.D., talk of the "dangers" visited upon women in the work force:

> *Work that entices women out of their homes and provides them with prestige only at the price of feminine relinquishment, involves a response to masculine strivings. The more importance outside work assumes, the more are the masculine components of the woman's nature enhanced and encouraged. In her home and in her relationship to her children, it is imperative that these strivings be at a minimum and that her femininity be available both for her own satisfaction and for the satisfaction of her children and husband.*[4]

As Helene Deutsch put it: "In my opinion the highest stage of maternal love, motherliness, is achieved only when all masculine wishes [meaning ambition, aggression, etc.] have been given up or sublimated into other goals."[5]

During this time the idea of the maternal instinct was promoted to convince women of the *inevitability* of taking on the mother role. Don't even think about going another route, the message held, this is the only right one for you. Writing in the early fifties, Therese Benedek, M.D., claimed that maternal behavior was rooted in woman's hormonal chemistry. "Normal motherliness is the result of specific biologic and psychic maturation," she wrote. Her view that this motherliness necessitated a certain degree of psychological "regression" on the woman's part, especially during the "crises" of pregnancy and menstruation, led her to assert that reverting to a state of emotional immaturity is "normal" for reproductively functioning women.[6]

In the postwar years, Margaret Mead's studies in cultural anthropology were widely read. As Betty Friedan points out in *The Feminine*

Mystique, Mead's observations on culture and personality could have had a liberating effect on women in that they revealed the variety of human sexual expression and the blurring of gender roles in many societies. But because of the ethos of the period and Mead's inability to escape it herself, the work came to affirm the *differences* between the sexes. Friedan quotes from *Male and Female* (1955):

> *In Bali, little girls between two and three walk much of the time with purposely thrust-out little bellies, and the older women tap them playfully as they pass. "Pregnant," they tease. So the little girl learns that although the signs of her membership in her own sex are slight, her breasts mere tiny buttons no bigger than her brother's, her genitals a simple inconspicuous fold, some day she will be pregnant, some day she will have a baby, and having a baby is, on the whole, one of the most exciting and conspicuous achievements that can be presented to the eyes of small children in these simple worlds, in some of which the largest buildings are only fifteen feet high, the largest boat some twenty feet long. Furthermore, the little girl learns that she will have a baby not because she is strong or energetic or initiating, not because she works and struggles and tries, and in the end succeeds, but simply because she is a girl and not a boy, and girls turn into women, and in the end—if they protect their femininity—have babies.*[7]

"Natural," native women, geared toward mothering, were celebrated. Women who felt otherwise, then, could only be denying their essential female function.

Margaret Mead's work was also applied to support the third maternal myth: that mothering fulfills a woman completely as nothing else can. To proffer women a satisfying role, Mead said, "it is only necessary that they be permitted by the given social arrangements to fulfill their biological role, to attain this sense of irreversible achievement. If women are to be restless and questing, even in the face of childbearing, they must be made so through education."[8]

Such "restlessness and questing," the experts had already made clear, would occur only among women suffering from "masculinized" ambitions. Women true to their sex would be content to revel in the fruits of their maternity. To a "feminine" mother, the authors of *Modern Woman* contend, "Having children is . . . the most natural thing possible, and it would never occur to her to have any doubts about it. When she hears someone question the advisability of having children she is bewildered unless she is told of some trenchant medical reason. Then she feels sorry for the woman deprived. If a woman does not have children, she asks ingenuously, what is everything all about for her?"[9] Some theorists of the period went so far as to say that bearing and breast-feeding a child provided sexual gratification as well, so totally did motherhood meet a woman's needs (a reassuring thought in an era reluctant to accept the "undomestic" aspects of women's sexuality).

From the vantage point of postwar America, it was important to uphold this motherhood ideology; there was a strong societal need at the time to keep women in the home. To ensure that women be willing to play along, it was important for them to believe that full-time motherhood was the task they were best equipped for and that it would complete their lives. One force driving this need was the patriotic fervor that led to pronatalist views. Feeling good about America meant feeling good about the American family which, in turn, meant feeling good about Motherhood (with a capital M). Another factor was the glut on the nation's labor market generated by the returning GIs. Women had joined the work force en masse during the war effort, and unless they made room for the men, the nation would have a staggering unemployment problem on its hands. Women had to be given the message that since the crisis had abated, they could best serve their country from the home front.

Pre- and postrevolutionary France serves as another example of how culture mediates the meaning of motherhood in women's lives. In 1980 Elisabeth Badinter, a French philosopher, published *Mother Love: Myth and Reality* (*L'Amour en Plus* in French), a historical inquiry that directly contested the validity of those lingering motherhood myths.

First, Badinter set out to clear up misconceptions about the past. While we in the twentieth century have been beset by a nostalgic wistfulness for the idyllic, familial ties of yore, studies of the past reveal domestic life to have been less than sublime. Until the eighteenth century and the attendant emergence of the middle class, Badinter stresses, the close-knit, nuclear family marked by a special, intimate bond between mother and children did not exist. As Philippe Ariès had originally pointed out in *Centuries of Childhood,* childhood as a distinctive phase of life was simply unheard of. Rather than being viewed as a crucial stage of development, childhood was seen as a "fallen" state; instead of being given sustained, focused attention, children were treated as miniature adults as soon as they could dress the part.

According to Badinter, the sixteenth-century view was that any expression of maternal tenderness spoiled the child and brought out his baser instincts. "Mothers damn their children when they nurse them voluptuously," wrote a Spanish preacher of the period, suggesting that women were thinking more of their own pleasures than their children's well-being when they "indulged" their offspring with affection. In the seventeenth century it became common for women of the bourgeoisie to send their infants out to wet nurses, and in the early eighteenth century women of all classes were doing whatever they could to shun breast-feeding themselves. Nursing was thought to mar the shape of the breast and soften the nipples, a deterrent in itself. And since nursing was so looked down upon, any woman caught in the act would risk a drop in status. It was also believed that a man's sperm would spoil the milk, meaning that any women who nursed would have to be celibate for the duration. Beyond that, social and cultural opportunities newly available to women made many eager to forego their domestic tasks, particularly those that interfered with their freedom to come and go as they pleased.

Badinter offers numerous examples of what she terms an "absence of love" among mothers in prerevolutionary France. The death of an infant or small child was accepted as an everyday occurrence. Frequently, the parents wouldn't even attend the funeral of a departed child. It was considered "unfashionable" to "seem to love one's children too much" and willingly devote valuable time to their care or education. When a mother did exhibit any affection, it was generally reserved for her eldest son, the heir upon whom she might later depend.

Such less-than-loving tendencies raise important questions about the twentieth-century vision of motherhood marked by the three maternal myths. If a woman's "love" for her children were natural, as later thinkers would contend, might she not have been tempted to love them all, instead of solely the one who might represent economic security? If women had an innate proclivity for self-sacrifice as mothers, why were so many unwilling to compromise their social and romantic lives for the good of their children? If women derived total fulfillment from mothering, why, as soon as broader options were presented to them, were they so anxious to shrug off their maternal responsibilities? Rewards for French women of the time were greater when they lived outside the bounds of our cherished myths, and accordingly, those who could sought to do so.

An abrupt turnaround in the maternal role occurred late in the eighteenth century. Mothers suddenly became important *as mothers*. "Mother love" was no longer viewed as a vestige of some uncivilized age but as a *force* to be harnessed for the common good. Jean Jacques Rousseau, who advocated a return to nature and rural values, articulated his vision of the significance of motherhood to society in his influential work *Emile:* "[M]en's earliest education is in the hands of women, as is their training in manners and morals. . . . Therefore to care for them as children and then when grown, to counsel them, to console them . . . such have always been the duties of women."[10] Because mothers held the future, opinion now affirmed, they must be supported in their role. Publications now encouraged and idealized maternal affection and sacrifice. In a marked switch, breast-feeding, previously seen as a nuisance and a potential threat to feminine beauty, became a *requirement* of any mother of moral worth: any who failed to nurse were allowing their milk to "dry up," which could result in illness or even death to the child.[11]

Obviously, Badinter argues, this shift did not come about because the nature of women or children had changed in the course of a few decades. In part, the impetus for the shift was political. In the move from an elite to a popular government, experiences that cut across class lines—like motherhood—had to be given added weight. Sympathies now extended to the underdog as opposed to the elite, so previously condoned acts like abandoning children and shipping babies off to wet nurses were no longer acceptable. The nation needed more subjects to replace those killed in the fighting, so bearing children was now a "good." Concurrently, so-called natural behavior was valued anew as the ideal of the "noble savage," also promoted by Rousseau, took hold.

But perhaps most important, the "new mother" standard appealed to the growing middle class. In Badinter's words, "Freer than many other women and unconsciously searching for an ideal, a reason for living, they were the first to be responsive to the arguments of the local authorities and doctors. They were the first to consider their children as their personal affair, as something through which their lives as women took on meaning."[12] As the emotional and spiritual anchor of the family, the middle-class mother assumed an elevated status, with her significance endorsed by public attitude.

The development of a universal maternal persona, which occurred in France and was later confirmed by Freudian theory and other ideologies in the United States, had mixed consequences, Badinter explains. On the one hand, it allowed women a certain level of respect and enabled them to find fulfillment and pleasure in their role as mothers. On the other, so strong was the pressure to be a certain kind of woman that those who didn't fit the mold were made to feel there was something "wrong" with them.

From a societal point of view, the beauty of the standard definition of mother is that it completely absolves the culture from having to take any measures to enhance women's lives. Women's lives are intact as is; motherhood is woman's fulfillment, her destiny. Once she has achieved motherhood, a woman's strivings are over. If there's anything lacking in her own life, the joy she derives from her child should more than make up for it. As Barbara Ehrenreich and Deirdre English observe in *For Her Own Good: 150 Years of the Experts' Advice to Women,* society's varying investment in the institution of motherhood has been part of an ongoing effort to resolve "The Woman Question," the dilemma of what to do with woman as the Industrial Revolution (and later the postindustrial era) transformed life as it was known.

As part of the tremendous changes of the nineteenth century, the home lost its value as a site of production: goods were now produced—faster, in greater quantities, and in a more uniform fashion—in the new factories and mills in the towns. Women's traditional contributions to family life, economic and productive, were no longer needed. At the same time, in part because the decline of the self-sufficient household precluded the need for large families, the number of children per home plummeted, and those that did arrive, rather than being put to work at an early age, remained dependent on the family for a longer period of time. With fewer children, each *individual* child was given greater importance and emotional weight. With the family's basic subsistence needs (food, clothing, etc.) increasingly supplied *outside* of the home (women no longer had to churn their own butter, weave their own cloth, etc.), the mother was assigned the crucial role of ensuring her children's moral and intellectual development. Women's "feminine" attributes were accorded special significance as they related to this role. Rather than the skillful, often physical tasks a woman had previously engaged in, childbearing and child rearing reflected her sacred calling. Woman Question solved.

The picture of the Victorian mother as a saintly, pristine creature also arose largely as a counterpoint to the vision of men of the period. To that extent, this image *served* the needs of men. Working for hire, capitalism, and urban life—all part of the new economic equation that prevailed as men left the home to seek wage opportunities—threatened the status quo. The stuff of daily life was split in two: there was the public sphere, where men operated, and the private sphere, tended by women. In this period, men's lives changed drastically while women's lives remained relatively stable. The industrial, urban world the men came to frequent was rife with temptations—commercial, recreational, and sexual. Man was citified, corrupted by commerce, tainted by the debased elements that lurked in urban alleyways. Woman was the link to a simpler, guileless past. To sustain the image of the family and maintain the integrity of men, women had to take up the slack. Society needed to view women as innocent and pure to stave off the assault on morality that industrial change had brought.

When *women's* lives showed stirrings of change, fears about the demise of culture again echoed through society. Around the turn of the century, for example, it became apparent that the growing numbers of women graduating from institutes of higher learning were *not* content to close their books and go home. The fertility rate of American-born, white women dropped throughout the nineteenth century, with the sharpest fall among those with a college education. This was an outrage, the guardians of American culture concluded. Above and beyond shaking up accepted middle-class norms, higher education for women was threatening the very *race*.

What followed were paeans to the glories of motherhood along with a flurry of diatribes against higher education for women. G. Stanley Hall, a prominent psychologist of the era, warned that book learning would ruin women for motherhood, leaving them "functionally castrated."[13] Since it was deemed impossible for a woman's mental and reproductive faculties to perform in tandem, women essentially had to make a choice. But with motherhood proclaimed to be woman's highest calling, there wasn't really much of a choice at all. President Theodore Roosevelt pronounced motherhood an obligation comparable to a soldier's duty and talked of bearing children as the greatest thing a woman could do.[14] According to Ellen Key, the Swedish author of the 1909 book *The Century of the Child,* "The mother is the most precious possession of the nation, so precious that society advances its own highest well-being when it protects the functions of the mother."[15] Women who failed to procreate were made to feel like criminals, key agents in civilization's demise. In President Roosevelt's words, "If Americans of the old stock lead lives of celibate selfishness . . . or if the married are afflicted by that base fear of living which, whether for the sake of themselves or of their children, forbids them to have more than one or two children, disaster awaits the nation."[16]

The tragic corollary to this recurrent view of motherhood is that women often unwittingly intensified their own oppression within the role by *perpetuating* the ideal themselves. With limited opportunities available to women, motherhood *did* frequently represent the most rewarding and enjoyable work they could look forward to. By taking pains to bolster mothers' status, and thus enhance their own standing, such women may have contributed to the scarcity of their beyond-the-home options. Similarly, movements that had their impetus in progressive ideals meant to promote women's choice and power often wound up in a stance that merely sustained the status quo.

The birth control movement of the late nineteenth and early twentieth centuries is a clear instance of this. In many regards, the quest was a radical one: the activists' case rested on the assumption that women's sexuality was significant in itself. The chief demand was to grant women control over their fertility. In the earlier period, this would be attained through the right to refuse unwanted sex; in the later period, it would be attained through contraception and sex education. Margaret Sanger, the leader of the birth control movement in the early 1900s who was sentenced to jail for running a birth control clinic, believed that women should be free to enjoy sex without being forced to endure repeated pregnancies. She argued that women of all classes feared unwanted pregnancies and thus feared sex itself.

Largely because it represented such a departure from prevailing views of sexuality and thus needed some legitimacy, birth control advocates increasingly sought affiliation with the eugenics movement. This school of thought, prevalent throughout the period, advocated the improvement of human society through selective heredity. In the earliest phase of this alliance, eugenic theory was employed in defense of women's rights. The claim was that children conceived against a woman's will would be flawed physically or in character and that the "highest quality" offspring would be born when their mothers chose to have them. As time went on, Linda Gordon points out in *Woman's Body, Woman's Right,* the ideas were used less to press for women's independence and reproductive choice than to affirm women's role as *breeders.* As Gordon says, "Every eugenic argument was in the long run more effective in the hands of antifeminists than of feminists" because many of the women opting *not* to have children were the most accomplished and educated—in other words, those with potentially the "best" genetic material.[17] The fear was that rather than "improving" the race, which was the eugenists' intended goal, birth control threatened to dilute it.

Women's expanded domestic role in the early twentieth century is another example of how a vision meant to *benefit* women ultimately limited their power. With women increasingly isolated in the home with less and less productive work (i.e., wage-earning work, like sewing, laundering, or keeping boarders) to do there, the resolution for their plight was simple: redefine child rearing as work. Raising children became a full-fledged career, backed by new scientific "disciplines" like psychology and child study and bolstered by an assembly of "experts." Books and pamphlets on child care were churned out; edition upon edition were sold. In everything from industry to medicine to hygiene, Americans had been putting a greater stake in science. Now it was decided that science held the secrets to optimal mothering technique, and only the professionals could translate this for the nation's mothers.

The new "scientific motherhood" had advantages for women in that it lent a new prestige to and justification for their work. It also, no doubt, gave some sense of assurance to women who lived many miles, if not a continent, away from their own mothers and grandmothers and lacked support. But, as Susan Strasser observes in *Never Done: A History of American Housework,* this trend separated mothers further from men and women who earned wages by binding them to full-time, nonpaying tasks. (This at a time when mothers were losing traditional ties to one another, as sewing circles, washday meetings, and midwife deliveries disappeared with changing technology and customs.) It also *eroded* women's expertise in an area where they had some autonomy. Women were now dependent on the experts to tell them what to do and on the products they were told to buy.

Possibly another more recent, and more contentious, example of campaigns that seem on the surface to affirm women's power but ultimately weaken it, is the current antiabortion movement. As Kristen Luker explains in *Abortion and the Politics of Motherhood,* although the embryo appears to be the central issue, "the abortion debate is actually about the meanings of *women's* lives."[18] After extensive interviews with activists in both the prolife and prochoice camps, she found that prolife women felt that "choice" undermined the integrity of motherhood, thus posing a direct threat to the meaning of their lives. By trying to preserve the inviolability of motherhood—which in their view means empowering women—the prolife movement in fact serves to *dis*empower women as a whole by urging a retraction of our reproductive rights.

Much of this century's maternal dogma is based on the theories of Sigmund Freud. As with the movements discussed above, early psychoanalytic thinking had contradictory, perhaps unintentional, results. Simplifying vastly, one might say Freud's theoretical work often reduced female behavior to manifestations of penis envy. The desire to have a child, in his view, derives from the female's distress at having been born without a penis. Getting pregnant and producing a child, then, satisfies her need for a penis substitute (if the child is a boy, then the quest is, literally, complete. If it's a girl, the mother can only pass along her sorrow about the lack of a male organ to the next generation.) Freud also believed that the wish to bear children could arise from a woman's early oedipal attachment to her father, which took the form of wanting to have babies by him.

It's important to remember that as brilliant and iconoclastic as he was, Freud was himself the product of a rigid, paternalistic society in which women were restricted to the role of obliging, obsequious hausfrau. The repression and thwarted aggression he saw in women, and which he thought posed a psychic danger to their children, were undoubtedly the product of this oppressive society. But such observations, based exclusively on late-Victorian, bourgeois culture, could not apply so neatly to another time and place. Freud's viewpoint was also a reflection of his own unique circumstances. Little Sigmund was the first and favored child of a young, beautiful, possibly flirtatious mother and a much older, distant, ultimately disappointing father. The tensions that were inherent in such a dynamic, and that laid the groundwork for Freud's major works, might have represented an exaggerated form of the complexes he insisted defined all families.

Freud was also approaching family relations from the viewpoint of a man. And in the period in which he was raised, women were regarded as the inferiors of men. To think otherwise would have meant overturning the beliefs of an entire culture. So Freud's assumptions about mothers cannot be separated from the ideas he *wanted* to hold onto as a male. The entire construct of penis envy, for example, is clearly a male fantasy. It took feminists to point out that, Freud notwithstanding, women are not all that broken up over their lack of a penis. It's the cultural and familial advantages the penis represents, not the organ itself, that women feel deprived of. Freud's views also suggest a discomfort with women's actual power. Deciding that women are drawn to motherhood because they cannot be men is, from the male point of view, far more comforting than regarding the act of childbirth as creative and empowering in its own right.

The problem with Freud's theories was not so much what he said about women (and perhaps the main point he had hoped to stress was that woman's essential nature had continued to elude his intellectual grasp), but how his ideas were interpreted in this country. Freud's works, which were and still are revolutionary, were in many ways a critique of society. They were *read,* however, as a critique of the *individual.* As Betty Friedan has pointed out, Freud was speaking *theoretically,* but he was often taken *literally.* With "penis envy" accepted as the basic female scenario, all female behavior was judged accordingly. (The idea of women's masochism grew directly out of this. If a woman exhibited any professional or intellectual drive, she was betraying her wish to be a man and was not fully accepting her femininity.) Also, with the mother's role in a child's early sexual—and thus personal—development established, any "problem" on the child's part could be directly attributed to the mother.

In the middle of the century a rash of mother blaming was unleashed when Freud's influence in this country reached its height. Shyness, failure, general unhappiness, or more severe disorders like autism, schizophrenia, and manic-depression (the latter three known today to have an organic element) were all traced to the miserable, malevolent mother, consciously or unconsciously taking out her frustrations on her child. Domineering or passive, overindulgent or rejecting, anything a woman was or wasn't, did or didn't do, placed her in the category of "bad" mothers. Part of Freud's legacy was that he popularized the language of pathology. Anyone who could read and talk became an amateur psychologist, and the easiest diagnosis to make was "It's all your mother's fault." And women, who truly did want the best for their children, couldn't help but take this endless censuring to heart.

In "Mothers: Tired of Taking the Rap," which appeared in *The New York Times Magazine* in 1990, Janna Malamud Smith, a clinical social worker and mother, describes how firmly ingrained this notion of mother bashing remains. She recalls how a child psychopathology professor informed a class that "Infant colic . . . develops when mothers are having problems with their maternal role." When problems arose, the experts would immediately set out to determine what type of mother was at fault. In a particularly chilling example of such thinking, described in Susan Brownmiller's *Against Our Will: Men, Women and Rape,* a committee of psychiatrists commissioned to help track down the Boston Strangler came to the conclusion that the fugitive killer was probably "consumed by raging hatred for his sweet, orderly, neat, compulsive, seductive, punitive, overwhelming mother." When the criminal was caught, it unfolded that his *mother* might have had little to do with his violent behavior, but that his cruel, drunken, wife-beating father undoubtedly did.[19]

The monolithic ideal of the perfect mother wrongs all mothers in that it denies their lack of power and resources in society and leaves them feeling guilty about their mothering behavior, regardless of intention or result, Smith contends. "I cannot remember ever working with a mother—wealthy, middle-class or poor—who did not have secret theories about how behaviors, or choices, or feelings of hers had deeply harmed her children." Mother was given so much power that she was ultimately rendered powerless. Women had become bound to their children by the enormity of their capacity to ruin them.

Articulating a meaning for motherhood has been a continuing challenge for the contemporary women's movement, especially as the task inevitably entails negotiating the stubborn myths. With the bursting out of feminism in the late sixties and seventies, it wasn't only blame women were tired of; the cultural mandate to mother needed a good airing out. Encouraged by new birth control options (namely the pill) and swept up in the momentum of the youth, civil rights, and feminist movements, more women were postponing or declining childbearing than ever before. There was, to many, an exuberance in the recognition that one didn't *have* to have children or be defined by one's childbearing status. The text most often cited as "representing" feminists' views of motherhood is Shulamith Firestone's 1970 book *The Dialectic of Sex.* The language is strong: The author calls for artificial means of reproduction, insisting that "pregnancy is the temporary deformation of the body of the individual for the sake of the species," and claims that "[t]he heart of woman's oppression is her childbearing and child rearing roles."[20]

Firestone's intention, however, was not to spurn motherhood per se, scholar Ann Snitow points out in a recent assessment of the feminist movement's approach to motherhood, but rather the patriarchal system that used motherhood to dominate women. Perhaps the best way to understand the period when feminists challenged motherhood outright, or ignored it altogether (the period of the "demon texts" like Firestone's, for which, says Snitow, "we have been apologizing ever since"), is to take into account how it paralleled the life cycle of the populous baby-boom generation. As young women were delaying childbearing and questioning motherhood in their own lives, they were scrutinizing the subject on a broader, societal level. When the group grew older and motherhood came to have a different meaning on a personal level, the content and tenor of feminists' analysis necessarily changed.[21]

By the late 1970s, the ideals of "equality" feminism (an attempt to minimize differences between men and women, or to term them irrelevant) were tempered by those of "difference" feminism. Many who became mothers found the intensity of the experience difficult to reconcile with the tenets of "equality." Perhaps by downplaying the uniqueness of women's experience, they were belittling women's unique power. Women's "difference" can be asserted, as long as women themselves control how those differences are defined.

Writers began to examine the emotional force of motherhood *(The Mother Knot)* and to situate the experience within social and psychological frameworks *(The Reproduction of Mothering, The Mermaid and the Minotaur).* Adrienne Rich wrote *Of Woman Born: Motherhood as Experience and Institution,* which explored the "power and powerlessness" of motherhood within the patriarchy through history, myth, literature, and personal experience. The book won the National Book Award in 1976.

To some extent, Rich's recast vision of motherhood grew out of the women's health movement, which had called into question the treatment of women by (often male) health professionals and the increased medicalization of childbirth. Just as women were reclaiming their bodies and declaring them healthful and beautiful, they were starting to reclaim *motherhood* and pronouncing it a significant, enriching part of a woman's life. Only by having control over our mothering experience can we attain equality and power in our feminine roles. As Adrienne Rich writes:

> *The repossession by women of our bodies will bring far more essential change to human society than the seizing of the means of production by workers. The female body has been both territory and machine,*

> *virgin wilderness to be exploited and assembly-line turning out life. We need to imagine a world in which every woman is the presiding genius of her own body. In such a world women will truly create new life, bringing forth not only children (if and as we choose) but the visions, and the thinking, necessary to sustain, console, and alter human existence—a new relationship to the universe.*[22]

Rich writes of an ideal of motherhood emerging. Even as she dignifies the perceptions and sensations of mothering, the shadow of maternal frustration, rage, and even violence—all stemming from woman's restricted role in what she terms "The Kingdom of the Fathers"—remains. Similarly, Dorothy Dinnerstein and Nancy Chodorow, in *The Mermaid and the Minotaur* and *The Reproduction of Mothering*, respectively, claim that our current, woman-alone form of mothering is ultimately destructive to those of us raised that way. Such mothering, they argue, merely perpetuates psychic imbalances in both the family and romantic relationships. As Nancy Chodorow explains, "When a mother's whole life and sense of self depends on rearing 'good' or 'successful' children, this must produce anxiety over performance and over-identification with children. . . . Such a situation, then, while producing femininity in girls, must necessarily also produce girls' resentment and conflict over acceptance of this femininity, and thus anxious and resentful behavior toward children in the next generation."[23]

These authors argue cogently for men's participation in child rearing. In like fashion, in *Maternal Thinking*, a philosophical exploration of motherhood (and its implications for child development and world peace), Sara Ruddick makes it clear from the start that when she talks about "mothers" she can just as easily be talking about men.

Such critics focus largely on the notion of maternal power and its lingering effects. If mothers are given complete responsibility for infants and children, they can only be perceived as all-powerful by those in their care. In an essay entitled "The Fantasy of the Perfect Mother," Nancy Chodorow and Susan Contratto state that the maternal myths support the individual's fantasy and lend justification to the *expectation* of perfection and subsequent disappointment that occurs when the mother fails to be perfect. As women, and as actual or potential mothers, we need, then, to separate our assessment of motherhood from the rage we still feel from being imperfectly (in other words, *humanly*) mothered. We need to distinguish our ideas of maternal responsibility (what woman today *doesn't* worry about inadvertently harming her child?) from the disappointments in life we still feel our own mothers are responsible for.

As weighty and relevant as such arguments are, some feminists have expressed concern that they can be interpreted as mother-blaming. There's also some doubt as to whether "inviting" men to participate in child rearing will have much effect as long as the social structure remains unchanged. Others question whether the focus on the joys of motherhood—and a reluctance to question their import—only plays into right-wing arguments and a resurgence of pronatalism in the culture, thus weakening rather than building the feminist agenda.

Motherhood presents some thorny problems for feminist thinkers: How can we rethink the institution of motherhood without seeming to attack mothers? How can we celebrate women's "difference" without allowing the ideology of difference to subordinate us and negate our rights (as has happened in the past)? How can we affirm the significance of motherhood while still trying to free women from the *obligation* to mother?

Certainly, none of this is easy to achieve in a society that insists on clinging to its myths of motherhood. The unfortunate truth is that any vision of motherhood that deviates from the standard is still considered a *failed* motherhood. Even if we don't believe that working or pursuing our own goals will deprive our children (and studies have borne out that it will not), we can't help but wonder: "What if everybody was right?"

One recent assessment of motherhood is Miriam M. Johnson's argument in *Strong Mothers, Weak Wives*. She sets out to reevaluate the modern assumption that women's mothering is an impediment to women which, by definition, puts us at a disadvantage. Rather than seeing mothering and marriage as part of a package, she analyzes each separately and concludes that it's the asymmetry in marital, rather than reproductive, roles that threatens women's status. Marriage in our society, she says, is "predicated upon inequality." This, of course, would not describe all marriages, but it does express the legal, economic, and cultural basis of marriage as an institution.

"Women become one thing when viewed as wives and quite another when viewed as mothers," Johnson writes. In viewing ourselves, she contends, the "difference" *we* see and celebrate relates to maternal thinking, the mothering aspect of ourselves. The "difference" society has projected on women, however, refers to women as wives, a way of seeing women that has then been extended to mothers.[24]

Perhaps in our own minds, the mother we're reluctant to be is the mother constrained by "wifehood," by the institutionalized subordination by men. The mother we aspire to be, then, represents maternal values unencumbered by the demands and dependencies inherent in the wife role. The restrictive motherhood myths, after all, served to affirm men's domination of women rather than the power of women who were to raise children. Paternity as the basis for patriarchy is driven not by motherhood but by men's "owning" the rights to children and the women who bear them. It's not that marriage per se is bad or that we shouldn't marry. But as we struggle with our own role definitions, and with the role definitions thrust upon us by others, it can help to clarify what our critique is directed toward.

Rather than acceding to the motherhood ideology, we need to continue to critique it. We must search for a balance that sacrifices neither our uniqueness nor our equality. We must make sure not to confuse circumstance and essence. While some ideas seem intractable, we're not in a stagnant situation; gender roles are more fluid than they've been in other eras, and the public is open to issues of parenting in general. There are opportunities for debate and we should seize them.

Chapter 3

THE BABY DIVIDE

One point of tension for women today is that while expectations for motherhood are great, so are our expectations for our lives *apart* from motherhood. Another is that while motherhood as presented to us has one set of meanings (celebrities photographed with their dimple-cheeked tots; couples reaching heights of intimacy by sharing the moment of childbirth), there's a contrasting vision that we know too well. The questioning of domestic roles in the sixties and seventies is too much a part of us. In many ways we've structured our lives to *oppose* those roles. We've been taught to fear becoming mothers.

The pressures that converge on the issue of motherhood can leave us with a great deal of ambivalence: We want to have children but are afraid to; we're not sure we want to be mothers but fear we'll regret it if we don't. Many of us hardly think about having children for much of our adult lives until, for whatever reason—a critical mass of our friends get pregnant, our partners express a desire for kids, we reevaluate what we want out of life—it becomes important to us. Even if we've always assumed we'd have children, we might say, "We'll do it differently." But this wish itself becomes a point of conflict when we realize there are few alternative role models and that society offers us scant room to maneuver.

In part because of the frustrations vented by those who were mothers in a less-than-liberated age, and in part because of the arrogance inherent in striking out on one's own, many of us came to view motherhood as a kind of psychic quicksand. Motherhood was not merely a variation on the kind of life we led, but its clear opposite. We became attached to our own autonomy, and motherhood came to represent the antithesis of what we had achieved. We thought in terms of polarities:

independence versus dependence; equality versus subjugation; sexuality versus asexuality; opportunity versus futility; fulfillment versus martyrdom; expressiveness versus silence.

Even when we do decide we want children, on some level we carry this split with us. No matter how committed we are, there's something we fear losing, something we fear we'll become. Having invested most of our lives in the nondomestic sphere, for many of us bearing a child calls to mind a sharp blow of the whistle and a swift about-face. It can be seen as the personal equivalent of a military coup, the overthrow of life and self as we know them.

We go back and forth on the issue. We move slowly. We erect *conditions* (when I turn thirty-two, when I start my residency); then tear them down and build new ones (when I turn thirty-three, when I *finish* my residency). We ask our partners to sway us either way, then get angry when they try to ("Easy for *you* to say . . ."). Weary of thinking about it, of trying to find The Correct Answer, we give our shoulders an uncharacteristic shrug: We'll deal with this later.

Or we tiptoe about it, approaching the issue in oblique, unthreatening ways. Aimee, a lawyer and at thirty-one the mother of a baby boy, recalls initial discussions on the subject with her husband: "We thought that maybe it was time to talk about thinking about the possibility of perhaps getting used to the idea of maybe starting a family." And often once we've slogged through the first round of maybes, what we find is yet another stranglehold of uncertainty.

We're comfortable with where we are now. We've worked hard to get here and we're not ready to give up our place so fast. We're nervous about letting a baby sabotage our ease with ourselves. When we regard our careers as a central part of our lives, chances are those we surround ourselves with have like priorities. Our bonds with others—our friends, our men—are based on our commonalities: our ambitions, our activities, our lifestyles. Any decision that stands to disrupt those ties threatens to deprive us of our base of security.

Often our experience leads us not to explore our ambivalence but to disregard it. "All of our support is for the adult, autonomous life," says Dana, a thirty-five-year-old single woman who works in the executive search business. "Our lives are structured around that world, around our purchases and our evenings out. You can start believing that's the entire universe since those are the concerns you and your network share. I've always felt a great deal of shame about wanting children because it just didn't fit. So I ignored it, repressed it, really. When you're working and keeping busy you're discouraged from thinking about it, so you don't."

Even when friends have signposted the route, parenthood can still seem like forbidding terrain. "I always thought I wanted kids. Then I met my husband, and all his friends had kids," says Melanie, thirty. "This has made me think seriously of *not* having kids. When they come over we have to move everything in the house, and sometimes I'm not in the mood to deal with it. It would change our lifestyle incredibly. Now we have the freedom to do what we want."

The baby is the divide. "One day it's not there, and the next day it is," says Tess, now pregnant with her first child. "It's scary being pregnant. I wonder, am I doing the right thing? Will I be able to handle it? I won't be able to take it back." The permanence of the fact may not hit at once. As one friend recalled, "We played with Jesse for the first few days and then, at the end of the weekend I thought to myself, 'Okay, that was fun. Now his parents can come and take him home.' Then it suddenly struck me: He *is* home. We *are* his home."

Much of our apprehension centers on the issue of control. We've come to expect a certain degree of mastery in our lives. When a child arrives, we have no choice but to loosen our grasp. The more a baby threatens to yank us from our realm of control, the more unsettling a prospect mothering may be. The world we've operated in is highly competitive and highly structured—the opposite of what we associate with being a mother. The thought of entering that emotional, intimate, boundaryless world leaves many of us terrified. We're afraid of having babies, those agents of chaos.

Randomness, spontaneity, those qualities of infants that can be so charming, can also be intimidating to us. The point is that you can't turn it off. You can't just be *reasonable* with them. You can't always deal with them on your terms. "I really dislike babies. I think they should come with directions," confesses Julie. "I've always had pride in my ability to handle things intellectually, to approach things in a rational, systematic way. You can't approach babies that way. They have different personalities, they scream and I won't always know why."

Basic baby care can seem like a war of wills. "I was watching a friend's baby," recalls Melissa, a thirty-two-year-old teacher who's pregnant with her first. "I wanted him to go to bed when his parents said he should. He refused. I held him, rocked him, walked him, and when I thought he was asleep he started wailing again. The way I saw it, the child didn't want to do what *I* wanted him to do. I get frustrated when I get beat out by a little kid."

Infants are mercurial beings with incomprehensible cravings and unpredictable urgencies; this can baffle us linear thinkers. "In some ways I feel like a man, the way our fathers must have felt," says Tricia, twenty-eight, a graphic designer. "Babies are for women. Give me an older child I can reason with. Having an older son or daughter, someone you can talk to and share things with, that's appealing to me. The baby, toddler, screaming, wetting stuff is not."

Many of us try to take control of the situation by fortifying ourselves with information. "Every mother I know has read everything there is about child raising," says Brin, twenty-nine, who has a two-year-old daughter. "You feel you need to learn about it, that it's something you can study for. Once you realize how much information there is and how much research has been done, you can't imagine how anybody could do it on their own. But because there's so much out there, you think you shouldn't make any mistakes—there's no excuse for doing anything wrong."

According to Eleanor Morin Davis, Ph.D., a psychologist and codirector of the New Center for Modern Parenthood in New York, women today want exact, guaranteed instructions for how to deal with babies. We feel entitled to this; we've been educated to look for the proper solution to any given situation. "Women today are less comfortable with reading their own responses and following their intuition. Trial and error is not enough. They want to find a problem-solving model to rely on."

Sometimes we may imagine having more command than we do; the language of expertise can be a substitute for actual experience. "I visited a friend when her baby was five days old," says Melissa. "She kept saying, 'He's this type of baby, he's that type of baby.' I wonder, how do you characterize a child after a few days at home? It's almost like they made a decision as to which category he fit into and stuck to it, that they had to pretend they knew exactly what was going on."

Under most circumstances we're likely to face, we consider ourselves fairly competent. We've gotten along pretty well with or without anybody else's help. We also feel we have to be competent in all things. Any lapse in our performance casts doubt on all our other successes, so the pressure is on. We don't like the fact that we're unsure of our mothering abilities, imagining that we should be as confident about caring for children as we are about the other things we do. As a professional and a potential mother, our status as a woman remains intact. But as a woman who attempts and has difficulty managing both, we've shown ourselves to be a failure: We've let everybody down.

We pump ourselves so full of expectations that there's no way we can possibly meet them all, and on some level we acknowledge this. The impulse is to avoid situations in which we fear we'll disappoint. As a marketing executive who opted not to have children told *Working Woman*, "I knew from the outset that being a mother was not a job that I would master. And I like to do things that I can do well."[1] We fear the baby, for he may reveal our shortcomings.

We see motherhood as something we should be good at, and dealing with other people's children can be a "test." When I confront a baby, I feel that I am supposed to perform somehow, that this is an occasion I must rise to. Part of me wants to flee, to bow out of the trial. Another part of me stands there stoically, acceding to the fact that I'm a woman, and women and babies are supposed to go together. When I touch the baby, or acknowledge him with a glance, I feel strangely observed. Even with the mother right there I can feel people looking at me, then at the child, wanting to put a frame around the picture of us; the attempt is to pair us off visually, a hypothetical mother-baby pair, the way couples try to match up single guests at a wedding. I feel at a remove, that it's not me talking, reaching, gesturing, but a representative of me.

What seems to be baby phobia may really be a kind of infant *illiteracy*. For many of us premotherhood, babies are utter strangers. If you grow up in a small family, go to college and then go to work, as many of us do, you may hardly run across them at all. "There are no children in my building, on my street, anywhere," observes Kelley. "There's no sense of children in my life. It's beginning to seem a bit unnatural to me, and I've been thinking about getting involved with a Big Sister program, to create that experience somehow."

In the past, most young women served a "mother-apprenticeship," learning to be comfortable with the role by taking care of younger siblings or other children in the community. Kids were always around, part of the neighborhood landscape. Families were larger; community life was more fluid. Women went directly from handling others' children to finding themselves with children of their own. Today we live in small, enclosed units distinct from other small, enclosed units. Our interactions with others are more structured, our borders more precise.

Many women note how little experience they've had with children. "I've changed maybe one diaper in my life," says Tess, gearing herself for the fact that she'll be changing many more. I know my own young-child experience is notably thin. I did baby-sit for a while, but my chief sites of exploration were the refrigerator and the bookshelf; the children I was paid to watch were only incidental. The best jobs were for late-in-the-evening affairs when you arrived after dinner and the kids went to bed almost immediately. Unless you had an unusually thirsty, restless, or dyspeptic kid, you hardly had to deal with your charge at all. I never baby-sat *babies* for the simple reason that none existed in my territory. Had I tried to sell my services to the newer, baby-laden families at the end of the block, I would have been edging into another teenager's turf.

Lee, who's thirty-five and divorced, comments on how alien the idea of babies has been to her social world:

> *A few weeks ago I went to a shower given for a woman in my yoga class having her first child. The odd thing was that of fourteen women, averaging in our mid-thirties, only one of us was a mother. The one mother had brought all the latest kid things for gifts, really snazzy stuff, and the rest of us couldn't help but marvel at them. None of us had any idea of what to bring. I think we were all pretty uncomfortable: having a baby was something we knew nothing about. Normally, you'd think that women go to a baby shower and talk about babies. But none of us had anything to say on that score.*

Lee sees this as being as much a reflection of society as of personal choice:

> *This is not a generation where people have always been handing babies around. As for me, I'd never held a baby until I went to Italy. There, you walk into a restaurant where there's a young family and the waiter yells* bambino *and starts handing the baby around. Here, the waiter would look at you and say, "Oh shit." It's a completely different attitude. There, babies are fun. Here they're an intrusion.*

Many women, of course, have always felt comfortable with babies and children. Others work to develop that confidence. "I never really thought about having children until relatively recently," says Karen, twenty-six. "I began working with teenagers and school-age kids and thought hmmm . . . I'm good at this. I started wondering how I would feel about having my own child and made it a point to baby-sit to get a sense of what it would be like."

Sometimes the confidence doesn't come until we have a child of our own. Says Becky, thirty-one, a new mother:

> *I never liked babies or children. They always turned away from me and went right to somebody else. I never picked up my sister-in-law's babies. It made me too self-conscious, the sense that family members were checking me out to see how I'd be as a mother. But it was different from what I expected. By the sixth month of pregnancy I was actually talking to the baby I felt so sure of her being there. Something takes over. I don't feel my lack of experience got in the way of anything.*

Beyond changing the structure of our life, having a baby promises to alter its emotional texture. We fear babies because we fear the feelings they'll trigger in us. "Infants tap parts of a woman's brain other than what she might be accustomed to using," says Dr. Davis. "Because of the rigidly scheduled, extremely demanding lives they lead, today's women aren't comfortable with the emotions that children induce, like frustration and rage. Similarly, they're wary of feelings of longing, dependency, and merging. We fear being overwhelmed by our emotional lives."

The specter of emotional anarchy frightens us, and the child's complete dependence on us only aggravates our own feeling of powerlessness. Because so many longings and impulses are awakened by the baby's presence, we identify with him and his helplessness. The very blamelessness of infants makes it yet harder. With their perfect, crystalline innocence, we know that whatever horrible feelings are provoked by a baby are not his fault but ours. For someone used to living among adults and keeping the chaotic, undefinable aspects of our emotionality under wraps, this can be threatening. Intuitively we know this, so we fear the baby and his impending challenges to our inner order.

"Our culture has a love/hate relationship with babies," says Susan Williams, Ph.D., a psychologist in Beverly Hills. "We love their newness and freshness, but we're uncomfortable with much that they represent: helplessness, dependency, mess, being demanded of. We may have internalized the hatred of the infantile we felt as babies—often from our parents—and project that onto our own babies."

Working through these feelings can encourage us to grow. "Becoming a mother brings us back to our own childhood and all those feelings we've had under control in our adult lives," says Dr. Davis. "It enriches us, expands our emotional range and our ability to deal with new experiences. It's scary coming across painful unmet needs, deep longings, and rages, but it can help us make peace with them."

We first experience infants when we are infants and children ourselves. We may have unconscious feelings toward siblings that continue to inform our attitudes toward children. "I think my dislike of babies goes back to my hatred of my younger sister," says Julie. "I was four years old and extremely resentful when she was born. I made myself very unpopular in the family by giving her chicken pox. It became part of family lore. To this day Mother will say, '. . . and then my beautiful baby was covered with scabs,' making me feel guilty, as though it were intentional. I have a fear that I'll hurt my own baby and I'm sure it stems in part from that." On the unconscious level, the baby may represent the sibling that kept us from being the center of our parents' lives.

The baby also threatens to destroy the exclusivity we enjoy with our partners. "The baby marks the end of you as the one and only," says Dr. Williams. "Before the baby you can be one and only to your spouse. The exclusivity brings a sense of security and control. Now you have to share it." Ruth, a doctor who's four months pregnant, is nervous about how the baby will affect her marriage. "It might not affect it negatively, but things will be different," she says. "I wonder, what if I have a little girl who will be Daddy's little girl? Will he pay attention to me less, need me less? You get a lot of mothering from your spouse. When the baby comes there will be another person competing for that mothering."

The baby also represents the end of ourselves as children. This can be a point of tension in a culture that idealizes youth and fun. Who wants to have to be the grown-up? "Does being a mother mean I can't be a kid anymore? That I can't listen to Bob Dylan and do zany things with my friends?" wonders Ruth. "Up till now I've been able to do what I wanted to do when I wanted to do it. I'll have to be more serious about my career and the future. I'm going to have to examine my behavior because there will be a little person observing me, modeling himself on me. I'm afraid I'll have to be more conservative, that I can't just be myself."

We're afraid of children because we're afraid they'll curtail our options. "I like to know that I can go get training in this or that, or to go to China for two years. With a child it's not so easy," says Marsha, thirty-two. Every decision that has come our way up to now has been fixable, has offered a way "out." Any choice that may preclude other choices is a difficult one for us to make. "When I think of having a child my fantasy is of being handcuffed to the crib, or of somebody holding my head under water," says Julie. "If you get married, you can get a divorce. You can never talk to your parents again if you so choose. But once you have a child, there's no socially acceptable way to get out of it."

Because we feel this way, we worry that we're selfish—the word other generations may use to describe our hesitancy about having children. But according to Dr. Davis, there's nothing wrong with being "selfish" if selfishness means being concerned about our own needs. "You need to be selfish," she says. "It helps you empathize with the baby. If you recognize what your needs are, you use that as a base to understand the baby. Some women say they're too 'selfish' to justify a decision not to have children, but even there, selfishness is not usually the issue. Selfishness is a label put on those who try to have their needs met. It's traditionally been used in rhetoric attacking women."

Having children also brings up our own mortality. "You can't see a brand-new pristine existence and not feel your own corruption and disintegration, that we're closer to death," says Dr. Williams. "The fact that you're carrying life makes you enormously sensitive to life-and-death matters," says Diane, thirty, who recently learned she was pregnant. "I feel incredibly moved by things like trees budding or birds building nests, and I almost break into tears when I see a 'possum or squirrel killed on the road."

While this engagement with mortality can be threatening, it can also confirm our sense of childbearing as continuity and renewal. "When my grandfather was dying, he was holding a picture of his great-grandchild, my sister's baby," says Ruth. "Having this baby means something to me about my family and carrying on something important. When I think about my grandfather and the carrying on of life, my other concerns begin to fade."

Another reason babies trigger apprehensions is that they threaten to oust us from a role we've come to treasure (or at least grow comfortable with): that of the daughter. When we have a child, we become more mother than daughter. Our status changes even in the eyes of our parents, whose daughter we'll always be. "I'm afraid I'm going to lose my mother, that she'll be focused on the grandchild," says Debbi. "Already she's completely focused on the baby. It makes me feel I'm just the vessel for this new thing."

We may not always realize just how much we get out of being a daughter, what it means to us. There's the perpetual fantasy of being special, of having our future be more compelling than our past. "My fear about having a child is that I'm not going to be the sexy one, I'm not going to be the ingenue," Dana confesses. "I like to be the favorite daughter. I know I've replayed this role again and again throughout my life and in my career, and I'm sure it's been an obstacle to my settling down."

A child would intrude on the special relationship with our parents that allows us to remain children in certain respects. "I think of being pregnant as a time when I can stay home and be pampered. But then the baby comes and that's the end of the dream," says Julie. Carolyn, thirty-three, says:

> *I know I make a good daughter. I'm not so sure what kind of mother I'd be. I can't deny that I enjoy the attention and pampering I get from my parents. I have my place already, it's secure. My older sister has a child, and she gets a great sense of joy when someone makes a fuss over him. She'd rather have someone compliment the child than herself. That's the difference between the two of us. I'd just as soon have the compliment paid to me.*

Another irresistible aspect of the daughter role is that it keeps us motivated. We're in a position to please. We have the advantage of doing what we want while enjoying the backing of others. "The fact is that women [today] are getting support from their parents, in both education and career, that they've never had before," says Dr. Davis. "The positive aspect of this is that it helps them to achieve. The negative is that it can make it difficult to relinquish the daughter role, because once you do that you won't be sure of where your support will come from."

A key element of this support as it exists today is that much of it comes from our fathers. "In the profiles of successful women we've run, over and over the women said that their parents—then it drops out and becomes their *fathers*—told them they could be whatever they wanted to be,'' says Kate Rand Lloyd, founding editor of *Working Woman*. There are men as proud to be known for their *daughters'* accomplishments as for their own. No longer do men concentrate all their hopes on their sons, regarding their daughters mainly as ornamental child-women destined for the domestic path. And because it's less burdened by the Oedipally derived competitive element that marks the father-son bond, a father's pride in his daughter may be experienced as purer, easier for both parties to accept.

It's probably no exaggeration to say that this has revolutionized father-daughter relations. ''The Oedipal pattern, where the daughter tries to secure her father's love, has been modified. The complex way of winning the battle has changed,'' says Dr. Davis. ''No longer does the daughter feel compelled to play the coquette, trying to act sexy, pretty, or helpless. Now, to make him proud, she can be creative, successful, and intelligent. This also works insofar as it gives her a different role than her mother, who may not have a career, so their competition gets played out on a different plane.''

The legacy of this dynamic can create anxiety for the woman considering motherhood. The father-daughter relationship that had worked so well for her in the past is bound to change. Because she had become so proficient at winning her father's affection and admiration, she may have aggrandized her sense of her own specialness and devalued that of her mother. In becoming a mother herself, she is now about to *join* the ranks of the supposedly devalued. A woman who has dedicated herself to fulfilling the daughter role may find the prospect of a change in work status particularly traumatic. She depends on her work to generate the support that sustains her self-esteem. She's terrified of losing it. Viewing motherhood as a daughter, we're afraid of the newborn child. He turns us into someone other than who we've been in relation to others.

Often what we fear doesn't come to pass: we find new sources of support; our families appreciate new sides of ourselves; we realize we're more adaptable than we thought. ''Surprisingly, I liked being home and being with other new moms,'' Nancy says of her time off from work. ''I thought stay-at-home mothers are all sitting around eating bon bons. But we were all professionals, all high-powered, interesting people. I had no idea everyone would be just like me.''

There's no way to predict how someone will react to being a mother—which is one reason it's so difficult to plan for it beforehand. ''In my residency I've seen it all," says Debbi. "There was one woman who got pregnant in her second year and expected to come right back to work. Then she called the week before she was due to return and said she just couldn't do it. She ended up dropping out of the program altogether. Then there was another who couldn't wait to get out of the house, she was so bored. I have no idea how I'll feel. It could go either way."

One woman recalls being stunned by how a close friend changed once the baby arrived. "To be honest, I was a little worried about how she was going to handle it," she recalls. "During the pregnancy it almost seemed she was denying what was happening. She was more focused on the changes in her body than on preparing for the baby. I couldn't imagine her being maternal at all. But now you can't get her away from her little girl. It's been a complete transformation."

While some underestimate the attachment they'll have to their babies, others are surprised to find that as much as they love their babies, they still need something more. "Before I had the baby, I thought that it wouldn't matter to me what I did professionally," says Angie, a new mother who has recently started to look for another position in her field. "I thought the child would provide enough fulfillment so that a merely decent job would be enough. I didn't think I would care about my work in the same way, but I do."

Navigating new emotional terrain absorbs a lot of energy, and it can be difficult to articulate our experiences. Women on both sides of the divide lament the breach that can arise between friends when one becomes a mother. "I've got a two-year-old, and my friends and sisters aren't even married yet," says Jane. "There's envy on both sides. They see me as settled and secure when I don't really feel that way. I wish I had the freedom they do to experiment with different careers. It's hard for me to share what I'm going through and what I feel."

Karen remembers how she felt when the first of her group of friends got pregnant. "There were different reactions among all of us. I was happy because I knew she wanted this, but I was also disappointed because it seemed too soon for her, that she hadn't really explored herself. Then there was a wistful feeling. The thought of a friend moving ahead like that makes you look at your own life and think: What am I doing? Is this really where I want to be?"

Some women resent it when their friends become immersed in motherhood at the expense of everything else. "I have a close friend with a new baby, and when we're together I hear nonstop about what the baby just did, what she needs to buy for the baby, how she wants another baby," says Ellie. "It makes me wonder, isn't there anything else we can talk about for a change?" Nonmothers may perceive this as an indictment of their personal choices. Ellie reflects: "About a year ago, another friend said she never could have grown as much as a person without being a mother. It left me feeling I was really in trouble, that I wouldn't live up to my potential unless I went out and had a child. I was really feeling the pressure. Only recently I've been able to say to myself, okay, so maybe I won't be so complete a person."

Some women are irritated by the weight new parents may give to having children. "At a dinner party last weekend a friend asked point-blank: 'Are you two trying?' " says Sharon, thirty-three. "These days it's one of the first questions people ask everywhere we go. It's heavy-duty pressure. I find it really distasteful. It's not something I care to be so public about or feel I have to defend. It seems some women want everybody else to become mothers so they can feel good about being mothers."

Part of the pressure women feel stems from the lack of role models. "My idea of motherhood is based on the nuclear, suburban family I grew up in. It's not very attractive to me," says Tricia. "I'm waiting to see if other women can do it and escape the patterns our parents fell into." Just as we long for positive examples of motherhood, we may have trouble finding *non*mother models. Julie says she considers herself lucky to have two such women in her life. "My roommate and my boss, both older than me, are not married and never had children," she says. "They live very full, satisfying lives. This has been really encouraging to me, as lately I've been wondering about how my own life will turn out. It makes me feel less frantic about getting married and having kids."

Our own conflicts about motherhood are compounded by the dichotomy that gets set up between mothers and nonmothers, a schism perpetuated by the maternal myths. As Dr. Williams points out in an essay, there have always been women who were mothers and women who had no children. But with broadened reproductive choices, the division between the two has become more marked. On the face of it, she writes,

> *the distinction between women as childed or not is natural and makes sense. The states of motherhood and childlessness are contrasted ubiq-*

uitously in the psychological and sociological literature, art, literature, poetry, and music. Historically, the joys and fulfillment of motherhood have been publicly endorsed to the extent of becoming dogma, whereas the failure and shame of nonmotherhood or infertility are viewed as a personal and social tragedy. Although the social zeitgeist seems to be changing to some extent, the polarization of mother and childless woman . . . prevails. This dichotomy serves only to describe an external condition, however, leaving much to be desired in describing a woman's internal, psychic condition.''[2]

Whether or not someone is a mother is presumed to say more than it possibly can say. The ideology of motherhood has set up a polarity in which having or not having children reveals certain qualities in a woman: nurturance as opposed to self-interest; maturity as opposed to immaturity; fulfillment as opposed to unfulfillment. When we fear not becoming a mother (fearing infertility or not being able to find a partner), we fear we'll never have a chance to experience nurturance, maturity, or fulfillment. When we fear becoming a mother, we fear we won't be able to live up to the ideal. The mythology traps us into self-doubt and a suspicion of others.

Aside from being unfair to both groups, the dichotomy is inaccurate and simplistic. As Adrienne Rich writes:

[I]s a woman who bore a baby she could not keep a ''childless'' woman? Am I, whose children are grown-up, who come and go as I will, unchilded as compared to younger women still pushing prams, hurrying home to feedings, waking at night to a child's cry? What makes us mothers? The care of small children? The physical changes of pregnancy and birth? The years of nurture? What of the woman who, never having been pregnant, begins lactating when she adopts an infant? What of the woman who stuffs her newborn into a bus-station locker and goes numbly back to her ''child-free'' life? What of the woman who, as the eldest girl in a large family, has practically raised her younger sisters and brothers, and then has entered a convent?[3]

Relying on the biological divide fails to acknowledge the emotional motivations and experience involved. Aren't there ways other than ''mothering'' that a woman can express her nurturing and creativity? Through friendships and professional relationships? Through work? Dr.

Williams points out that men aren't arbitrarily categorized as "fathers" and "nonfathers." Why shouldn't women be granted varied means of achieving growth, expansion, and creativity? Why should women be subjected to the split?

The greatest problem with the false dichotomy is that we often apply it to ourselves. We must find a way to bring aspects of nurturance into our lives without letting that nurturance define us. We need to be comfortable with both our independence and our connection to others. We need to reach out across the divide and empathize with other women's experience. We shouldn't let motherhood be a barrier between women, or a barrier within ourselves.

Chapter 4

THE DAUGHTER'S VOICE

Two major contemporary books on the mother-daughter relationship begin with virtually the same scenario. In *My Mother/My Self,* Nancy Friday envisions this "little scene":

> *In her kind, warm, shy, and self-deprecating way, mother calls me into the bedroom where she sleeps alone. She is no more than twenty-five. I am perhaps six. Putting her hands . . . on my shoulders, she looks me right through my steel-rimmed spectacles: "Nancy, you know I'm not really good at this mothering business," she says. "You're a lovely child, the fault is not with you. But motherhood doesn't come easily to me. So when I don't seem like other people's mothers, try to understand that it isn't because I don't love you. I do. But I'm confused myself. . . . You can't expect me to be all the mother you need. I feel closer to your age in some ways than I do my mother's. I don't feel that serene, divine, earth-mother certainty you're supposed to that she felt. I am unsure how to raise you. . . .*

As we're immersed in this heartfelt unburdening of truth, taken in by it completely, Friday declares it "[a] scene that could never have taken place."[1]

In her introduction to Judith Arcana's *Our Mothers' Daughters,* Phyllis Chesler writes:

> *I took this book home to my mother.*
>
> *"Please mother read this book. It will make everything*—every-thing—*clear. Then, you'll say you love me. Only me. For my strength. For all the ways I'm* different *from you. Then, we'll embrace. Prodigal Daughter, Prodigal Mother. We'll speak only words*

of love to each other. Nothing superficial will ever pass our lips again."
"You're so melodramatic," she says, putting on her glasses.

With her mother now appropriately bespectacled, Chesler concludes: "(This conversation didn't take place. But we're closer to it every day, my mother and me.)"[2]

In *Of Woman Born* Adrienne Rich recalls that she, too, had had fantasies of "some infinitely healing conversation . . . in which we could show all our wounds, transcend the pain we have shared as mother and daughter, say everything at last."[3]

There's something very powerful here: the truths between mothers and daughters that never get voiced. The daughter yearns to hear them, yearns to *have heard* them. Though we might, on the whole, enjoy rewarding relationships with our mothers, all too frequently there's an unsettling gap. Often it takes the form of silence, a breach of language, that plunks itself down between us. How many of us have not dreamt of a cathartic outpouring of honesty between our mothers and ourselves? How many have not longed for an intimacy that surmounts the battles and banalities that can seem to define our relationships? Whether or not we feel close to our mothers, there is a closeness. There's the sheer fact of proximity, eroding our boundaries over time, the biological bond, the love. The connection between us has such vast potential that it can't help but disappoint. Our mothers present us with one way to live in the world, then we find we must reject it. We grow up believing our mothers, then at some point we start disbelieving them.

When it comes to learning about life as women, our mothers are our chief guides, or at least the most immediate ones. According to writers like those mentioned above, this is where we feel they've failed us. Unclear about their own place as women, they can't hope to offer much in the way of clarity to us. Afraid to express their own doubts, they're rarely in a position to offer us assurance about ours. We know there's more depth and complexity to their lives than what they reveal to us. In their attempts to protect us from the realities, they leave us unprepared for them. In their wish to convince us that everything is okay, they invalidate our fears. Inevitably, we feel betrayed.

These issues—the disappointments and angers that try our bonds with our mothers—are always important to us. They track us throughout our lives, building and waning as crises come and go, as we learn or forget. But once we address the idea of becoming mothers ourselves, they reach a roaring crescendo. The fact is, we are about to become what *she is,* whatever that may mean to us. Up till now we've reached something of a truce, a laying down of arms. We have staked out our territory; she has marked out hers. There's a comfortable, if tenuous, status quo. But now our paths are going to converge. No matter how far we may have wandered away from her, we've turned back and are heading toward her straightaway.

Like other aspects of our relationship, the fears about mother newly awakened by our own thinking about motherhood are complex. On the one hand, we worry about being too much like her, a fear we might not have had when we were (safely) ensconced in our careers or romantic affairs. We ask ourselves: If I become a mother, will I become my mother . . . and do I want to be like her? (Adrienne Rich informs us that the word *matrophobia* means not fear of one's mother or fear of becoming a mother, but fear of becoming one's mother.)[4] At the same time we fear we can't be enough like her: "How can I do what my mother did (bear and raise a child) when I've made myself into someone completely different from her?" In our minds we have defined motherhood in a way that unavoidably reflects a vision of our own mothers. And much of this is negative (what we *don't* want to be). How can we expand our working definition to include ourselves and what we'd like to be?

As we take our turn in the generational cycle, mother becomes important to us in new ways. Whether it's in communion or rebellion, we think about her. Memories get stirred up; she may make regular appearances in our dreams. Old feelings about her we thought we had outgrown come hurtling back at us. As we recognize that she went through the same things we're either going through or are about to, her life (meaning her *subjective* life, not merely her life as it pertained to us) becomes less remote. We may want her help, her advice, her encouragement. Identifying with the mother who was young like us, we may wish to offer the same to her retroactively.

Even as we begin to assert ourselves as mothers, we can be overwhelmed by our needs as daughters. We're afraid of repeating old patterns: Will she be open with me about what to expect, or will she shut me out as she's done before? Ellen, thirty-two, says she can hardly think about having children without being saddened by her lack of closeness with her mother. "My mother was never comfortable talking to me about physical things, practical things, sexual things," she says. "She would always change the subject as soon as she could. Now I know I'm going to have questions about pregnancy, breast-feeding, and everything else. So who am I going to talk to? My mother-in-law? Even though she's easier to talk to, that wouldn't feel right somehow."

Other women wonder, Will she interfere to the point where I feel it's not my life, but hers? "My mother tends to be a little intrusive, and when I suddenly need her more, how will I be able to set limits?" asks Ruth. "I'm afraid I'll lose my sense of myself, that the boundaries between us will get all fuzzy."

Our mother's past experience also takes on an immediate relevance to us. Our mother's body—the unclothed version of which we may never have seen—is the one most like our own that we know; from her we may inherit our body's tendencies and predilections (we generally start menstruating at about the same age as she did; more often than not we're of a similar size and shape). We pore over family stories for clues as to what we may confront. Did she have any trouble conceiving? (She got pregnant right away—we are relieved.) Were there any difficulties in her deliveries? (More than twenty-four hours each—expect a long haul.) She becomes something of a biological template for us. We ask her, Is there anything about you that could also be about me?

Perhaps inevitably, how a woman feels about her mother can affect her attitudes toward motherhood. For some women, this lends clarity to the issue. "I've always been close to my mother, and I never had a doubt that I wanted to be a mother myself," says Gina, twenty-nine. Other women, often those who were witness to their mothers' unhappiness, are less sanguine about motherhood and may choose not to mother at all.

Though the effect isn't quite so linear (neither pursuit nor avoidance), I can see that my own feelings about motherhood do mirror my feelings about my mother. These feelings couldn't be quite described as either positive or negative, but are rather feelings of vagueness, or disbelief. It's difficult for me to picture myself as a mother in precisely the same way that it's been difficult for me to see myself as my mother's daughter.

I feel a sense of estrangement from my mother that has plagued me as long as I can remember, only mildly disconcerting but disconcerting nonetheless. My inability to *know* my mother has been an endless source of frustration to me. She presents herself as a neat, harmless little package. ("Oh, *I* would never say a thing like that . . .") She is a stable figure, resolutely—if not infuriatingly—so. I've refused to accept this picture. I've sneered at it. No one could be so neat or so benign, I've felt. From stories about her childhood that have circulated through family lore, I know she has a wild, mischievous side, and sometimes a flash of that shines through. That side intrigues—even thrills—me. I've always had this idea that one day, without warning, she'll throw off her domestic chores, write dirty novels, and go off to dance with the Rockettes. I've retained this fantasy, although I've yet to see her practicing any high kicks.

I feel with us that there's something deeper than a turf skirmish, with her insisting that life is simple and me insisting that it's complex, something, perhaps, related to this elusive detachment between us. Whatever it is, it somehow touches upon the discomfort I've had about motherhood, the discomforts I've had about myself. Recently, I've thought about a story I've heard many times, the story of my own arrival. My mother describes the moment when, lying in her hospital bed, still weary from her ordeal, she first saw me. My grandfather, never one to be left idle, carried me into her room, flanked by nurses on either side. "I took one look at you, this long, skinny kid," she'd recall, chuckling, "and I said to myself, this one can't be mine."

For a long time, I took this anecdote at face value. Since within my family, being short and stocky has been such a part of our collective identity (and despite my original dimensions, believe me, I got there soon enough), I thought her reaction was a matter of body type. Coming from an endomorphic gene pool, an ectomorphic newborn simply ran counter to her expectations. But now, reaching back toward this moment—knowing what I know now about me, her, and us—I've come to believe it was something else. That little jolt of surprise was fear: I think I terrified her. As someone who stressed her naiveté over her competence, who was invested in being childlike (sweet and never threatening) and cherished for it by those around her, having her own child must have been jarring. No doubt she also had her own apprehensions about becoming a mother, which, given the social climate of the early sixties, she wasn't supposed to have. In retrospect, I can see that it was not so much my shape as my existence that unnerved her.

I think that initial encounter set the tone for the relationship that ensued. My mother never got over it, never got over me. Somehow, by being born and being who I was, I had disappointed her. I began as a threat (to her innocence, her protectedness, her control), and I became more of one as time went on. Colicky, a screamer, ever anxious to air my discontents, I was exactly the wrong kind of baby for a woman who thrived on order and predictability. That dynamic has always persisted with us. I was always too demanding, too vocal, too much. Since day one, it has been me challenging my mother, her backing away.

Aside from me and whatever I represented, I believe my mother was afraid of many things, as perhaps all of us are. In response, she has structured her life to avoid whatever might upset her. In her daily life she is utterly unafraid; she has everything under her command and is proud of it. I've inherited my mother's fearfulness without her defenses. Her way of making peace with the world was to accept it without delving too deeply; mine has been *not* to accept anything until I understand it.

And so we've clashed. My mother could never tolerate my fears, since they cut so close to her own, and so she denied them. I was left with the feeling that my perceptions were wrong. I felt alone in my fears, thinking that my mother, having repudiated my vision of the world, wasn't with me, never realizing how with me she actually was. I always believed that if I could somehow make my mother understand me, I would know I was okay, that the ground would stop shaking beneath me. My thoughts had to be approved by her, as though, like myself, they had to gestate and be born through her in order to exist at all. But everything that I was desperate for her to acknowledge, she was desperate to refute. No matter how finely I could tune my voice for others (as a student, as a writer, as a friend), I could never express myself effectively with my mother. I was always too abrasive. The words would come out shrill. I could never be tactful enough for her; she could never be truthful enough for me.

Unable to truly identify with each other, we couldn't quite separate from each other either. Still longing for what I've felt was never given me, I've seen myself as incomplete. I think this is the dilemma the three authors who opened this chapter were talking about. We crave that rapprochement with our mothers. We need to affirm who we are so we can go on with our lives. We need the truths that we live with confirmed. Our mothers' attempts to avoid those truths, with the intention of protecting us or protecting themselves, stall us; they make us doubt. When we're unable to find a meeting point, we imagine it's our fault.

This pattern replicates our feelings from childhood: mother is grown up (therefore she knows), and it's our task to grow toward her. Her approval lets us know we're moving in the right direction. In terms of our becoming mothers, we need to see ourselves as complete women, women who have enough to give and have the strength to give it. We need to see ourselves as whole. There's no one, we feel, who can give us that wholeness except for our mothers, the ones who originally pointed out to us our lack of it.

According to many feminist writers, this failure of honesty among women derives not from any failure on the part of individual women, but from our culture. The inability to achieve truthfulness, it has been argued, is inherent in a patriarchal society in which women are assigned total responsibility in one sphere—the home—when in fact real power lies elsewhere. In many cases, says Judith Arcana, "the reason for [mothers'] silence is their own ignorance, compounded by inexperience, shame and discomfort. Generally, however, they seem *not to remember* the painful, frustrating aspects of their living as women. In their struggle, they have lost sight of their doubts and desires, and so present to us the apparent facts of their lives as if that were all there was to see. They've learned to glorify the minimal place women occupy, and offer us sorry vanities or bitterness in place of the information we seek."[5] To maintain both their integrity and peace within the family, generations of mothers have been reconciled to the demands and limits put upon them. The anger emerges only erratically, in language difficult to decipher.

As Adrienne Rich points out, the roots of our disappointment in our mothers often are set outside the actual mother/daughter relationship. Mother blaming is easy, she says, for it distracts us from our anger at the way women as a whole are treated in this culture. As a girl grows to see the restrictions society places on those of her gender, her resentment focuses on her mother. Indeed, Rich cites the example of women who had been sexually abused by their fathers and then blamed their mothers for *allowing it to happen.*[6] In a society like ours, she argues, women can't afford to get angry at those who hold power—the men—but express it toward other women instead.

The result, argue Judith Lewis Herman, M.D., and Helen Block Lewis, Ph.D., in their essay "Anger in the Mother-Daughter Relationship," is a "chronic anger" plaguing women on both sides of the maternal equation. This anger, is, however, dangerous to express. It's held back because women lack the means to confront it at its source (society) and are dependent on those who may provoke it (men). This strains the mother/daughter relationship because the anger may be displaced toward each other (a safe target) *and* because it conflicts with the nurturing and affection "that have been the most consistent basis of women's dignity and power."[7]

We're ambivalent toward mother since we are to become like her (our biology has programmed it to be so), and this means taking on the same dubious role in society. Psychological theorists have suggested that, because of contemporary gender roles, mother tends to represent passivity, emotionality, and dependence, while father symbolizes the opposite: activity, rationality, and achievement. Identifying with mother is difficult for us, for it means envisioning ourselves in a devalued role. If we resist this role, however, we imagine we've deceived her and added to her sorrow. We also, then, must relinquish the fantasy of reconciliation.

Yet mother is equally ambivalent toward us. The daughter she has engendered is bound to suffer the same indignities she has suffered as a woman, which she can't hope to protect her from completely. At the same time, we may have greater opportunities than she did. She may resent us and yet may want to experience the broadened possibilities vicariously through us. Just as mother may be conflicted about what she wants and what she has, she may be conflicted about what she wants for us. As Simone de Beauvoir explains, "In her daughter the mother does not hail a member of the superior caste; in her she seeks a double. She projects upon her daughter all the ambiguity of her relation with herself."[8]

Mother reexperiences all of her frustrations through us yet sees our ability to transcend her situation. She may be shaken up by the conflicting feelings that emerge, which may or may not be conscious. To mother, our independence may seem treasonous. She may want us to go out and take on the world in a way that she wasn't able to, yet she may also inwardly hope we will follow her, for indeed that would justify her choice, or, perhaps, her absence of choice. If she worked, she may be disturbed if we start to question our careers. Either way, we represent new realms of possibility, so she's both threatened by us and reluctant to let go of us. We're unsure of where we stand in the world; we're afraid of her crowding presence yet fear giving up her protection and support.

These issues seem to have become heightened in recent generations. In *The Hungry Self,* a perceptive analysis of eating disorders, Kim Chernin explores the contemporary mother/daughter relationship, which she contends is inevitably a "fateful encounter between a mother whose life has not been fulfilled and a daughter now presented with the opportunity for fulfillment."[9] The tension produced by the stark discrepancies in our lives can be profound. It leaves us daughters "hungry" for the closeness we might have with a mother who could identify with our lives and appropriately prepare us for what we might face. We feel a lack in our mothers, and we know that we, with our relative freedom, serve only to point up their own deprivations to them—deprivations that they may not wish to be made aware of. Chernin writes: "We are a generation who, with every act of self-assertion as women, with every movement into self-development and fulfillment, call into question the values by which our mothers have tried to live."[10]

The result (which Chernin says is a key factor in eating disorders among young women) is a form of "survival guilt." Mother doesn't personally benefit from our successes; on the contrary, she loses us to them. We conclude that we've been selfish, that we've overindulged. We worry that we have taken mother for granted, taken our opportunities for granted. But we didn't know how else to live. Both our mothers and the opportunities were presented to us. Should we have taken it upon ourselves to enforce self-denial in repentance? In protest? As we separate from mother we feel guilty, because we feel we've left her behind. As we experience success we feel guilty, because we feel we've gained where she's missed out, gained at her expense, in essence. As we build autonomous lives we feel guilty, because we feel we're breaking the great chain of female commonality by going out on our own. There's the belief that the realities our mothers dwelled in reflected the reality that always was.

Many women have the fantasy that they have somehow "ruined" their mothers. Our mother's opportunities were limited, we conjecture, because *we* chose to be born. She got married, she quit her job, she got fat because of the pregnancies that produced us. We kept her bound to the house by our unappeasable demands. As we recognize our own fears about the constraints of motherhood, we're appalled by what we "did" to our own mothers. In a vicious cycle, this, in turn, contributes to our own mothering doubts. "I feel my mother always regretted my turbulent personality, that if she knew and had the choice she wouldn't have wanted me," says Julie. "I fear I'll have a mellow child that I'll overpower, like I overpowered my mother, or that I'll have one even wilder than me and won't be able to handle it."

Kim Chernin concludes that fantasies of harming our mothers haunt many women with troubled relationships with their mothers, notably women with eating disorders:

> *Virtually every woman who has come to me about a serious eating problem believes that her mother experienced stress so severe in mothering her that between us we are forced to wonder whether it was a breakdown. As daughters, it is difficult for us to acknowledge this. It feels as if we are revealing the most strenuously kept secret of our childhood and family life. It feels, merely in acknowledging the fact of our mother's crisis, that we are betraying her, we who know how militantly she struggled to ward off her crisis in mothering and to keep it hidden.*[11]

If we can't see our mothers as the kind of women we want them to be, we fantasize that at some point they were. Jenny, whose mother committed suicide when she was a child, was raised exclusively by her father, a man she holds dear. She has few pleasant memories of her mother, who was frequently institutionalized and beat her three children when she was home. But as for her mother *before* she was born, Jenny imagines her to have been a different woman altogether. "From all the stories, she had been vibrant and creative before she had children," she says, with combined wistfulness and pride. "I think it was the stresses of motherhood that did her in."

These fantasies help connect us to mothers we might otherwise have trouble identifying with. But the higher we elevate their potential, the more guilt we feel about having thwarted it (whether or not in fact we did). I know that while growing up I focused on my mother's mischievousness, her athletic ability, her spunk, even though I rarely *witnessed* these traits; they were chiefly brought to me in legend. I boasted not of her domestic skills (which, I can finally appreciate, are considerable), but of the fact that in college she had been a promising student of anthropology and sociology and had been offered the chance to go to New Guinea with Margaret Mead.

I'm also well aware that she chose not to venture into the wilds of native cultures because she thought she should get settled in her own culture first. And that then she got my father, and soon afterward she got me. Then I started screaming, impossible child that I was, and her ambitions, dreams, and confidence were forgotten in the din. When I plead with my mother to get out there, to do something that will build her sense of self and empower her, part of me is saying, "Please, don't let me feel that I'm the one who stopped you. You're freed from having to mother me now." At the same time, I'm asking her to be more of a model for me, so *I* can be freed from an example that I dread.

As we enter into motherhood, our need to see our mothers as models intensifies. Frequently, as our own priorities get shuffled around, and different sides of our selves get tested, we appreciate her where she used to disappoint. "Growing up, my mother didn't seem as smart as my father," says Kelley. "My father is logical, mechanical, precise. He would never get lost on the road, knew the answer to everything, and could do the crossword puzzle in pen. As an adult I see how intelligent and competent my mother is, how perceptive about people, and now I value that."

But what we often get is two sets of realities crashing into each other. When we become mothers, we imagine we're going to step into our own mother's reality because that's the only mothering reality that we know. That also means we must give up our uniqueness, because our lives were designed in contrast to hers. The adjustment is made yet more difficult by the fact that the statements she offers about her experiences as a mother differ from what we intuitively *feel* she believes. And our very confusion is problematic because she has claimed that there is no confusion to begin with.

We remember the tensions between a role resented and a role glorified. Many of our mothers were led to believe that caring for us and tending to our environment would bring them fulfillment. We felt their pressure; it put pressure on us. If we weren't perfectly happy then they had failed, and we had failed them. Feminists have pointed out that the domestic ideal of the fifties and sixties locked mother and child in a war of nerves, the expectation that each should fulfill each other totally leaving them both estranged and enmeshed. In *The Second Stage*, Betty Friedan describes how this claustrophic environment, in which the mothers clutched onto their children for some meaning in their lives, has affected the now-grown daughters: "The scars that female power in the family left . . . create some of the exaggerated fears women experience as they now confront the reality . . ." of creating their own family lives.[12]

The mothering ethic of the period was so strong that women raised by working mothers may have felt *un*mothered. "I was definitely aware that my mother was a different kind of mother from other mothers who were at home and took their kids to the park," says Barbara, thirty, a lawyer. "She wasn't necessarily available when I wanted her to be. But even though she wasn't waiting for me at the door, I did know where she was. And because her career had helped put us in a good economic situation, my parents could create a support network for me—the doormen, people to call—which helped."

The absurd demands of the maternal legacy also serve to justify our disappointments in our less-than-perfect mothers. According to Nancy Chodorow and Susan Contratto in their essay "The Fantasy of the Perfect Mother," many feminist writers have tended to identify with the "angry child," the daughter who has been unmothered or incompletely mothered, and have failed to move beyond this viewpoint in their own analyses of the mother/daughter relationship. As a result, a clear discussion that draws on the legitimate needs of both has yet to be established. In *Maternal Thinking,* Sara Ruddick quotes peace activist Ynestra King:

> *The feminist movement has spoken in the voice of angry rebel daughters. Even when mothers join the movement it is often the wronged daughter in them who speaks. Each of us is familiar as daughters with maternal practice, but most of us . . . have rejected the self-sacrificing, altruistic, infinitely forgiving, martyred unconditionally loving mother—for this is how I saw my mother—have rejected that mother in* ourselves *as the part of ourselves which is complicitous in our own oppression.*[13]

When women regard their independence as something won as *daughters,* they're ambivalent about becoming *mothers* because that implies a loss of independence. It also makes a meeting of mothers and daughters more difficult.

In the past, such disparities and discrepancies were less of an issue. Literature from previous eras reveals that mothers and daughters tended to be extremely close. Building their own "female world" apart from the world of men, the women of one generation lived lives barely distinguishable from those that preceded them. With their alternatives so confined, women were highly supportive of one another. Women had productive skills that were valued, and these were passed on to their daughters. With industrialism, the stability of the women's world shattered. Skills that had given women integrity were either appropriated by male professionals (physicians, educators, manufacturers, etc.) or trivialized. Families moved for reasons of commerce, not kinship; generations were split up. The nuclear family, with father at the center, tightened its grip on its members. Female bonds were downplayed while a woman's status with regard to the man of the house—the source of power—was given great importance.

Today, any vestiges of a female haven for the most part dissolved. Many mothers and their adult daughters feel they are living on different planets. The world changes so constantly and drastically that it's hard for information to get passed on, or to remain relevant when it does. And the "flow" of culture doesn't always run from older generation to younger, keeping family tradition and wisdom intact. Today, mother may turn to daughter as often as vice versa. As Christopher Lasch has pointed out in *The Culture of Narcissism,* in a marked departure from previous norms, today's adults may look to their children for clues as to what to wear or how to act. A society that values youth over experience erodes the sources of power and self-respect mothers have had within the family.[14]

The daughter then feels disdain for the mother (who's clearly "out of it"), as well as disillusionment: "You mean you don't know these things?" For the woman striving to maintain a close relationship with her mother, this can be frustrating. "I know what my mother does in her life, because I grew up with her," says Ruth. "But she has no idea what I do. She just doesn't get it." For many women, this independence is both a prize and a loss. There's no comforting body of accumulated knowledge to fall back on; they're on their own.

That's where many contemporary mother/daughter pairs stand: rather than binding them in loyalty and love, the isolation they lived in has pitted them against each other (angling for father's attentions and for power in the house); rather than identifying with the other, mothers and daughters polarize each other. As Dr. Davis says, "In the minds of many daughters there is a split: mother is the perfect mother and she is the perfect career woman. Mother represents everything maternal, and she represents everything professional. The daughter projects all her unmet emotional needs onto the image of the perfect mother. Then when she becomes a mother she feels she has to live up to that image. This becomes a point of conflict since she had so vehemently rejected that role for herself."

With an ideal as our standard, we're doomed to fail. "For me, the question 'Can I be a mother?' means 'Can I live up to my mother?' " Catherine, a thirty-year-old professor, confides. "I worry that I'm much too selfish to be the kind of mother she was. I would never be able to sacrifice the way she did." Some women carry their doubts so far as to question their ability to conceive and bear children; others worry that they'll harm their children or in some way be harmed themselves.

"The image of the idealized mother, an image that forms at a very young age, is like a hot potato in the unconscious. Sometimes it is projected onto the self, sometimes onto the mother," says Barbara Counter, Ph.D., a clinical psychologist in Los Angeles. "Once a woman realizes she can't live up to this idealized image—as of course nobody can—she might panic or become depressed. It's an extreme reaction: the feeling is, if I can't be the ideal mother, I can't do anything. I think on some level this happens to every woman who brings her first baby home from the hospital."

For many women with truly formidable mothers, the vision of mother goes beyond fantasy. You could call it the "superdaughter syndrome": women who fear they can't make the leagues of their high-achieving mothers. Molly recalls that after her parents divorced, her mother more than met the challenge of being a self-sufficient, single mother:

> *My mother had clearly been running the house all along, then she went on to become a lawyer on top of that. My mother was the first generation of supermoms, so I don't feel that I have to rebel against her to have a career. My response is more like, god, I'll never be able to do all she did. I know it's doable because I've seen it done, but it seems an incredible amount to live up to. Whenever I have a problem managing things, I think something's wrong. This shouldn't be. I always stop and say, "Wait a minute, my mother never had a problem doing everything."*

Women who had looked to their mothers as models might feel confused if they choose to depart from her example. Emily, thirty-five, whose mother had a career in publishing during her childhood, reflects: "I always really admired my mother. I used to show off about her at school, telling everybody how my mother went into the city every day. But when I became a mother I'd be there, cradling my daughter, and think: Why didn't she want to be there for this? It made me wonder about her, it made me wonder about me. I felt like a real throwback because it was important for me to be with my child. Now that I'm past the baby-love stage, I turn to Mom for inspiration again."

Whatever our take on her mothering performance, our own mother is our measure. "After the birth there was a period of redefining the kind of woman I want to be, always in relation to my mother," says Erica, whose son is not yet a year old. "I don't want to be the mother she was, but I do need to give her credit. I'm trying to figure out just where I'm comfortable, how different I want to be."

Even before we become mothers, we're sidling up to her, comparing. Looking at this literally, many women see their mothers as an internal guide as to when one should have children. Most women I talked to were highly aware of their mothers' ages when they had children, and how they stood in relation to that. Women often seemed to feel they had to justify why they were becoming mothers at a different age (usually older) than their mothers did. "When my mother was my age, she had me and my sister and my brother was on the way" a woman might say, somewhat incredulously, somewhat defensively.

"At one point in my early thirties, I started imagining every month that I was pregnant, even though I was using birth control," says Annette, now thirty-five. "Then my periods started getting especially painful and I started imagining that all sorts of things were wrong. Finally, I realized that something was saying to me, my *body* was saying to me, that I wanted a baby—now. My grandmother emigrated from Sweden at twenty-seven and had my mother at thirty-three. My mother had me when she was thirty-three. And *I* was thirty-three when my son was born. To tell the truth, I was hoping I wouldn't have a girl because that would have been too Freudian."

This mothering timetable suggests a hereditary component to the so-called biological clock, attesting to the strength of our identification with our mothers. Even something as seemingly uncharged as timing becomes a reference point. If her mother had children late, a woman might not be concerned. "My mother had me when she was forty-five, so I don't feel that there's much of a hurry for me to have children," Abby, a thirty-five-year-old yoga teacher, told me. If their mothers started their families younger, they can feel themselves aging beside her. I can't believe that it's a complete coincidence that I started this book when I was twenty-nine, my mother's age when I was born.

No doubt for all the reasons of conflict discussed, many women see their mothers as models of what to *avoid* in life. Most women, I've found, harbor some mothering fantasy that directly counters the kind of mothering they received. Even when they were basically happy with their mothers, women often see one area, one lack, that becomes the center of their own mothering philosophy. It could be a matter of roles

("I don't want to be too tired to talk to the kids after coming home from work"), lifestyles ("I saw my mother struggle as a single parent, and I think I'd like to give my children the structure of a family"), or something deeper and more personal.

"I hope my relationship with my daughter is better than the one I had with my mother," says Tricia.

> *In our rare talks about our relationship, my mother tells me that it's a lot better than the one she had with* her *mother. When I think about what a good mother/daughter relationship means to me, I think of closeness. And what comes to mind here is being comfortable with physical closeness, with each other's bodies. I'm terribly uncomfortable with my mother's body, and with my own body when I'm with her. I'm usually quite comfortable with nudeness, with my boyfriend, with my friends, but with her I'm not. I don't like her body. There's an almost physical revulsion I have to it, which is sad to me because that's the body I came out of. I'd like to be comfortable with my daughter. I'd like to feel we could take showers together and not be self-conscious.*

In Nancy Friday's *My Mother/My Self,* Helen Prentiss, a pseudonymous source who is identified as a child psychologist, describes the makings of her mothering fantasy:

> *As a child I always felt I was getting only my mother's "official" emotions—what she thought would be good for me. Not her real emotions. And so I learned to show her only what she wanted to see, the daughter in me—not the full person. The result was that while we were loving, it was not very honest. This is what I wanted to make up for in children of my own. Especially a little girl, because I could understand a girl's feelings.*[15]

My own mothering fantasy runs along similar lines. My imaginings are varied and unclear, but what they have in common is some expression of honesty. I picture being with a child—a son, a daughter, they alternate—walking, playing, doing something together spontaneously, usually outdoors (as opposed to in an airtight suburban home). I envision myself explaining things as completely as I can, waiting to change the subject until the last question runs out. My voice is level, not singsongy with condescension, not coy, or with the air of having been rehearsed.

Unable to give up my dream of honesty between my mother and myself, I re-create it as my vision of mothering. (As perhaps I have re-created it in becoming a writer—what better way to play out the need to be understood?) The danger, of course, is taking such a corrective plan too far, resulting in generation reacting against generation, perpetuating frustration and dissatisfaction among those who try to love.

For some women the deprivations of the past are so profound that they choose *not* to become mothers. Victoria Secunda, author of *When You and Your Mother Can't Be Friends,* says that most of the women she interviewed were terrified they would never be good mothers because of their emotionally incomplete childhoods. Some chose not to become mothers for this reason.[16] At the close of her book, Nancy Friday says that the memories lingering from her childhood have all but ruled out motherhood for her: ". . . I did not want to turn into the kind of nervous, frightened mother she had been to me. Alone, I can control the helpless mother who lives inside me. A mother myself, I would become just like her."[17]

Bearing sons seems the best solution to some, a way of having children yet avoiding the emotional turbulence stemming from one's own daughterhood. "I'm scared that as a mother I'm going to have to relive some of my painful experiences, especially if I have a girl," says Ruth. "What if she gets teased in the eighth grade? I couldn't take it. I think a son would be easier in that way."

In *Every Mother's Son,* Judith Arcana explains that when she decided to have herself sterilized, she had to give up her "daughter dream":

> *Some part of the desire for a daughter had been to do it right—make a "new woman," another part was to make a person who would be like me, and a third was to have a child with whom I could be intimate. I see that my reasons were, respectively, egotistical, doomed to failure, and questionable—to say nothing of an awful set of expectations for any daughter to face. Of course, I have come to see that my son is very like me, and we are intimate friends. And making a "new man" is much the same process of politically conscious mothering. Besides, the greatest part of the daughter dream had been the desire to reraise myself. The little girl I had wanted to raise was me.*[18]

From our vantage point, mother is static and we are the change. She represents not only what is but what *has been.* It's easy to forget, however, that she went through the same separation and individuation processes that we have, albeit in a different time and with different pressures. She, too, was no doubt anxious to "improve upon" the restrictive, unrealistic, or annoying child rearing of *her* parents. I remember when a friend of mine was going through a crisis because her parents disapproved of the younger, not-quite-settled man she was living with. In that inimitable way that sobbing gives way to laughter, she burst out with the realization that, some thirty years back, her *mother's* parents had initially been opposed to the marriage between her mother and father. We went around the group of us, and sure enough, more often than not our parents' marriages were considered radical at the time: wrong religion, wrong part of the city, wrong physical type ("Do you really want short kids?"). So our own parents' choices, which we regard as institutions, were often acts of defiance.

When I stop to think of it, my mother's life path could be seen this way. My mother and my uncle were raised primarily by governesses. Their relationships with their parents were far more formal than what we're used to today; aside from special occasions, they rarely had meals together. My grandmother was a gifted artist, and someone who viewed life as a spiritual quest, turning at various times to such sources as psychoanalysis, meditation, and alternative medicine. She and I were extremely close while she was alive (she died when I was twelve), but I can't know what it was like to be raised by her. My grandmother's tireless pursuits into art and mysticism were to me fascinating journeys, secrets I felt honored to be let in on. To my mother, however, they may have represented abandonment, or irritating distractions at the least. "I'm much more down to earth than Granny," my mother would say proudly, asserting her difference.

When my mother's turn came around, she made family, rather than her personal interests, the center of her life. She wanted to have control over the cooking and cleaning in the home and not have to be dependent on household help. There are similarities between them—devoted marriages, family loyalty, generosity—but in terms of their daily lives, my mother and grandmother could not have been further apart. Every afternoon my mother spent mastering a casserole or putting in calls for some charitable organization—which to my mind merely betrayed a lack of imagination—was her way of saying to *her* mother "I want my life to be different from yours"—the same refrain that echoes in my mind.

With all the yin and yang, action and reaction of mother/daughter relationships, we're often more alike than we think we are. When I'm listening to someone and my mind wanders, sometimes I can feel my mother's polite smile sitting on my face. Like her, I have the knack of finding things everyone else is convinced have been lost. Certain similarities may emerge when we become mothers. "My mother was very self-sacrificing, and I always promised myself I would never be that way," says Erica. "But now I can see that's what I do in my marriage and with the baby. It's too easy to just give and give and give." When we catch ourselves acting just like our mothers, sometimes we're appalled; sometimes we're inwardly proud.

Becoming a mother does present opportunities for reconciliation with one's own mother. "The particular empathy you develop with your mother is something you can never have until you have a child, until you stay up all night and clean up nasty messes," says Dr. Williams. "It can be a time of forgiveness. Pregnancy may help reorganize identification with the feminine."

The desire to make peace with one's mother, so strong in all of us, often gets played out in our vision of motherhood. The wish can become particularly intense once the baby is actually underway. "Pregnancy is a time of enormous idealization," says Dr. Counter. "Women often see themselves as being wonderful mothers, their mothers as wonderful mothers, and might well regard their relationship as having been wonderful too. One consequence of this fantasy is that the woman and her mother are poised for greater closeness."

Or poised for disappointment. Says Anita, thirty-four:

> *I had hoped having the baby would change things between me and my mother, put us on more equal footing. Actually, our relationship hasn't changed that much. Her harping and trying to control me has carried into whatever I'm doing, and now that happens to be caring for my baby. She loves buying clothes for the baby. This could be a nice thing, but in fact it's annoying. Luckily, I like her taste. But she determines what this baby wears. I let her have her fun, but when she starts saying, "Why is she wearing this and not that?" it gets ridiculous. I still feel like the daughter being told what to do.*

Just as motherhood offers possibilities for connection, it sets up the chance for a rift. "If the mother feels threatened by, or envious of her daughter, or if the daughter is determined to outdo the mother, the problems can be difficult to work out," says Dr. Williams.

> *Sometimes, a mother who devoted her whole life to her kids doesn't want to get involved with the grandchildren because she ''did that already'' and wants to have fun herself. What this communicates to the daughter is ''I paid my dues, now it's your turn,'' giving the impression that motherhood is terrible. Or, the mother might want to do everything, which undermines the daughter's confidence. What's helpful is the mother who's involved but not overwhelming, who acknowledges the daughter's competence but offers to give her a break. This way the daughter feels nurtured and the baby gets nurtured.*

Such nurturing can be healing to the relationship. It can help us get beyond the barriers that have arisen between our mothers and ourselves. As time goes on, the changes in women's lives may begin to bring mothers and daughters together. With more mothers having experience in the professional world and asserting control over their lives, moving into mother's realm might feel less like falling into an abyss. But roles are only one point of tension. The relationship is riddled with nuance. Entering motherhood is but one episode—potentially rich, potentially disheartening—in what is always a lifelong project.

Chapter 5

THE CAREER CLOCK

At some point in her career, about the time when children enter the mental picture, many a woman hits upon a jarring realization: her choices have run down. She has no alternative but to work, yet she is also to be the primary caretaker of a child. Her husband tells her how much he values her career, yet he won't sacrifice time from his to care for a baby. She needs the money, but she doesn't want to be forced to squeeze in time with her child like one more client appointment. Her employer expresses great sympathy yet can't come up with a viable compromise.

Choices? We were the envied generation, the first group of women able to do it all simply because we happened to be born at the right time. "Sure you have choices," the great corporate bosses of the world promise, putting a pin-striped arm around our shoulders reassuringly. "You can be with us, or you can leave." After being taught that in business dealings we should always strive for "win-win," we learn that when it comes to our own lives, the decisions are more like "either-or."

What's most curious about this is not that the situation exists (since when has the business world been such a good friend to women?) but how reluctant we are to see it for what it is. Even as we're straining desperately to do everything and stay sane, we're on our knees in gratitude to our employers for the privilege of lending them our gifts. We don't question the system but rather ourselves for not having strategically planned our lives better. But how could we have planned better when we so wanted to think that all was planned well enough for us already?

Not long ago I met two women, both unmarried, well situated in their businesses, and somewhat past forty-five, for a professional lunch.

Each ordered a salad—a light dusting of greenery that seemed more inspired by a decorator than a chef—since they both had business dinners scheduled a few hours later. At one point our conversation veered to the subject of working mothers, although none of us were.

"Every time one of my employees tells me she's going to have a baby, what I'd really like to tell her is to forget the job," said one woman, a successful literary agent. "No matter how good she is or what she says, I know she's just not going to accomplish the same amount."

"I'm running into this right now with a researcher, and she says she wants to work part-time," said the other, a marketing consultant. "We have such a small, close-knit company that I feel that I can't just abandon anyone, but at the same time I know it's going to cause a bit of a strain."

"Part-time is meaningless, and someone who runs out at five to pay the sitter isn't much better," the first agreed. "You simply can't be effective unless you go to the extra dinners, the meetings, the parties where deals are made, and almost no new mother is going to do that. If I hear that someone I've worked with is going to work at home, I basically give up on that connection. It's not the same."

I sat there quietly, painfully aware that I was potentially one of those obsolete workers who so infuriated them. My mood plummeted. I had enjoyed being on the inside of this select little group, and suddenly, by dint of my age and fertility status, I was thrust outside. How could they say these things, trashing my life plans, basically relegating me to a good decade of professional paralysis? I had thought that women who had worked to carve out a place for themselves would stick up for those of us who came along afterward.

My mind resisted any anger toward them or toward the rigid, efficiency-driven corporate world their views represented. The truth is, for the most part my career has treated me pretty well. Most of my creative and economic rewards have been filtered through my work. It has lent me an identity that has served as an open ticket wherever I travel: I am a writer. I have a business card that says so. I belong. To acknowledge that this has been just an arrangement of convenience, that in business you either fit the slot or you don't, is too disturbing, and therefore I've been unwilling to do so.

Although we may not have seen it that way, our generation has pretty much bought into the corporate world. Travel, deal-making, bottomless expense accounts, all the perks and paraphernalia of the working life beckoned to us. The working women older than us seemed to be having interesting lives, more interesting, certainly, than many of the suburban housewives we knew growing up. When I graduated from college in 1983, the business world was the place to be. In those days being "glamourous" wasn't lounging about scantily clad; it was wearing a drab-colored suit and some manner of tie, spouting MBA jargon in a corporate boardroom. Office romances were big. Those who couldn't find romance at the office could at least have a romance *with* the office: talking on a Watts line from work at 10 P.M. was cool; being at the movies at the same hour wasn't. If your speech sounded like excerpts from a macroeconomics textbook, if you networked in your spare time, if you partook of power meals, you were "in." Our response to the recessionary economics of the seventies, when huge numbers of corporate employees were laid off, was twofold: to compete to ensure we'd be too valuable to let go; and to make certain we were paid *at least* what we were worth.

The same way that buttoned-up junior executives were scorned as out-of-date in the late 1960s, in the 1980s, counterculture types were seen as living in the past. Going *beyond* the corporation and becoming an entrepreneur was admissable, and even admirable. But that required some background and backing from business, so one didn't stray too far. Completely bowing out of the corporate structure was more than a little peculiar, it was dumb. Especially for women.

We had just been let into the boys' club and were still on a high from it, wearing its uniform with pride. We were appreciative of the invitation; we were continually *told* we should be appreciative. Still feeling guilty that we could do what most of our mothers couldn't, still feeling the burden of having to prove our gender's seriousness and merit, we've scarcely allowed ourselves the luxury of being angry when we feel we've been screwed.

For myself, to try to challenge the system, or even to *question* it after I've dug myself in so deep, is too overwhelming a task. The automatic response, instead, is to challenge *myself* within the system. So, still at the luncheon from which my mind had wandered, an internal dialogue—the ongoing dialogue that I may pick up or drop at any given time, depending on my level of anxiety about how I'll manage my life—goes ahead at high speed: In my head I figure out how I'll piece together a work week that comes in distinct, previously claimed segments. I imagine that I will get up early, stay up late, twist the day into all shapes and contortions. I imagine that I can hustle enough so that I can solve the problem, so that there *is* no problem and no need to be angry. In order to come to terms with the situation, I create a fantasy where all is resolved.

Most women I know who haven't yet faced the motherhood/career dilemma retreat into similar fantasies. (Those who *have* faced it harbor few such illusions.) With imaginative flights once reserved for romantic reveries (watching sunsets on the beach, holding hands in the park) women today are conjuring visions for their work/family lives. Linda: "Maybe I'll redeem my shares in the company, have a nice chunk of money, and by that time John will be a practicing physician, and we'll move to the country, and . . ." Gina: "I'll marry somebody who makes a good income so the pressure will be off me, so when I'm a mother I can do all the things I've wanted to do . . ." Ellen: "My company will be going well enough so I can control my hours, and we can move to a place that's healthy for kids . . ."

Nice dreams, with lots of "ifs" attached to them. Counting on all the parts to converge neatly, we're forced to play military commander with our own existences: "Okay, we'll have one career milestone detonate here, and we'll hope to have the baby about the time he arranges a transfer out of the city, assuming he can . . ." We forget small details, like the fact that babies and pay raises don't always arrive on command. We feel we have to be incredibly in control, because once we lose control our entire future will simply collapse.

The movie *Baby Boom* from 1986 presents a Hollywood version of many women's collective fantasy. Diane Keaton plays a high-level, high-strung advertising executive who suddenly inherits the full-time care of a baby girl. She says good-bye to her job, moves to rural Vermont, and lives in tree-studded maternal bliss. When she starts to pine for a little of that office-hours activity, she develops a line of natural baby foods, which is, of course, a tremendous hit. (In the meantime, Keaton has found a sensitive, intellectual country gentleman, played by Sam Shepard, and fallen madly in love.) When the credits roll, she is a successful businesswoman *and* earth mother, living happily, wealthily, and romantically ever after.

This idyllic version avoids the conflicts, the guilts, the constant pulls and tugs of most women's reality. But perhaps more subversive than this omission (this is the movies, after all) is the underlying message: if you're resourceful or exceptional enough, none of these issues matter. Whether or not the business world addresses women's needs is irrelevant, because you can *transcend* the entire problem. That is in itself encouraging (and the daydreams reel away on our own private screens), but the implication is that if the compromises don't break as neatly as planned, then it's your own fault.

Our predicament is that what we want for ourselves is by definition contradictory: We want to devote time both to a career and to our children when we have them. The ideals we've grown up with demand that it be so. For many of us in our twenties and thirties today, our personal values mandate having a career. Even if jobs alone don't define us, work is at least an important piece of the definition. "There's a part of me that thinks being a housewife isn't enough, even though intellectually I think that should be okay," Melissa confides.

For us work is more than something to do, or even a way to generate income. It's a source of self-confidence and identity. In past generations, the span of a woman's career was usually a transition period, a brief spell of autonomy between moving out of her father's parlor and into her husband's kitchen. By contrast, we've worked since the day we graduated. Our jobs have had more of a chance to become entwined in our lives. The independence they afford has become far too precious. "My clients say to me, 'Go home. It's not worth it,' " says Laura. "But I've been raised with the Protestant ethic, that you work hard and do your best. I never thought I wouldn't be working."

But many of these same women who regard work as inseparable from life *also* have the conviction that a mother should be there for her child. In a study at Brown University of 3,000 college students, conducted in 1980, many women said that in their experience, children with working mothers were less well adjusted—a conclusion no research has ever borne out.[1] "I thought it would be no big deal to work," says Erica. "I figured, I'll get child care. It's only money. But I don't want to turn him over to another person. On Monday mornings I go to work and my husband stays home. If the baby's fussy or acts up, I imagine it's because he senses I'm not there. I believe he's good-natured and content because usually I am there."

Whether or not we had round-the-clock maternal care ourselves, we grew up in a time when that was considered the norm. As for those of us with mothers at home, our family lives were organized around full-time mothering. Often we absorbed the belief that this was the correct—the moral—way to raise children. True, we avidly rejected the stay-at-home lifestyle and put great stock in—not to mention time into—our careers. But we launched those careers as individuals, not as mothers or even, planning ahead, as future mothers. What would we do when we found ourselves with a child? Funny, many of us didn't think of that. It somehow seemed a life apart, as if what happened then would be happening to some other person.

Lately there's been much talk about child-care arrangements, as well there should be, but the subtext to this discussion is that many women aren't at ease with child care either. Viscerally, most Americans reject the notion of bringing up children en masse. We're not a socialist country, and few of us have a true "kibbutz" or communal mentality. According to the American mythology, the highest cultural virtue is individualism, and one aspect of individualism is having the opportunity to raise *your* children in whatever manner *you* choose. Any third-party involvement detracts from that right (unless, perhaps, you hire a qualified individual to handle the charge on your behalf, though to many even this is suspect). The point is that while many are actively working to develop child-care alternatives, a societal ambivalence toward third-party care has created barriers to progress on both the governmental and private level. There's also a measure of elitism involved. In eras past, group child care was the alternative for those who couldn't provide care themselves—the destitute, the dissolute, the desperate. Despite the daily stresses, and despite the lack of any evidence that good-quality group care hampers development, to many women farming children out for the day smacks of neglect. In *Backlash,* Susan Faludi describes how an onslaught of alarmist reports on the dangers of day care picked up on and perpetuated women's fears.

For some women, none of the choices available is sufficient. Concentrating on work at the expense of mothering means slighting the children; mothering at the expense of work means forfeiting independence and autonomy. Yet at the same time, attempting each task partway isn't good enough. Unlike most decisions, in this case compromising is not merely a matter of give and take. It inevitably means compromising oneself.

Even after a decision is made, few women seem satisfied with their own efforts. "I find all the switching back and forth very frustrating," says Nancy, thirty-one, a banker with one child. "I wasn't prepared for the feelings of being torn, of feeling that I'm not spending enough time with my daughter and that I'm not doing enough at work. I had always had the belief that if you just try enough, work hard enough, everything will be fine."

Their own uncertainty can leave women defensive, feeling suspicious of those who've opted otherwise. "I have two friends with children, Elizabeth and Terry. One works and the other doesn't," says Janice, twenty-eight, a lawyer. "Terry will say to me, 'Elizabeth stays home all day with her children. Can you believe it?' Then Elizabeth says, 'Terry works all day and is never home with her child. Can you believe it?' It seems neither of them is terribly comfortable with what they're doing, and both are working very hard at convincing themselves they're doing right."

A few years ago the media "discovered" a battle being waged between stay-at-home housewives and on-the-job women. Each group apparently saw its integrity threatened and felt the need to justify its position. Articles appeared with titles like "Why Working Mothers Make Me Mad" (*McCall's*), "The Mommy Wars" (*Newsweek*), and "The Maternity Backlash: Mother versus Mother" (*Working Women*). While this conflict has been hyped up (as one commentator put it, "You can always sell tickets to a female catfight"[2]), perhaps of greater concern to women now confronting the issue is that we've *internalized* the conflict.

I remember talking about these matters with a suite-mate back in college, in one of those rare moments of clarity when it dawned on us that someday we'd have to leave school and support ourselves. Andrea, an industrious premed student, asserted that when she had a baby, she'd be back in her white lab coat within a week. From the conviction in her voice it seemed she had given the point some consideration. I was appalled. What a horrible attitude to take, I thought. What a hypocrite, supposedly dedicating her life to human need, while not caring a bit for her child's welfare. What did she think an infant was, someone you could just discharge, like a patient, or send off silently with a prescription: take two glasses of milk and call my answering service?

Yet I recall being equally stunned a few years later when a coworker, a talented woman about my age, told me that she would leave her job in a second if she got married and had a baby. Is that all this place is to you, I wondered to myself, a way station before you throw yourself whole into some man's life? Doesn't your work mean more to you than that?

The contradiction between these two views never became apparent to me. Nor did the possibility that I could confront the same contradiction head-on in my own life. With the inexhaustible naiveté of youth, I had always assumed everything would fall into place. I wasn't forced to fight to *have* a career, so why would I have to scramble to keep it alive? After all these years as a professional, haven't I earned some right to *be* that professional, whether or not I exercise my professionalism forty hours a week? Why should growth as a woman necessarily entail a retreat in one's career?

When we don't come up with answers, we stop asking the questions. We go on in our careers—because we need to, because we want to—and rely on the fantasies we create to inspire us. But, since our life scripts aren't sketched out in Hollywood, any fantasy that includes babies sends all those other dreams ricocheting against one another. And the pieces that bounce the most usually include those connected to work: The position work assumes in life is bound to change. It needn't be supplanted entirely, but priorities inevitably shift.

Some women find this threatening. Intuitively, they feel that when they have a baby, their work drive will falter. Once they step past that invisible dotted line that marks the entry into a new life (they can pass through one way but it's impossible to pass back), they'll lose their "edge," whatever it was that kept them motivated and moving. Or their identity will simply dissolve. It's not that motherhood and its distractions aren't appealing; merely that the change of focus—which means a move away from the familiar and toward the unknown—is disconcerting.

Sometimes the fear is more tangible, often related to a specific goal. In the same way that some men feel they need to "establish" themselves before getting married, many women feel they should reach certain milestones before they conceive. "I know it's time that I start thinking of having children, but if I do now, I'm afraid I'll never get to where I need to be in my business," says Natalie, thirty-three. "I've been working toward this for years, and now that I can see things coming together I'm afraid I'd regret it if I let anything get in the way."

According to Dr. Davis, "career can sometimes be used as an excuse to avoid doing the thing you fear doing the most. A woman might say, 'I can't be a perfect mother until I'm a perfect scholar, lawyer, whatever.' " Unfortunately, she says, while waiting for the perfect moment to arrive, one can fall into a kind of emotional paralysis. In certain ways, the analogy with men postponing relationships holds: "Men reluctant to commit feel they have to develop themselves enough to feel they can give themselves to another without losing themselves," she explains. "What they fear is the merging of closeness, the longing, need, and dependency. Quite similar, in fact, to what many women today fear about having a baby."

Often, however, it's the idea of work rather than the work itself that's hard to relinquish. As priorities naturally rearrange themselves and work is less prone to cry out for attention, many women feel liberated. "I felt so differently about my job after I got pregnant," says Aimee. "I would sit in my office with my hand on my belly. Someone would be yelling at me on the phone about something and I would think, what's the problem? Why are they making such a big fuss about this piece of paper? A few pieces of paper maybe, but it's really all so irrelevant."

Others, who have managed to keep their work selves and their "self" selves from getting hopelessly intertwined, or are able to see aspects of work as emblematic of one stage of their lives, have fewer qualms about cutting back at work. "I don't feel my job is that important, but then I never did," says Tammy, a physician who recently had a baby. "I never believed I was that indispensable to my employer. I don't work to achieve or to climb the status ladder, but to socialize, to be where things are happening, and to have some intellectual stimulation. Those things I can get by working part-time. Working and being with the baby give me very different kinds of satisfaction."

But forgetting for a moment the financial imperatives (which can be considerable), lots of mothers feel that their careers are too much a part of their lives to give up with ease. "From the time we started talking about children, I've said I was willing to make the compromise in my career," says Nancy.

> *Whenever I complain about it, my husband says, "But you* said *you didn't mind." Well, that's true. In one breath I might say that and mean it, but in the next I might be worried about being promoted. In banking the place you want to be is vice-president. At this point I don't see that happening, and I'm conflicted about it. I've been so trained to be career-oriented, I'm not prepared to let it go. Even though consciously I made the decision to slow down at work, emotionally I wasn't ready to.*

Many professional women who plan to become mothers at some point are clearly unnerved by the idea of stopping work. ("I'd go *nuts!*" is the frequent rejoinder to the suggestion.)

Although we know that in terms of actual toil and time mothering stands up to just about any job, many of today's women have trouble accepting full-time child care as a valid way to spend the day. Often they accept it in theory, but not when it comes to themselves. The common feeling is that they must *do* something, and doing means taking part in some activity that is acknowledged and economically rewarded by society. No matter how much they may *do* there, staying home inevitably falls under the category of "not working," something that doesn't always sit well with us. To many, staying home implies passivity, backwardness, inertia.

Melanie reflects:

> *This month I've been between jobs and I've felt lost. Last night I went out to dinner with two friends, both engineers, and I felt I didn't have anything to talk about. They in their crisp little work clothes, me in jeans. I felt out of it. I can't wait until I start up again. Then I'll have my sense of purpose back. The funny thing is that I never really thought about my career as a career. I always thought I'd marry and be taken care of. But now that I've married someone who can take care of me, I'd feel guilty if I didn't work because all this time I've been taking care of myself.*

In all of my visions for my own life, work figures prominently. For me, trying to imagine not working is like trying to picture myself living in an igloo: a prospect so remote as to seem ridiculous. Work is a matter not only of schedule, but of identity. It's part of an overall response to life, an engagement with the world around me. Even when I've worked in an office as opposed to at home, as I do now, my work has refused to be conveniently partitioned into appropriate chunks of time. Rather, it sprawls out languidly across the day like a landscape, marking either foreground or background, but one way or other setting the mood. Sometimes it nags like an inner voice; sometimes it cheers with its rewards. Welcome or unwelcome, work manages to creep into every nook and cranny, justifying the time, defining it.

At times it chills me to acknowledge how important work is to who I am. Intuitively, I feel it shouldn't be that way. But if I opted out of work, what kinds of thoughts would fill this mind, which up to now has been so contentedly occupied? All I can envision is some sort of blank where my sense of self had been.

In her study of sex roles, Margaret Mead suggests that the essential difference between the genders is that in order to achieve their role identity, girls and women can "be" while boys and men must "do." In *Male and Female,* she writes:

> *Women's biological career-line has a natural climax structure that can be overlaid, muted, muffled and publicly denied, but which remains as an essential element in both sexes' view of themselves. . . . The young Balinese girl to whom one says, "Your name is I Tewa?" and who draws herself up and answers, "I am Men Bawa" (Mother of Bawa) is speaking absolutely. She is the mother of Bawa; Bawa may die tomorrow, but she remains the mother of Bawa; only if he had died unnamed would her neighbors have called her "Men Belasin," "Mother Bereft." Stage after stage in women's life-histories thus stand, irrevocable, indisputable, accomplished. This gives a natural basis for the little girl's emphasis on being rather than on doing. The little boy learns that he must act like a boy, do things, prove that he is a boy, and prove it over and over again, while the little girl learns that she is a girl, and all she has to do is to refrain from acting like a boy.*[3]

As long as a woman produces offspring, her place in the world is confirmed and she need do nothing else. End of anthropology lesson. Well, Mead's observation may have been apt for Pacific Islanders in the 1940s (and subsequent scholars have questioned even that), but it certainly is not universal among American women in the 1990s. Countless women, it seems, are betraying their gender by forgetting how to "be."

This is not surprising, says Dr. Davis, since today "women do not have that part of themselves that involves being with the child and being available to the child affirmed by society. In rhetoric, perhaps, but the real rewards are reserved for the structured, career-oriented life."

The incentive to work comes from men too. Whereas in the past women "got" a man by being delicate, passive, and noncritical, and avoiding being competitive or intellectually threatening, today we may seduce men with our brains, success, and earning power. Some women feel that the promise of continued success and earning was inherent in their wedding vows. Without that, are they still worth the love? Some have their doubts: "I'd lose respect for any man who didn't lose respect for me if I stopped working," Julie asserts.

Often women hesitate to introduce such a change in the marriage. "I met my husband, an attorney, through work, and most of our friends are people we've met together through business," says Nancy. "We relate a lot on the level of understanding each other's jobs and knowing the same people. If I stayed home, I would be nervous about him not perceiving me as being in that world. He has voiced concern about my being home too long, saying he was afraid I would have nothing to talk about except the baby. I think it threatens him to think that I wouldn't be a peer. We've never talked about it in those terms, but I think it's part of my decision to work." Annette, who has been keeping her business going at home, says of her husband: "I don't think it's fair to lock him in the breadwinning role. I don't like the idea of swindling a man who thinks he's getting an ambitious career woman."

Many women feel assailed by conflicting signals, telling us alternately that as women we should do *and* we should be. "People are saying to us we shouldn't get carried away with our jobs, that we should be content to be mothers," says Melanie. "But then there's the message that if we want professional parity with men, we have to be out there and not at home."

Recognizing how unsettling it is not to actively "do," many women have expressed the idea that as mothers they'd be more comfortable working and wishing they had more time than actually having the time. Often, says Dr. Davis, this push-and-pull enacts the pushing-and-pulling feelings a woman has about her own mother. In wishing she had more time, she's wishing she could be ever-available the way her mother had been (or the way she *wished* mother had been). But she may be scared of that very availability. "The mothers of today's women were caught on the cusp of social change, and many were fighting the restrictions of the mother role," she says. "The daughters picked up on that frustration. They might have gotten the structural mothering, but often they didn't really get the nurturing mothering." The thought of taking on that role themselves terrifies many women because it stirs up the frustrations their mothers felt and that they felt regarding their mothers.

The majority of women today work, but society has been somewhat slow to accept that professionalism and femininity are not mutually exclusive. Feminist psychologists have pointed out that successful women often feel that the qualities that brought them professional success—aggressiveness, ambition, etc.—are marks of their *failures* as women. Some women feel that in order to preserve their femininity they have to get out of the business world altogether.

"My last boyfriend said to me that at the rate I'm going, I'll end up with a pet dog instead of a baby," says Kelley. "That was pretty harsh. I got really defensive about that, because I was scared he was right. Work was everything to me, even though I said it wasn't and I didn't want it to be. It got me thinking, and I realized I can't even do basic feminine things. I do a lot of microwaving and very little cooking. It's the environment I'm in. Women aren't women at work. I'm afraid that if I stay here much longer, I'll completely lose that in myself. I wear more dresses than I ever did, probably as a symbolic way of maintaining my sense of femininity."

Kelley said she was seriously considering making a change and had thought of moving to rural Spain. "When I was there last year I saw women who stayed home and loved their kids. I saw the most incredible children. I met this guy who delivered his own child. It made me think of how far away from the natural, family side of life I am."

Because society presents the notions of "working" (professionalism) and "not-working" (motherhood) in such a polarized way, many women have a hard time reconciling their own desires to do and to be. As a result, some women experience wide swings in the way they see themselves, moving from hard-core career woman to mother-goddess in one sweep. Sometimes this is a way of overcompensating for their own ambivalence—about either motherhood or their own ambition. Although Kelley says that it would be difficult for her to stay home with a child in the city where she now lives and works, she imagines that in Europe domesticity would be fulfilling. Maybe it would be. But might she be perpetuating the split by turning herself into two women: the "career" woman at home and the "natural" woman in Spain?

Our crazy maternal myths still maintain that once a woman thinks about babies, the clouds part overhead and she glows and hums and starts knitting things for junior's feet; that she becomes a fount of serenity. Somehow, society wants to erase the ambitious, businesslike aspects of the woman from view. So fierce is this fallacy that many women who have children yet feel the urge to work are ashamed of it. According to Arlene Rossen Cardozo, author of *Sequencing: Having It All but Not All at Once,* many are afraid to realistically assess their own options for this very reason: "Some women resist exploring their finances because they suspect that they could manage without the money and don't want to admit to themselves that they work primarily to meet psychological needs . . . If they evaluate the financial situation thoroughly and find that they are working *primarily* for psychic rewards with money a secondary factor, they feel guilty."[4]

Women shouldn't have to feel apologetic for wanting to work—especially given that we're continually reminded that men and women alike are measured by their professional status. In social situations, in order to make that leap from talking about the weather to talking about anything else, someone will invariably ask what you "do." The response provides an anchor for the conversation. It determines whether you talk about the quirks of the economy, the splendors of the Far East, or recent scientific breakthroughs, and, to some extent, whether you'll become friends. It's almost as if the professional world were one giant college campus, with each profession a separate fraternity or club. There's advertising and media (throw great parties), medicine (think they're absolute gods), and sales (don't let them start talking). And just like in school, not to be a member of any group is the worst fate of all.

Many mothers who don't work are resentful of this. "I don't like being typecast as just a breeder," says Jane. "When people ask what I do now—and people always do ask—I say I'm a mother. They say, 'Oh, a housewife?' And I say, 'No, not a housewife. I'm a mother.' Then they say, 'Oh, that's good for you.' It angers me, because they say it with such condescension."

The phrase "just a housewife" sends a shiver down most women's spines. It conjures up images of a hapless woman mindlessly running a vacuum cleaner across a single spot on the carpet, with diapers and dishcloths draped about the house like flags at the U.N. The trouble is that many people have the idea that you can judge a person's mettle by her title, and they don't know what to make of smart, accomplished women who opt to commute down the hall to the nursery rather than to a high-rise office space. Nor can others always accept that making this choice does not mean making the choice *forever.* In what can only be society's projecting its doubts about women being in the work force, a mother's taking a few years off is often interpreted as a major social statement.

Women who choose to stay home as their children grow do not see their task as a sorry substitute for a paying job, and it infuriates them that some people do see it that way—and that other people's views can undermine their confidence. Although she has come to grips with the notion of staying home, Linda is apprehensive of how *others* will handle it. "I'm not sure how I'll feel in the future when some people will start to see me as the doctor's wife," she says. "I don't think I'll react to that very well, not after I've made a professional name on my own. I'm not the little girl who went out to find a husband with good prospects and now gets all her ego satisfaction from him."

All of these issues form the emotional backdrop for our own battles between the career clock and the biological clock. We're at an odd juncture because neither working nor nonworking mothers are getting true support from the culture. Underlying the personal confusion is society's chronic confusion about women and paid work. Looked at historically, the conflict is clearly artificial: women have always done productive work apart from child care. The problem seems not to be work in itself, but a combination of corporate intransigence and residential planning (suburbs were designed with the idea that people would *leave* them for their jobs).

According to sociologist Jessie Bernard, the role of full-time mother is "the product of an affluent society. In most of human history and in most parts of the world even today, adult, able-bodied women have been, and still are, too valuable in their productive capacity to be spared for the exclusive care of children."[5] Indeed, one study of 186 societies found that mothers were the primary caretakers of children in less than half. After infancy, the figure dropped to less than 20 percent.[6]

When money-earning work took place in the home, women's participation in it was not questioned. Then, as home-based tasks were moved to factories and commercial centers in the nineteenth century, woman was, essentially, laid off from her job. A new job had to be found for her—and that was taking care of children and the household. Women, of course, had always done this, but in the late nineteenth century domestic duties were accorded supreme, even mystical, importance. As the number of children per family fell, the emotional investment in each rose dramatically. Woman's role was to instill moral purpose in her children and maintain the moral character of the home. To allow anything to intrude on this was not only a failure on the woman's part but a threat to society, which looked to the institution of home for a sense of stability and continuity.

The late nineteenth century also saw the growth of popular science, and one of the scientists' favorite preoccupations was noting how ill equipped women were for anything but domestic tasks. Severing "women's work" from that of men was considered an evolutionary milestone.

Women who sought to work (or vote, or study) were "promoting *'anti-differentiation'* "—and moving society "a step backward toward savagery."[7]

As Barbara Ehrenreich and Deirdre English point out in *For Her Own Good,* women were thought to be "ruled" by their reproductive organs. Since it was believed that the human body had a certain amount of energy that had to be carefully rationed, it followed that woman's reproductive function had to be fiercely protected from the potentially corrupting influence of the brain. The hysteria that raged rampantly through the upper-class female population only confirmed that women were at the mercy of their capricious ovaries and uteri and were thus unfit for work.

Even though working-class women were laboring long hours under difficult conditions, experts clung to the notion that femininity was a fragile state and that too much mental or physical exertion put a woman—and her present or potential children—at tremendous risk. One turn-of-the-century physician contended that higher education caused women to "overdraw their reserves," leading to the loss of mammary function or fertility.[8]

In her 1909 book *The Century of the Child,* author Ellen Key asserted that the right of women to work infringed on the rights of their future children. She called women's employment a "crime against their feminine nature" and denounced women who hindered their mothering capacity by "excessive study, excessive work, or staying up nights."[9] Even as recently as 1943, a popular child-care guide urged the prospective mother to avoid mental activity during pregnancy, lest she produce a nervous infant.[10]

Throughout this period, the number of women employed outside the home rose steadily. The growth of towns and cities, the arrival of immigrants, and the development of power-driven machinery that relieved physical labor all contributed.[11] Most women, however, did leave the work force when they married. This was in part a reflection of societal expectation but was also due to the fact that the conditions of work available to women might have made marriage appear a relief. As long as women stayed in their own employment corner (as teachers, servants, laundresses, seamstresses, or salesclerks), there was little fuss. But whenever women were seen to threaten men's jobs, all the old rhetoric about women was hauled out. As an example, one labor leader warned in

1897: "The demand for female labor is an insidious assault upon the home; it is the knife of the assassin, aimed at the family circle."[12]

As the twentieth century began, women were increasingly combining work and marriage. Once the depression hit, however, married women were encouraged, or even ordered, to leave their jobs. But in what has proved to be a pattern with women's employment, popular attitudes had little bearing on what women actually *did*, for in the interwar period the number of women working increased. Similarly, after the Second World War women who had been working were urged back into the home, but the number of women who left the work force was just about matched by the number who joined it at about the same time.[13] Public opinion seemed to endorse or condemn women's work of its own accord, ignoring reality yet influencing how people regarded the issue.

This was precisely the case in the fifties: Women were continuing to enter the labor force even as they were told how "dangerous" working was. An ever-growing band of experts claimed that women were supposed to be satisfied by mothering and housework; if they, even unconsciously, desired anything more, their children would suffer. Theories from the young sciences of psychology and sociology were used to convince women that this was the case. Women were warned that an interest in joining the professional world called their femininity into question (and certainly every child deserved to have a *real* woman as his mother). And any woman who took a job stood the risk of "unmanning" her husband and thus destroying her marriage.

One potential barrier to such ideas was the fact that more women now had access to education, and thus, presumably, greater ambitions. The academic establishment responded by trying to impose domesticity upon the curriculum. One (male) college president asked, "[Is it] impossible to present a beginning course in foods [that is] as exciting . . . as a course in post-Kantian philosophy?"[14] Housework was presented as though it demanded the intellectual rigor of any other postcollege pursuit. A marriage guide from the war period asserted: "A woman who is an effective homemaker must know something about teaching, interior decoration, cooking, dietetics, consumption, psychology, physiology, social relations, community resources . . . housing, hygiene, and a host of other things. She is a general practitioner rather than a specialist."[15]

In the early sixties, the rise of the single, urban culture, glorified in

Helen Gurley Brown's *Sex and the Single Girl,* announced to the world that not only was the employed woman not miserable or maladjusted, she *enjoyed* her work and the freedom it gave her; not only was she not masculinized and coarse, she reveled in her femininity and sex appeal.

Women came to be split into two camps—career women and mothers—each with its own set of stereotypes. Housewives were depicted as pathetic, outdated creatures. The popular culture seized on this, churning out books and films about housewives who were mad, sex-starved, or hopelessly addicted to drugs. Career women were cast as icy, aggressive, soulless characters, secretly lonely and yearning for love. As for the working mother, no one knew what to do with her, so for the most part it was still assumed she didn't exist.

But she did exist, for the reality was that many women *had* to work. With businesses busy selling and everybody busy consuming, the American standard of living—the level that was considered the middle-class norm—had crept up beyond the point where one income could sustain a family. The continual increase in the number of working mothers was ignored because it belied the assumption of American prosperity. Mothers "helped out" by taking on jobs on top of their child-rearing responsibilities. The economic recession of the 1970s accelerated this trend, and as we moved into the 1980s *two* well-paid professionals sometimes struggled to support a family comfortably. What is more, with increasing rates of divorce, single motherhood, and male unemployment, many women were supporting entire families on their own.

This is not to say that the importance of jobs to women began and ended with the money; nor that there weren't plenty of women who, often at some financial sacrifice, opted to stay home with their children. But the ambiguity of the situation added to the tension. Women weren't supposed to have to work. If a woman felt she needed to work in order to pay the bills, what did that say about her family? If she had taken on a career to "tide over" her family and the rough times had eased, was it okay to *want* to keep the job because she *liked* it? Could a married woman with children ever be as interesting as a career woman? Could a single woman with a career ever have the feminine integrity of a full-time mother?

In the early 1980s, the working mother burst upon the scene in the form of a new image, the Superwoman. This turned the questions about work and family into a nonissue: the Superwoman could do it all. This was a manipulative image in that it presumed it was up to the *woman*—

as opposed to her husband or her employer or society itself—to ensure that everything was doable. As long as she could buy the right products and services to keep her going, that is. The Superwoman (also known through other media incarnations like *Redbook's* "Juggler" or *Good Housekeeping's* "New Traditionalist") was a marketer's dream: here was someone to whom you could pitch clothing, cars, and business equipment in addition to all the cleaning and cooking standards.

Nurturing both a family and a career can be stressful, but it's not a stress most women can simply consume their way out of. The constant shifting of roles can in itself be wearying. Nancy describes how she had trouble bouncing back and forth:

> *When I went back to work I was still nursing and had to pump according to the baby's eating schedule. That meant pumping three times during the day and storing the bottles in the office refrigerator. I would be negotiating some loan on the phone, look at my watch, and think: Oh no, I have to pump. I would have to walk down to another office, close the door, and call a friend to talk about mother things for a while to calm myself down. I just couldn't pump when I was in the work mode.*

Motherhood can also be a rude financial awakening. Many women, used to coasting along on a decent salary or raking it in after the merger of assets that was marriage in the eighties, are stunned by the costs of having a family and the potential hardship of trying to get by on one salary. "In retrospect, I would have made different decisions. I don't think we would have bought our house if I knew how important the work flexibility would be to me," Nancy reflects. "If we had kept our old place, there'd be less financial pressure now." For many mothers, any relief the paycheck provides is nearly offset by the cost of child care. Other women feel trapped in their jobs because of insurance and other benefits, or because they fear that once they leave they'll lose their spot for good.

Lots of women lament the lack of backing for mothers among *other* female professionals, who they had hoped would be more sympathetic. "From the instant my pregnancy started to show, I started to feel how little female loyalty there is in my profession," Laura says of the stockbrokering business. "The older women, those who broke ground for us, were not in any way mentors for the younger women; they were still struggling to create their own business relationships. When I voluntarily left the profession, they took offense. Oddly, the senior men nearing retirement were more supportive. I think it has a lot to do with their own daughters being professionals."

According to Aimee, who now works part time, the moment she heads for the door is the most awkward of the day: "I can feel everyone glaring at me. No matter what you do when you're there, other people don't think it's enough. There's this machismo thing where the later you stay the more valuable you are. The women who are unmarried and childless are the harshest critics. They make it a point of saying goodnight to me. They say, 'Oh, you're leaving. It's that time. Good night.' "

But perhaps the biggest shocker is the degree to which the business world has failed to accommodate women—something they might not have had to face before the issue of motherhood arose. According to a report in *The New York Times,* companies tend to favor men who are married, while women who aren't married and don't have children get the nod over women who either have children or are perceived as a reproductive risk.[16] "It takes women a while to tune into this," says psychiatrist Carol Nadelson. "There may be women at their level, but when you look a level or two up, where people are making the decisions, it's still mostly men. I think it's harder for women today than it was for me, because I knew what the score was. These women didn't expect the double standard."

We hid these truths from ourselves for a reason: because they're potentially devastating. So devastating, says Dr. Nadelson, that the disenchantment may tip the balance of a given woman's work/home decision:

> *The issues women in careers deal with now are draining, time-consuming, and confusing. It makes many women want to just forget the whole thing. A woman may decide she's tired of hitting her head against the wall without getting anyplace. Her attitude is "I'm not going to get the promotion anyway. The child will be more rewarding." It's a retreat, but it's more discouragement than an actual lack of courage. Women may not articulate this, and may not even be aware of what's prompting them to leave. The myth is that women are making choices that are free and independent choices. In some ways they are free, but often there's this frustration in the background.*

In spite of all the difficulties, many women find that having children is far from the worst thing for their careers. Women who had been immersed in work talk about "balance." ("I'm just not as interested in staying hyped up all the time. Before I was probably out of control and didn't even know it," one woman confessed.) Those who hadn't settled on a path say mothering has helped give them a focus. ("I sometimes think that if I hadn't had my daughter, I would have been an academic drifter. Instead of bullshitting around for years, I've raised a child. Now I appreciate the value of time," says another.)

Other women talk about unexpected career pluses as mothers. "Here in the suburbs, I've met a lot of high-powered women simply because we all have children," says Annette. "Having kids makes things more egalitarian. I would have done anything for these same contacts a few years ago. People who wouldn't have talked to you because you weren't at their level suddenly become your buddies."

There do seem to be some positive changes. More companies are offering—or talking about offering—flexible schedules for women, and often for men. It would be too optimistic, however, to conclude that this reflects any great shift in attitude. More likely the cause is economic: businesses are waking up to the fact that working women are too valuable to lose from attrition. Training new employees is a very expensive undertaking. Companies are beginning to look at the long-term contribution a woman can make. Some appear willing to work a little harder to keep employees who will produce for them over the years.

This is happening faster in some fields than others. "When firms came to interview us, the women in my class let them know up-front that flexible leave policies would be attractive to us," says Chloe, a lawyer and mother who is working three-quarter time. "Perhaps a few years ago women felt they had to pretend they weren't interested in time off. Here, they were bending over to accommodate us. With our training, we're not so easily replaced, so we do have the power. I've noticed, though, that the secretaries in these same firms are not treated so generously."

We can't just wait for employers to decide that reaching out to families is good for the bottom line. The commitment has to be larger than that. And some of that commitment has to come from us, as we're closest to the issues. Part of this involves remembering what we went into the workplace for. "In the sixties, the hope was that as women got powerful jobs, the business world would become a more humane place," says Isobel, a researcher and teacher who started her own career at that time. "I don't see that happening. I see frustration, but not enough of the anger that can be turned toward challenging the system and working to help other women."

Society's failure to support women has thrown us in upon ourselves, leaving us preoccupied with our own lives, with little energy left to raise questions and make demands on behalf of women as a group. Society's refusal to embrace the working mother has provoked in us insecurities and doubts, so that we don't feel justified in making such demands. We accept society's definition of the problem (whether or not an individual mother should work) rather than tackle the real problem—that our economic structure is incompatible with raising children.

In an essay written in 1986, Barbara Ehrenreich discusses what she calls the corporate woman's malaise. She examines the latest crop of literature aimed at working women and finds a lot of advice about "moving" within the corporate world but little mention about what this mobility means save for professional advancement. Instead, she reports, "we find successful corporate women asking, 'Why am I doing what I'm doing? What's the point here?' or confiding bleakly that 'something's missing.' "[17]

The answer, she concludes, is not to pack up and become a homemaker (although that is a decision a woman can make). Rather, it is to question the values of a system in which ladder climbing is the only thing that matters. To reduce the dilemma to working versus not working or even work versus family is to miss an important point. Work *is* part of our lives. Even if we take a few years off, we're undoubtedly going to work again. Thinking about motherhood prompts us to rethink what's important to us. Maybe we can bring some of that rethinking to the workplace with us.

Chapter 6

SEX, BABIES, AND ROCK AND ROLL

A few months ago, a friend and her husband came to spend the weekend with us. As we were driving back from the airport, commiserating on their long flight delay, we learned that Anne was expecting. (Actually, the way it was put to us was, "Marc is going to be a father," but we made the connection quickly enough.) This was the first time that a close friend I had grown up with—been through college with, shared boyfriend horror stories with—was pregnant. Something about the way I identified with Anne—the way our lives had paralleled each other's—and about the intimacy of the weekend, made me incredibly conscious of my own body as a potential baby carrier. It was the small resort town's last big weekend of summer, inns and restaurants were full and thriving, and I could envision a bold VACANCY sign tacked up on my abdomen. Glimpsing Anne in her bathing suit, I noticed a slight, unfamiliar thickness around her middle. I privately took pride in the spareness of my own shape but somehow felt that this vanity would be fleeting, just as the chill in the air told me I wouldn't be swimming much longer. My body felt less mine, yet more so; I felt exquisitely aware of my own femaleness.

This feeling triggered something in me. It started as a low, rolling hunger, and by evening I felt inordinately amorous. Somewhere in my mind the link was made: if you have sex, you can become a family; you can take this wild, intriguing step that my friends had chosen to. Intellectually I knew all that, but my body, which seemed to have forgotten it, was apparently recognizing the equation anew. I had always been able to think of my husband as a father in the abstract, picturing him doing wonderful things with children who had sprung into my imagination already born. Now I acknowledged the brute biological truth of it all: he had sperm. And any one of those frantic, microscopic things (I've seen them darting about in science films) could transform my body completely. So there he was, innocently flossing his teeth after a long evening of hosting, while I was eyeing him strategically, having predatory thoughts about his sperm.

Looking back on this, what's odd is not that stirrings of wanting a baby and stirrings of wanting sex had converged but that it had seemed to me that I had made some great discovery. That it takes egg and sperm to make a baby is among the more obvious facts we live with, yet somehow we don't live *it.* We learn that sex is about making babies, then learn that it's not about making babies but about a whole lot of other things. Ours is the first generation to grow up with the pill and legalized abortion—to come of age when the consequences of sex had become more manageable (not that we can take our reproductive choices for granted today). In the past, a woman's initiation into sex often coincided with her initiation into motherhood; as soon as she was paired off she went straight to the task of producing children. By contrast, women of our generation might be sexually active for years before even thinking about family. For a good chunk of our adult lives, the sex we experience is alienated from its basic, species-preserving function. When today's woman decides to become a mother, sex and babies have been so far apart in her mind that she may have the feeling of having to "relearn" this aspect of what intercourse is for.

Changing attitudes toward sexuality have benefitted us greatly. As the daughters of the sexual revolution, we've had the freedom to acknowledge and articulate our desires in a way not available to women before us. But in celebrating the importance of this new expression we've let sex and reproduction be dichotomized in our own minds and experience. The link to fertility is only part of our sexuality, but it is a part of it—one that's connected to fears and longings that may not always be apparent to us. Even if we try to ignore it, on some level the association is there.

Possibly the most profound effect of the sexual revolution is that it drove fertility underground. When the pill was introduced in 1960, the severing of sex and fertility was complete: the means of forestalling pregnancy was detached from the sex act itself. A woman could have sex without being reminded of her fertility and regulate her fertility without being reminded of sex. All she had to do was add one tiny step to her daily regimen—swallowing a pill so small it's barely felt as weight on the tongue—and she would be safe, totally freed from the burden of her fertility. For women this was indeed liberating. Up till then, sex invariably brought with it the brooding possibility of pregnancy, which meant risking one's life with an illegal abortion or being ushered into a rigid social role. The pill was empowering to women in that it gave us control over our bodies. Women could now enjoy sex for its own sake, as men had long been able to do.

For those of us who grew up in the post-pill era and had yet to learn the secrets of the bedroom, the new rules may, in retrospect, have been somewhat confusing. I remember, as a child in the sixties, having the idea that there was some kind of wild party going on. There was something daring and thrilling about being an adult, I could only conclude, although the adults I knew seemed as oblivious to it as I was unenlightened about it. It didn't take much television watching to figure out that the "something" was sex. In that tantalizing world beyond my sleepy neighborhood, sex was everywhere. Sex was what made you want to buy things. Sex was why you wanted to look good. Sex had something to do with the music my parents said was "junk," songs with driving rhythms and vocals that were gritty rather than sweet. Sex was about wearing skirts that crept high at the leg and pants that slipped low on the hips. Sex was about staying up late.

I knew sex fueled the world long before I knew what sex was. In those early sexual-revolution days, when a bared belly button could still prompt a wink, being the oldest child in the family was a distinct disadvantage. There was no one to translate for me; I missed all the innuendos.

At one point I heard an older girl describe how her mother told her "the Facts of Life." She spoke in a "*you* know what I'm talking about" tone of voice that told me this meant sex. The next day, when I had my mother conveniently cornered at the kitchen table, I asked her to tell me the Facts of Life. I leaned forward on my elbows, anxious to be let in on this vital secret once and for all. My mother was visibly shaken by the question, but recovered quickly enough to inform me that the Facts of Life were "to do unto others as you would have others do unto you." I was horribly disappointed; everybody knew the Golden Rule. "That's just one fact," I prodded, having pushed the issue this far. "How about the other facts?" "That's all you need to know," she said, rising to do the dishes.

Sooner or later I figured out that sex was how you made babies. I used to look at women with babies and be embarrassed for them because now other people would know that they'd had sex. It seemed odd to me that these were people who "did it," yet they they didn't seem in the least bit sexy, at least not in the white teeth, hip-hugger, go-go dancing kind of way. Women with babies drove station wagons, collected money for good causes, and wore straight-lined clothes. They were a lot like my mother. The sexy world where you danced and flipped your hair seemed much more fun. And that had nothing to do with having babies.

As I got older I found out that sex was about belonging, about being liked, about knowing that you were grown up. Babies were still far down there on the list, if they made the list at all. Of course I used contraception, but even that failed to truly bring home the connection between what I was doing and the possibility of pregnancy. Contraception always seemed more along the lines of hygiene. You bought diaphragm cream in a drugstore, where you also bought toothpaste and soap. Using contraception meant being a responsible sort of person. Because I was diligent in my diaphragm ritual, I could assure myself I was a "good girl." Before the sixties, perhaps, a good girl was someone who didn't have sex. From what I could tell, being a good girl in my time meant you could do anything you wanted as long as you "took precautions."

For many women in the post-pill age, sexuality remains far removed from the notion of pregnancy. "Today's young women didn't grow up with the idea that you can't have sex because you can get pregnant," says Dr. Nadelson. "They've grown up with the idea that you can control it, and if that fails, you can fix it anyway. Sex is a lot more connected to relationships than it is to procreation. When I talk to young women, I see that it does eventually dawn on them what sex is all about, but it's a slow dawning. Often it takes a pregnancy scare or a friend having an abortion to jolt them into reality."

Ellie recalls that for most of her adult life, sex and babies were poles apart:

> *The first thing I thought about sex as a teenager was: I could get pregnant. But soon that became a much more minor concern. What mattered far more was the quality of the sex, whether I'd be satisfied and satisfying, whether I'd be attracted to the man and he'd be attracted to me. I got pregnant once and really flipped out, almost*

like I had forgotten that could happen. It was a shocker, and sex was a serious thing for a while. I call that my "holy period." But then I lapsed back into having sex because it was fun, because it was good for the relationship.

That's the way sex was sold—it was supposed to do good things for us. If we were insecure about our bodies, sex would make us like them better. If we were insecure about a man, sleeping with him would boost our confidence in the relationship. Sex was supposed to make us feel good, and if it didn't we would have to assume there was something wrong with us. There was no encouragement to question what sex meant to us, what intimacy meant to us, what we might be afraid of. Sex was lavishly available, and we were supposed to partake of it, as though we had stumbled into some sort of overstocked all-you-can-eat meal.

"Everyone else was having sex and talking about sex," recalls Cathy, thirty-two, who owns an arts boutique. "Everyone seemed to be totally fulfilled by sex, so you pretended you were, too. Actually, I wasn't always comfortable with that level of intimacy, and it made me terribly insecure. Now I realize that a lot of other people were feeling the same way I did, wondering if they were normal."

Magazines that told us how to put on makeup and how to lose weight also told us how to have good sex, in terms that were every bit as clinical as a calorie-counting guide. Having good sex was integral to being a healthy person, just like diet and exercise. Good sex was in fact *a part of* diet and exercise: I remember reading that semen is chock-full of protein (don't just rush to spit it out, the article advised) and that a rollicking session of lovemaking burns upwards of 300 calories, about the same as a brisk-paced one-hour walk. One of *Esquire's* "Ultimate Fitness" columns asserted that vigorous sex offers the "benefits of aerobic exercise" and may, for the truly driven, produce "some of the physical and psychic effects of a four-minute mile."[1] We were given the impression that someone who didn't have sex was not only prudish and uncool, she wasn't taking care of herself.

All the "fun" aspects of sex were played up, at least in an upbeat, sanitized way, while the physical, emotional, and reproductive consequences were played down. It was like in the movies, where the only aftereffect of sex was the urge either to discuss the meaning of life or to smoke a cigarette. Even to think about the possible fallout meant that you were uptight, so you trained yourself *not* to think about it.

In college, sex was taken so lightly it seemed almost to be some kind of campuswide extracurricular activity, like an intermural sport. At University Health Services antibiotics were handed out like penny candy. "Burning while urinating, you say? . . . Take this." The administration might as well have given each student a "ration" of Tetracycline the way they allotted library privileges and computer time. When I think of all the organisms left festering in our systems after incomplete or improper treatment, I get a bit queasy. But then I realize I shouldn't complain; the diseases have gotten far worse since then.

Several years later, what's striking is that no one I knew *questioned* any of this. No one I can remember said, "I don't like putting these antibiotics in my body. I don't know what they really do to you," or, "I've had infections two months in a row. Is there something going on?" Sometimes, the health staff would hint that there were other factors in these magically appearing and disappearing ailments, asking questions like "Did you tell your partner?" or "Have you changed partners?" making it sound like we were engaged in some huge square dance. But most of us wholly believed in the powers of medicine, accepting that it was gone if the doctor said it was gone, that pills cleaned up everything, like white-out or a good rubber eraser.

There was no reason at all to think twice about sex. If we had doubting voices murmuring in the backs of our minds, we knew it was neurosis: maybe our parents had gotten us hung up about it. Since we had no reason to say no to sex, we had a hard time justifying it to ourselves when we wanted to decline. We had sex because it was *there.* We got the idea that it was more important to go with the flow than it was to know where we were going. Often the feeling was: Why ruin a perfectly good evening with a perfectly decent guy by spurning his advances? If we think back, with brutal honesty, how many times did we go to bed with a man out of *politeness?* All those lines men once used to get women in the sack—age-old refrains like "Everybody's doing it" and "It'll be fun"—we were using on ourselves.

In recent thinking about the sexual revolution, some feminists and historians have claimed that the new sexual freedom chiefly confirmed the status quo by giving men perpetual access to women's bodies. I don't know if I'd go that far. I think it has given women the chance to explore our feelings and assert our needs. And the effects of this far transcend the sexual. Also, I'm not so sure *men* haven't been more than slightly confounded by the change. "When a woman threw her body at you, often you wondered, 'What's this about?' " one man in his thirties recalls. "Does she like me? Does she just like sex, and I just happen to be there?" Sometimes men have felt pressured or exploited themselves.

One thing the sexual revolution has done, I believe, is bring men and women closer together in their approach to sex—at least on a superficial level. For men, sex has always had lower costs than it has for women. Even when there have been broad social or religious deterrents to sex, the rules were always stricter for women. The advent of the pill and a more forgiving morality minimized the costs of sex for women. Women were encouraged to enjoy this free, or at least cheaper, ride.

"In terms of sex, women have been told to be more like men," says Brenda, thirty-three, a fitness instructor on the West Coast. "After making love, a guy would typically roll his eyes and think, 'Oh boy, now she's going to want to get married.' Women desperately want to avoid letting a man think that is automatically what they're after. So a woman will go out of her way to convince men that having sex is not that big a deal to her."

Convincing a man is one thing. All you have to do is sleep with him and not make too many demands. Convincing ourselves is something else. For us to be carefree about sex it *has* to be separated from procreation in our minds. The cost of sex itself may have been lessened in recent decades, but the cost of *reproduction* is still high.

Because the male model of sexuality has become accepted as the post–sexual revolution norm for both genders, many women have strived to apply this sex/procreation split to themselves. "Men have always had this Madonna/whore thing, where there are some women you bear children with and some women you screw," says Cathy. "Now I feel women are told to play the Madonna/whore game with our own minds. We're told that we can be sexual or we can be maternal, but not both. I want to feel that I can bring all of myself into the act of making love, but there's a part of me, part of my feminine, giving side, that I feel I have to hold back." In past eras, women were supposed to think about babies but not about sex. Now, it seemed, we were supposed to think about sex but not about babies.

Looking back, I wonder if in the past we repressed the link between making love and making babies. Part of it was, no doubt, not being in a situation where we wanted babies, either in terms of timing or the man. But I feel there was something beyond all that, and much subtler: that we were somehow curbing an awareness of fertility because to acknowledge it was dangerous.

On one level, the fertility side of sex was threatening to us as individuals. "We're afraid of connecting sex and fertility because in the past fertility restricted women," says Susanne, a thirty-two-year-old writer. "If we could keep the sexuality without the fertility, we could keep ourselves free." We also no doubt picked up that reining in such thoughts kept us "in the running" romantically. "To come across as desirable, you have to be cool and fun-loving as opposed to serious-minded," says Brenda. "Thinking about the possibility of getting pregnant is definitely serious. If you want to be considered sexually attractive, it doesn't jibe."

The ideals of the sexual revolution maintain that the freer and less inhibited the sex, the better. Unless a couple wants a baby and thus procreation is a motivation for sex, fertility is going to be an inhibiting factor. As a way of keeping the man, a woman may, consciously or unconsciously, suppress feelings that threaten to stifle her abandon. Who knows? Another woman may be unencumbered by such constraints. Alas, the sexual revolution has not eased sexual competition between women, and women still feel the onus is on us to prove ourselves worthy of men's erotic intentions.

The matter of fertility is held to be so hush-hush that often, when going to bed with a man, women feel apologetic about even dealing with it. When she gels up her diaphragm or asks him to get a condom, she is the killjoy: "Oh no, the fun's over. And it's my fault." So fierce is the pressure to separate sex from fertility that to raise the issue—as certain means of birth control demand—is thought to be *detracting from* the sex. But when you think about it, it's ridiculous that in the context of sex we should feel compelled to *apologize* for being fertile, which in effect means apologizing for being members of our sex.

The man himself may not help, as many men make no secret of their revulsion toward contraceptive matters. "There have been men who have helped me put the diaphragm in," says Ellie. "I've always thought that was sweet and romantic, turning it into a part of making love. But other men have just turned aside so they wouldn't have to look. They wouldn't seem to see that what I was doing was preparing myself for them, that it was part of my giving to them. It's made me shy about the whole thing." And of course, we're always being told that to appeal to men, any sign of our fertility (menstrual blood, body hair, body fat, stretch marks) should be camouflaged or removed. According to today's aesthetic, in order to be sexy we should look more like sub-fertile adolescents than grown women.

For our own sexual survival, we went along with the idea that sex existed in its own realm, freed from other biological and emotional realities. Any feelings or doubts we had related to our fertility were mere vestiges of a less enlightened age. But what do men think women are? Many somehow expect us to be these ready vessels, fused with electricity but otherwise inert. Considering how some men tend to respond, it's understandable that women might decide that their fertility is something unappealing about themselves, something to deny. When we're not with someone with whom we plan to make a baby, it's only the frolicking around part of ourselves that's fun and attractive. The potential mother in us is not. A holistic expression of ourselves, which fuses both elements, may be more threatening still.

When we deal with birth control, we often see it in terms of our relationships rather than our fertility. Contraception is unappealing because it involves planning ahead, and the culture of sex stresses spontaneity. "I've always felt kind of resentful about having to use birth control," says Brenda. "I've never liked the unspontaneity of it. You have to think about it, stop, put it in. It takes away from that feeling of going for the moment."

The planning part of birth control poses a problem for many because society is still puritanical with regard to women and sex. It's okay for a woman to have sex when she's "swept away with passion," but for her to knowingly *equip* herself for sex is suspect. In the first case, the indulgence is not her "fault." The erotic fantasies enacted ad nauseam in books and films show women "giving in" to a man's ardor and "becoming helpless" in his embrace. The idea is that the man is in charge and the woman is but an innocent player. For the *woman* to take control of her situation by being responsible for her protection runs counter to the dream.

Men, too, have bought into these myths about women's sexuality. Some are turned off when a woman carries birth control because they consider it "calculating." There's also a bit of male ego involved: Any man would like to believe that it's *his* incredible magnetism melting his partner's will, and not that she keeps condoms in her purse and can therefore sleep with anybody, any time. Lots of women feel torn in that they want to protect themselves but don't want anyone to know they're doing so. Some women like to say they're on the pill "for medical reasons." That solves the problem all around: you're safe from pregnancy *and* suspicion.

Research on women and birth control use indicates that this ambivalence toward planning ahead is pivotal in whether or not a woman chooses to protect herself. In *Taking Chances: Abortion and the Decision Not to Contracept,* sociologist Kristin Luker says that women "weight their own costs and balances" with contraception.[2] One of the clear costs of birth control in young women's views was that of acknowledging intercourse, she found. "Many women said contraception is 'unnatural.' This implies that sex is natural, but planning for it is not," she reports. In certain situations the costs of acknowledging that she intends to have sex may seem too high to a woman. If, for example, a woman ends a relationship, continuing to use birth control suggests that she expects to continue being sexually active regardless, which may not be the impression she wants to give. The unspoken rule, Luker contends, is that it's acceptable to have sex with a committed partner, but not when you're between committed relationships. That is, of course, a value judgment. The physical reality is that you need to be as protected during a one-time fling as you are in a stable relationship.

Even though birth control has become increasingly available to young women, the incidence of unwanted pregnancies has remained high. According to the Alan Guttmacher Institute, a nonprofit organization that studies reproductive issues, 82 percent of pregnancies among teenagers are unwanted. It's estimated that 46 percent of American women will have had an abortion by the time they reach forty-five.[3] The separation between sex and fertility in women's minds may play a role. In explaining how reproductive decisionmaking works, Kristen Luker differentiates between "risk" and "uncertainty": "A 'risk' is a probability of known magnitude: there is a consensus as to the likelihood of a given event. An 'uncertainty,' on the other hand, is a probability of unknown magnitude." To the medical and family-planning community, a woman's failure to use contraception represents a clear risk. But to a woman for whom the link between sex and fertility has not been experientially confirmed, it may represent merely an uncertainty.[4]

The birth control method a woman uses can affect how she perceives the link between her own sexuality and fertility, says psychologist Susan Williams. With barrier methods, a woman literally creates a block, not only between herself and the man who could make her pregnant, but between the self (which is choosing not to conceive) and the body (which could potentially conceive). Methods like the pill or IUD, on the other hand, actually change the body into a body that can't conceive, thus incorporating the meaning of contraception rather than confronting it on a conscious level. "When women use the pill or an IUD, methods where you don't have to connect it with sex, the attitude is often, 'I don't want to think about my fertility,' " she says. "Many such women are clearly uncomfortable when they return to a diaphragm or condom for medical or other reasons."

But according to Dr. Williams, sex-independent birth control does not truly split our sexuality from our fertility. Despite what we may have tried to prove to men, to our peers, and to ourselves, the two are inextricably linked. "With the pill or IUD you don't have to think about the connection. You can magically be okay. But that's only consciously," she says. "What shows up in dreams and on the couch is that the two are tied. A decade or two ago it was blasphemous to suggest that anatomy is destiny. But the fact that a woman can get pregnant from having sex changes that act forever in the unconscious, no matter what technology we apply. The technology may help us deal with certain problems, but the unconscious conflicts are the same."

In other words, on a conscious level we've been running around and having a good time, while on an unconscious level we've been struggling with what it all meant to us. As Gail Sheehy wrote in *Passages:*

> *Roughly 400 times in her life a woman must make a sober choice. Either she will leave herself open to pregnancy, or she will deny her uterus its animating powers. For a woman there is no such thing as casual noncommitment. If she wants to wander free, it requires an act of negation every month. And a good deal of psychic energy is involved in that denial. She can never simply not think about it because that in itself is a way of tipping her destiny.*[5]

But we tried to act as though we were *above* that destiny. "Back in the sixties, we made this agreement that random sex was fun," says Dr. Williams. "Many women have decided in retrospect that it wasn't all that much fun. What I see today is a lot of confusion. Women are wondering what sex is about. Is sex about two people creating something transcendent, whether it's love, a baby, or a relationship? Or is it about lust, which means experiencing sex as isolated from these other things?"

Fertility itself is a metaphor. On the unconscious level it can mean creation, expansion, self-fulfillment, worth, or connection. "Motivations related to such fertility needs show up in our actions, our sexuality, our efforts to live a 'fertile' life," says Dr. Williams. "The splits that get created, between sex and reproduction, love and sex, men and women, do cause conflict for us and inhibit our growth."

If we've been confused we're not alone: Society has long been baffled by how to handle the link between sexuality and motherhood. Men have always been uncomfortable with woman's power—embodied in both her sexuality and her fertility. Men's efforts to control women and assuage their own fears have led to gross inconsistencies in their assumptions about women and sex: At different times, women were thought to be saturated with sexual desire or immune to it; women's seductiveness was men's downfall or their purity was men's salvation; motherhood depended on women's sexual satisfaction or precluded their need for it.

Perhaps the clearest example of ambivalence toward women's sexuality is the Christian notion of the Virgin Birth. This improbable construct simply had to be invented; sexual pleasure, and women's sexual pleasure particularly, was considered physically and spiritually enfeebling for men and was thus deemed evil. It was bad enough that ordinary women who bore children had given in to their lusts, but for the Holy Mother this was inconceivable. The ideal mother had to be chaste, innocent, and above the tainting influence of carnality. Early Christian thinkers, recognizing that some sexual activity was needed in order to propagate the species (not to mention perpetuate the faith), determined that intercourse was permissible only when procreation was the intent.

The common historical view is that female sexuality took a nap around the beginning of the Common Era and didn't wake up until the Renaissance. According to Thomas Laqueur, author of *Making Sex: Body and Gender from the Greeks to Freud,* despite the admonitions of religious leaders, up until the last few hundred years women were assumed to take pleasure in sex. It was thought that a woman couldn't conceive unless she experienced orgasm, and that the "titillation and delight" was a sign that conception had occurred. Without orgasm, one commonly read text explained, "the fair sex [would] neither desire nuptial embraces, nor have pleasure in them, nor conceive by them."[6]

In the eighteenth century it was determined that women could get pregnant without "the telltale shudder." (The evidence, of course, had been there all along. The fact that it wasn't applied until this time, Laqueur says, suggests the social construction of sexuality.) At this point, orgasm, "[p]reviously a sign of the generative process . . . a feeling whose existence was no more open to debate than was the warm, pleasurable glow that usually accompanies a good meal . . . was relegated to the realm of mere sensation, to the periphery of human physiology—accidental, expendable, a contingent bonus of the reproductive act." The break in the link between generation and pleasure, he explains, presented the possibility of female passionlessness and "created the space in which women's sexual nature could be redefined, debated, denied, or qualified. And so it was of course. Endlessly."[7]

Which brings us to nineteenth-century sexuality, or, perhaps more precisely, nonsexuality. At this point, intercourse was considered an indignity women had to endure as martyrs to the cause of reproduction. Female sexuality was completely edited out of the generative story while the womb and ovaries took center stage. Not only were women thought not to take pleasure in sex, they were to be *protected* from such pleasure as it might destabilize their fragile reproductivity. If hyperactive reproductive organs left a woman with no energy to read, write, and think, as was the belief, they certainly didn't allow for the flowering of feminine sensuality. In the words of one nineteenth-century British physician, "The majority of women (happily for society) are not very much troubled with sexual feelings of any kind. . . . Love of home, of children, and of domestic duties are the only passions they feel."[8]

That "happily for society" suggests the source of Victorian repression. As noted before, the idea of women's purity was a stabilizing factor in an era of rapid industrial change. Linda Gordon points out that the attributes promoted in the sexual arena—self-denial and delayed gratification—were those demanded by the new capitalist expansion. Nineteenth-century thinkers waged a valiant campaign to create order out of an increasingly complex world. Women's sexuality, along with the passions it stirred in men, was seen as an entropic force, so it had to be suppressed. Women's reproductivity, however, did fit neatly into societal ideals, so the maternal role was urged and exalted.

The strict antisexual beliefs of the nineteenth century did not succeed in promoting sexual moderation. On the one hand, not everybody truly believed them. Men were obsessed by women's sexuality, which they imagined to be a mighty and terrifying force once unleashed. Everywhere, doctors of the period found evidence of rampant desire among women, which was by their definition a clear abnormality in itself. Some went so far as to claim that female patients longed for the speculum as a means of procuring sexual fulfillment.[9]

On the other hand, some people, chiefly women themselves, believed these repressive views too well. The sexual mores were so restrictive that women were expected to be virtually numb. Masturbation or free sexual expression was thought to damage future offspring and induce mania and idiocy in the offender. Women were warned that having too much sex would leave them not only feeble but infertile. Some doctors advised intercourse once a month as an appropriate amount; others suggested once or twice a year for purposes of procreation only. Any more might overwhelm the delicate female circuitry.

These attitudes, it should be noted, were applied only to white women of the middle and upper classes. Among this group, a near-epidemic of hysterical illnesses left women too fragile to submit to their husbands' advances. Their declining sexual vigor and physical stamina were supposed to attest to their higher level of civilization. Lower-class women, however, were purportedly seething with lust. It was as though the collective sexuality of the female gender was concentrated in one social group.

Throughout the century the birth rate among white American women fell steadily, from 42.8 in 1855 to 28.5 in 1900 (measured in births per 1,000 women per year).[10] Many theorize that the antisexual atmosphere was a direct cause. But it's also possible that women took to their beds not only in response to their fettered instincts but to avoid childbirth, which at that time was quite a hazardous prospect to both the birther and the born. So what seemed like repressive behavior on women's part may actually have been self-preservation.

Freud's revolutionary theories of sexuality gradually took hold in the early twentieth century, but by midcentury this had proved less than liberating to women. Freud took the conflict between women's sexuality and women's reproductivity to a literal, physiological level by pitting one organ against the other: the clitoris versus the vagina. The clitoris is a nonreproductive organ; the vagina reproductive. By terming the vagina the "mature" female sexual organ and relegating the clitoris to "immature" status, Freud made the case that female sexuality had no justification without its link to procreation. Freud conceded that female sexual pleasure was healthy, but he posited that there was one "good" way to achieve such pleasure: via the vagina. A clitoral orgasm revealed a woman to be neurotic, unadjusted to the notion of childbearing, and envious of men—which left a great many women feeling shameful and confused about their sexuality.

With every decade, new experts on sexuality came on the scene. In the 1940s it was believed that women were biologically and sexually fulfilled by mothering. Giving birth, breast-feeding, and snuggling one's baby were thought to be just as satisfying, if not more so, than marital sex. The authors of *Modern Woman: The Lost Sex* claimed that women who didn't want children were condemned to a "sexual limbo." Their rule was: "The less a woman's desire to have children and the greater her desire to emulate the male . . . , the less will be her enjoyment of the sex act and the greater her general neuroticism."[11]

Healthy, "feminine" sex was seen as the glue in a marriage. As Betty Friedan pointed out in *The Feminine Mystique,* women depended on sex with their husbands to make them "feel alive."[12] Women's consolation for being stuck in the home all day was that the home was a place of boundless erotic possibility. Women were so sold on sex that many simply interpreted their dissatisfactions (with their marriages, with their limited opportunities) as sexual frustration.

In the late forties, pleasure returned to the scientific picture with *The Kinsey Report's* announcement that sexually, men and women were more alike than not. The focus here was on orgasm. An experience women were once assumed to be exempt from now became obligatory. Frigidity was seen as a crucial health problem that could result in a number of female ailments, including infertility. One early report from the Kinsey experiments concluded that women with higher education had fewer orgasms. Although this was later refuted by the researchers, it caused quite a stir, raising all the old concerns about women's education and employment detracting from her reproductivity.

The 1960s saw the dawning of the sexual revolution, but there had been hints of an insurrection brewing; direct references to sex in the popular media doubled between 1950 and 1960.[13] The idea was, anything goes, as long as the result is pleasure. Suddenly *quantity* of sex outweighed the *quality* of relationships. Whatever was "fun" was permissible; it didn't matter who (or how many) you did it with, nor how you did it. Sex had become yet another standard for people to measure themselves against. If the suburbanites of the fifties had been concerned about keeping up with the Joneses materially, now they worried about keeping pace with them *sexually.* People tried to show how modern they were by having the latest sex bible prominently displayed on the bookshelf. The truly hip got into swinging and open marriages.

According to contemporary critics, the rise of the commercial culture has been instrumental in popularizing sex. The consumer economy depends on the quest for personal gratification, self-expression, and, to a certain extent, hedonism. From the sixties onward, the most promising group in the eyes of marketers comprised independent, financially privileged youth. The emphasis had completely shifted from marital to personal fulfillment. Sex fueled the consumer economy, creating a huge demand for fashion, cosmetics, and sexually suggestive entertainment. In turn, the consumer economy generated interest in sex. As a vehicle of the market economy, sex was completely stripped of its reproductive elements. In the jargon of Madison Avenue, sex meant "image" and "aspiration."

Throughout the period, sexual liberation increasingly became linked to women's liberation. Women's sexuality had been suppressed for so long that to celebrate it was to take a stance against the patriarchy. In 1966 Drs. Masters and Johnson published *Human Sexual Response,* which reduced sex to a clinical tally of orgasmic tremors. According to their theories, women were naturally multiorgasmic and didn't need men at all. Feminists seized on this as proof that women were the sexual "equals" of men. The stress was on orgasm, and the clitoris, having finally emerged from its post-Freudian disgrace, was seen as the equivalent of the penis. Women's "potency" was expressed by her ability to climax, not in her fertility. Women's sexuality was not regarded in reproductive terms, for that would have accentuated the *differences* between women and men. And focusing on difference was the opposite of what women at the time were attempting to do.

Disillusionment with free sex set in during the 1980s. Detached from childbearing, emotion, and intimacy, the celebrated act began to lose its allure. The rising incidence of sexually transmitted diseases, first herpes then certainly AIDS, left women asking themselves: Is it worth it? The popular media announced "the New Celibacy." Stable, monogamous relationships and having children began to be seen not only as safer than casual sex, but more fulfilling. This in part reflected a rethinking of values, but there was also the factor of ennui. Sexual attitudes had come full circle: In the past, sex had been so forbidden as to be exciting. But by this time, sex had become so acceptable as to be banal. Sex therapists report that the most common complaint they hear today is a lack of sexual desire. Some 20 percent of Americans are estimated to have lost the urge.[14]

Feminists have also begun to question their earlier exuberance about sexual "liberation." Different time periods had been looked upon as "antisex" (repressive) and "prosex" (progressive), but many were wondering if it was indeed that simple. British feminist Sheila Jeffreys noted that in "freeing" their sexuality, women were told to conform to male sexuality, thus perpetuating the male-dominated system and keeping female sexuality subordinate. In *The Joy of Sex,* for example, women were urged to accept the male tendency to objectify women: ". . . the most valued thing from you in actual lovemaking is . . . being an initiator, a user of your stimulatory equipment."[15] Author Dr. Alex Comfort even suggested that, for the sake of good sex, women learn to objectify *men.* Feminists also began to look more closely at male sexual violence against women—rape, domestic violence, child sexual abuse, and the association between sex crimes and pornography—in the context of sexual liberation and decided that not all freedoms have brought equality.

In some respects, things haven't changed all that much from the height of Victorian morality. For one thing, society is still obsessed with sex. The difference is that in the nineteenth century everyone pretended sex didn't exist while we in the twentieth century broadcast it everywhere. And secondly, the fear of women's sexuality remains. As the authors of *Re-Making Love: The Feminization of Sex* write, "the fear of women's sexual independence has become a major theme of the 80s, one that indicates not only the growing strength of the Christian right, but the powerful, lingering influence of sexism in American culture."[16] The authors argue that the sexual revolution had a greater impact on women's sexual behavior than that of men. Therefore, efforts to curb sexuality and go back to a "purer" age—as present-day conservatives, the ones opposed to abortion, sex education, and access to contraception, plead—really means that *women,* not men, should concede their sexual freedom.

It could be argued that severing the connection between pleasure and fertility that contributed to the sexual repression of the nineteenth century has a parallel today in the severing of sexuality and fertility (through contraception as well as reproductive technologies). The result is a general befuddlement about sexuality and its relationship to childbearing.

So this is the sexual reality we walked into. Sex, as it was presented to us, was separate from that which had previously sanctioned it: childbearing, marriage, and often love. What meaning did sex have for us? What did it mean to us as women? "When I grew up, there was total women's sexual liberation, but for no explained reason," says Dana. "By the time you got to high school you knew it was okay to sleep with a variety of people, men or women. This didn't give me much of a sense of being female or being anything in particular."

In the past, fertility was the constant and sex the variable. Today, sex is the constant and fertility the variable. Because of the confused meanings, today's women often have trouble coming to grips with strong feelings in which the two are merged. "I made love with someone new recently," one woman confided. "I cried. I had this sense of vulnerability, of feeling 'I really need you. I want this act to mean something.' Part of the meaning I wanted it to have was for it to be connected to having a baby."

Women (and men) frequently do have fantasies related to fertility. It could be a fleeting thought that you and a partner would have cute children, or an actual fantasy of making a baby. "Sometimes women are troubled by these fantasies, especially when they appear in dreams or while [they are] making love and getting pregnant is not the conscious goal," says psychologist Eleanor Morin Davis. "But the fantasy can be symbolic, such as revealing a desire for a closer connection with someone. Trying to deny the meanings and value of fertility actually makes a woman more of a prisoner of it, more likely to struggle with it on the unconscious level."

Annabel says that it wasn't until she had a boyfriend who expressed that fantasy that she "allowed" those thoughts to surface.

> *At about thirty-one or thirty-two, I began wanting to have a child, but I still kept those feelings away from sex. But then I started seeing George, who had very different feelings about sex. While we were making love he'd tell me how he'd like to make a baby with me. He didn't like it when we used birth control. If I stopped and said, "Let me go get my sponge," he'd get upset and try to discourage me, promising that he'd pull out. I knew this meant taking a big risk. But then the risk itself became exciting to me, too. Now there was this big new angle to sex. Because of George, I began to connect sex to making a baby. I said to him, "You really think about this, don't you?" I used to fantasize about having his child and about how happy that would make him, until I realized, because of other problems in the relationship, this was out of the question.*

Many women don't make the connection in their own minds until they've decided to try to get pregnant. Abandoning birth control once and for all can be somewhat jarring to women who have over the years trained themselves not to associate sex with babies. Women who have long cursed contraception may be surprised by how "strange" it feels to go off it.

"It was really weird to start having sex with the thought of having a baby, to consciously take away birth control," reflects Annette. "It seemed almost unnatural to me, when it was, of course, the opposite. I felt a certain trepidation. There was a contrived feeling about it. I felt less like a physical woman, more like someone producing something. I'd think about the sperm and think, 'C'mon, get in there!' It's strange, but the fact that it can happen—and that it *does* happen—does make you realize the power of sex."

Some women feel a release when sex and making babies converge. "I've heard women and men say sex is never better than when they're ready to get pregnant," says Dr. Davis. "The awareness of a possible conception taps into fantasies of unmet emotional needs, and of the need to merge." Sherrie, twenty-nine, who recently had her first child, says there's a liberation in feeling that the two of you can give wholly to each other. In her experience, this enhances the closeness. "I think it's a deeper feeling of commitment to each other, of trusting," she describes. "You're venturing into the unknown together. It's a special bonding, an overwhelming feeling of security and trust in each other."

Carol, a thirty-five-year-old mother of two agrees:

> *When you're actually in the act of what might be procreation, it's more meaningful. It's not just for the moment—suddenly there's this* momentousness. *Sex takes on this whole new aura. I'd be really aware that* this *is the man who will be the father of my child. I wouldn't be thinking about some fantasy or movie star. My timing could be off, but I think I felt when my daughter was conceived. I got the sense the connection was made. In general, I'm not a spiritual type about these things. But I felt something had transcended the act of intercourse.*

At the same time, letting go of one's consciousness of fertility can be healing. Couples experiencing infertility, for example, may start to regard sex as more work than play. Deciding not to worry about conceiving for a change can be healing to them. One woman who recently had a miscarriage recalls, "I remember the first time my husband and I made love after the surgery. It was an important part of getting over the sadness for me. I needed to forget about the baby and learn to live in my body again. I needed to see there was something between us besides what we had lost. There was something defiant about allowing myself pleasure, a feeling that I was going to get through this."

A few years back, Germaine Greer, author of *The Female Eunuch* and self-styled sexual revolutionary, published *Sex and Destiny,* a book arguing that sex has all but lost its meaning. Bringing in historical evidence and cross-cultural testimony, she made a case for reevaluating the separation of sex from its reproductive function. "Most of the pleasure in the world is still provided by children and not by genital dabbling," she wrote.[17] Her suspicion that we have been oversold on sex and undersold on children came from watching her own female cats, "who wept piteously when it was time to undergo the gang rape which is feline intercourse, and purred continuously while in labor, even when the labor was obviously painful, and purred all through their suckling, not stopping till the kittens were weaned. The triumphant tomcat may have enjoyed his brief ejaculation, but the female purred for eight weeks."[18]

An intriguing argument, especially coming from someone who made her name by saying things like "Lady, love your cunt." But in the same book Greer waxes rhapsodically about the dignity of the veil that women in several Muslim countries are forced to wear. She wrote about how women in various parts of the world maintain their integrity by spending their days apart from men, and about how this enhances the sense of "mystery" and attraction between the sexes. Probably not the arrangement most of us have had in mind.

Keeping female sexuality distinct from fertility, has, in the view of Greer and other recent critics, served male interests because fertility suggests a potentiality men don't have, and the very inconvenience it presents challenges the authority of the male model. But what we need to ask ourselves is: Must sexual liberation inevitably lead to alienation? Does sexual equality mean we should deny the uniqueness of our experience as women? Shouldn't we be able to acknowledge the feminine aspects of ourselves without relinquishing all our autonomy?

And if female sexuality is inextricably linked to procreation, what does that mean to us? Does this in any way invalidate nonreproductive sex, which most of our experience of sex will be anyway? Absolutely not, says Dr. Williams. "In Freudian terms, sex is linked to the life force, which means procreativity and *creativity,*" she says. "If a couple is having sex not for the purpose of having a baby, it's for some creative expression between the two. Something new comes from this: love, understanding, or a relationship is born. That's its link to procreation."

If sex is, in essence, among life's more elusive mysteries (and despite efforts to address it clinically, and to quantify behavior and response, it remains mysterious: What triggers an attraction between two people? How does a physical connection bring a couple closer?), then isn't its ability to generate life one element of that mystery? Whether or not we're conscious or choose to avail ourselves of that ability, isn't it a part of us?

Chapter 7

PHYSICAL BAGGAGE

Sara, a bright woman in her early twenties, was reasonably well adjusted but for a preoccupation with her weight. No matter what the scale, her friends, or her doctor told her, she remained doggedly convinced that she was too fat. Francine Baras, her therapist, was listening to Sara, trying to learn what fears bore so heavily on her that she had shifted them, in fantasy, to her body, when she noticed her patient had chosen a rather odd position in which to sit. "Look at what you're doing," she urged Sara, pointing toward the young woman's lap. Sara looked down and saw that her hands were clasped several inches in front of her abdomen as though they enclosed an invisible cushion. "You're pregnant! You're sitting as though you were pregnant!"

When I heard this story, the emotional truth of it jumped out at me. While Sara's case is an extreme acting out of it—reflecting rage toward her mother, who had several children after Sara, and a near-frantic fear of becoming like her—the link between expectancy and obesity is quite basic. Fat. Mother. Ugliness. Loss of control. Loss of self. As much as we may assure ourselves that there's a difference between justifiable, "good" weight (There's a baby incubating in there. What do you expect?) and plain, old unremarkable flab, the association is probably more vivid, and more troubling, than many of us would care to admit.

And no wonder, with images of the ideal female body plastered all over our psyches. Women have always been judged more by appearance than performance. As Joan Jacobs Brumberg points out in *Fasting Girls: The History of Anorexia Nervosa,* the body has supplanted the face as the focus of female beauty.[1] Today's women have been raised with the idea that thinness is the ultimate measure of self-worth. "She has such a pretty face," someone might say, with pity, about a pleasant-looking woman who is overweight. How often do you hear the reverse: "Such a shame that she's so plain. And she has such a nice body"?

We learn quickly that the fat girl is unpopular at school, the glamourous movie star is slender. We're bombarded with pictures of thin, perfect bodies on television, billboards, and magazines—a regular ambush of exquisitely sculpted images. In order to be able to reproduce, a woman needs fatty tissue comprising a certain percentage of her body weight. Yet to many, and certainly according to the physical ideal that's been sold us, that is considered "too fat." Looking at it in those terms, any society that calls a body capable of reproducing an undesirable body is likely to breed conflicts about childbearing among women.

Pregnancy alters your contours, stretches them, distends them. There's just no avoiding that. When pregnant, you will have to bolster your wardrobe with items designed for the swollen belly, even if you're an enviable size 6. Granted, on a conscious level most of us accept that to have a child you have to carry the baby and his supporting apparatus for a while. In rational terms, that's no big deal, just a minor inconvenience in the transition to motherhood. And on many levels, the process is quite beautiful. The body expands, becomes something larger than itself, the new mother filling up with the new life she is nurturing. But in our society, putting on weight is simply too tied up with women's self-esteem, social status, and attractiveness to be regarded an emotionally neutral event.

In *The Beauty Myth,* Naomi Wolf makes a compelling argument that as the tyranny of imposed social roles has faded, an analogous pressure to be thin and attractive has emerged in its place. "The more legal and material hindrances women have broken through, the more strictly and heavily and cruelly images of female beauty have come to weigh on us. . . . As women released themselves from the feminine mystique of domesticity, the beauty myth took over its lost ground, expanding as it waned to carry on its work of social control," she writes.[2] I think hers is an important message. The compulsion to diet and the chronic hunger in its wake exhausts us, both physically and spiritually. Our attention is continually drawn inward, to the minutiae of body variability, rather than outward, to the institutions and ideas that oppress us and cause us to question our worth.

But I would argue that it's not a simple matter of substitution. Even if today's women have been spared the "happy housewife" image, we're still mothers and nurturers, and society expects that of us. The "beauty myth" and its implausible standards of slenderness have not replaced but have been *overlaid upon* the traditional attributes of femininity. The mandate to rid oneself of curves and flesh (in symbolic terms, to transcend one's reproductivity) *coexists* with society's assumption that women are not only the bearers but the caretakers of children (meaning that a woman is subordinate to her reproductivity). We are to strive for all that thinness represents (equality with men, control over our bodies, eternal youth) and yet submit to the physical, emotional, and societal demands of maternity. And herein lies the tension.

The body at odds with itself. The public (androgynous) self at odds with the private (reproductive) self. We want to experience our femininity, yet we also want to hold onto our self-mastery and control. We want to feel good about pregnancy and motherhood, yet we are terrorized by the physical chaos it represents. We are told that as mothers and pregnant women we will be valued regardless of body size but, looking around us, we believe that is a lie. We see that having a slim body is not only an aesthetic but a *moral* imperative. We want to grow as women and mothers but see that the culture, literally, has not granted us the room to do so. We fear people looking at us and thinking we look fat because we know we've thought about others that way.

I know that for myself this issue doesn't sit too well. I grew up overweight. You would never have called me fat—the operative adjective was "plump"—but the three-letter word was ever lurking in my mind. I dragged my body around with me like a sorry relation in my charge, ashamed, appalled, and annoyed by its very presence. My pudginess was a constant reminder that I was condemned to a life of mediocrity and oblivion. I could feel myself lurching toward it with every laden step. There was a chubby boy about my age in my neighborhood. He would usually sit placidly by the group, like any overweight child who knows his place, without saying much of consequence. I remember thinking that some day when I grew up, I would probably marry him. The prospect was none too appealing, but he was harmless enough. And being chubby myself I figured I should at least be resigned to my fate.

If childish baby fat was bad enough, female *womanly* fat promised to be even worse. The distaste with which my mother carried her own heavy frame confirmed that impression for me. Sometimes I'd stay in the room as she was getting dressed. Her underclothes were broad swathes of diaphanous fabric that to me resembled plastic wrap more than any identifiable article of clothing. She would walk about self-consciously, trying not to betray her discomfort, with her head hanging down, as though by not looking at me she could pretend I wasn't watching.

My mother with her head hanging down. That picture of abashment stayed with me. It told me that one's female physicality should be admitted only grudgingly, that to be ample was to be too much. My mother in her prediet days had ponderous, low-lying breasts and generous hips and thighs. Whatever all this flesh meant, it was something shameful. *She* clearly wasn't happy about it. As my mother's daughter I was stuck with this unfortunate body of mine, doomed to be defined by its dimensions.

In private moments, I used to fantasize that somewhere on my body I'd discover a secret zipper that ran the entire length of me. Then the true, slender me could step out of its blubbery cage, liberated at last. Or, I'd dream that I'd find a jar of magic disappearing cream under my bed. Just a few well-placed smears, and my flabby excess would dissolve into air. Then I'd be thin and live happily forever after.

In my freshman year of high school I went on a diet and lost a good bit of weight. It started more as an experiment than as a decisive, positive step because, at that time, I held little hope for thinness. But bit by bit things began to change. As the pounds slipped off, I became less shy with the new people I met. I said good-bye to the stores that sold chubbies and bought my own clothes in the junior department. People I knew couldn't get over the difference in me. I now merited a more appealing adjective: "petite." The broad swings in other people's responses and in my own self-confidence were confusing, and I spent years struggling with them. But the only possible conclusion I could draw from the experience is that weight does matter and that, as a female, being heavy is a tremendous handicap in life.

That's a hard lesson to unlearn. To this day, I have the sensation of being at a perilous edge. Somewhere inside I believe that the weight could all come back, and that if it did, whatever self-assuredness I'd managed to build up could crumble. Even though I'm not consciously worrying about my weight, sometimes, without thinking, I'll check my profile in the mirror. I want to make sure that everything's okay, that no fat has mysteriously snuck up and attached itself to my unsuspecting body.

In the same way, while I no longer shirk away if another person—my husband, a girlfriend changing in the same room—glimpses too much skin, I'm still not at peace with my body. In an odd way, I've separated myself from my body. It's not my *being* that's in view; it's an accomplishment. I've chiseled that body down to tolerable size. It's something I've made, just as I might write an article or concoct a fancy dinner.

Regardless of the cause or the promise that it's temporary, a swelling stomach is bound to be unnerving to me. I don't think this would dissuade me from getting pregnant or lead me to regret it, but I know that the sight of my bloated self will send some painful associations charging after me. All sorts of psychic bells will go off, alerting me that I'm getting fat, I'm helpless to stop it, I've failed. After years as a miserable, awkward, blob of a kid, I've vowed to myself I'd never let it happen. My acceptance by other people depends on it. My new acceptable self depends on it. This attitude isn't something I'm proud of. I would like to think I was strong enough to be above the issue entirely. But I know that it's something I'll have to contend with.

Many pregnant women today feel there's a conflict between what's good for them, which is to stay thin, and what's good for the baby, which is, of course, to gain weight. Carole, thirty-five, a marketing executive, admits that the inescapable weight gain has cast something of a shadow over her otherwise rewarding pregnancy:

> *When I was younger I was overweight. Then when I got married, I put on more weight. Last year I went to a serious, medically supervised weight loss program and took off thirty-five pounds. So now, when I'm supposed to gain weight, it goes against everything I've learned. When I went in for an appointment early in the pregnancy, my doctor said, ''You should put on thirty to thirty-five pounds.'' My response was: ''No way.'' My intellect and my emotions are at odds here. I do feel I'm in control of what I'm putting on now, and that I have the tools to take it off when it's time. But it's still difficult. It's harder in part because of where I am. At four and a half months, I don't think I look pregnant yet. I'm thinking, people must think I'm fat. They must think I'm out of control.*

Not all women grew up as chubby children and are burdened with the same blubbery baggage. But we've all grown up with the fear of fat. Each magazine we buy tells us a new way to slim down. There are diet centers or weight-loss studios at every suburban mall. We've seen sugar-free sodas, fat-free ice creams, and a whole slew of diet products edge out other goods for space on the supermarket shelves. Any woman who hasn't worried—or at least wondered—about her weight either has a superhuman ego or is oblivious to her surroundings.

Although she has never had a serious weight problem, Tricia concedes that watching the numbers on the scale creep upward would give her pause:

> *When you're pregnant you have to eat a certain amount, you can't deny yourself. I'm much less into denying myself these days—I guess you could say I'm getting more used to my body—but even a couple of years ago it would have really concerned me. I would have thought, "Oh no. I have to eat enough to feed another body. How am I going to lose weight? Maybe I won't eat breakfast. Maybe I won't eat dessert." Still, I do worry that on some level I'll resent the pregnancy for making me gain weight.*

The tension during pregnancy may be especially acute today because the guidelines for weight gain in pregnancy have recently been revised upward, from around twenty pounds to closer to thirty pounds, depending on the individual. "Many women find this extremely disconcerting," says Francine Baras, a therapist in New York. "Their idea had been, 'I won't gain more than fourteen to eighteen pounds. I'll work out and not eat too much. Actually, I'll be quite attractive.' They're disappointed to learn that they do need to gain more for the health of the baby. It throws them off."

Many women who never had to worry about weight before become concerned when they get pregnant, says Ruth Striegel-Moore, assistant professor of psychology at Wesleyan University. "Everyone knows at least one story of someone who did experience serious weight gain and worries that it will happen to them," she says.

Often it's not just the image in the mirror that troubles women, but how they look to their men. Some men are put off by their pregnant wive's bodies, and make no secret of it. "A man might not say it directly, but joke about it, or say that it will be different when the baby is born and she's back to 'normal,' " says Dr. Striegel-Moore. "This puts pressure on the women, who are probably already sensitive about their weight. Even the backhanded stuff is powerful. Women worry that they'll never return to their original size."

These concerns raise the specter of other women. As we learn to measure ourselves by our body shape, we are conscious of how we measure up against everybody else. Pregnant women—who may in fact be seen as particularly beautiful by others and could be the object of envy—may feel unattractive about their globular bellies since everyone else is staying lean. "Gaining weight was my biggest fear about pregnancy," says Connie, twenty-nine, whose daughter is four months old. "The worst part was being pregnant during the summer. My friends were getting thinner and I kept getting larger. I couldn't even bear the idea of food after a while, seeing how large I was getting."

For some women, an excessive concern about getting fat can threaten the health of the pregnancy. Teresa, for example, is worried about her younger sister, who boasts that no one can tell she's pregnant at six months. "She doesn't want to look fat," Teresa explains. "Her doctor yelled at her when she had gained only four pounds after five months. And the funny thing is that she's a nurse herself and should know what's healthy and what's not."

Aimee notices that a pregnant coworker has nothing but diet soda for lunch, and that when she stays in the office until ten or eleven at night, as she often does, she orders in a salad. "I think she's had a weight problem before," Aimee suggests. "She's definitely not handling this well at all. I don't think she has fully accepted that she's going to have a baby."

Lynn Jaffee, program coordinator at the Melpomene Institute, a women's health/fitness organization based in St. Paul, says she often gets calls from women who are having trouble conceiving. "The first thing I do is ask how much they weigh and how active they are," she says. "The sense I often get is that they're exercising a great deal and don't have enough body weight. They may not be ovulating regularly, if at all. The problem is they complain about not being able to get pregnant, but they don't want to give up their shapes. They're torn." Thirty percent of all women with infertility problems have a history of eating disorders.[3]

According to Margaret Edell, a nutritionist in San Diego, these conflicts frequently arise in treatment. "Many women I've worked with try to control their weight during pregnancy," she observes. "Even if they're gaining far less than they should, they can be absolutely panic-stricken over the little weight they *did* gain. I've had patients who decided to quit breast-feeding early because they were anxious to lose weight and didn't want to take in the calories needed to nurse."

There's also concern that some weight-conscious parents are projecting their own dieting behavior onto their young children. According to Fima Lifshitz, M.D., chairman of pediatrics at Maimonides Medical Center in Brooklyn, this has been a factor in cases of delayed development and failure to thrive. "Some parents put children on low-fat diets, not realizing that young children do not have the same food requirement [as adults]," he says. "Vegetables may be a sufficient snack for an adult trying to lose weight, but a small child needs more energy to grow." As we move into the next generation, the mother-daughter-food triangle that we see in anorexia becomes the mother-*infant*-food triangle, with potentially dire consequences for infant health.

What's going on here? Certainly, there are plenty of women today who revel in the physical flowering of pregnancy and are comfortable with the nurturant qualities of food. Many enjoy their new, buxom shapes. But it's the number of women who are troubled by the changes, despite their stated desire to have and raise children, that's worth noting. Women have been putting on belly weight in order to reproduce since we became a species. Why do some of us feel compelled to fight against nature now, and why are so many others made uncomfortable by the requisite bodily changes they must endure? How is this tied to other issues women are facing today as we begin, or contemplate beginning, our families?

According to O. Wayne Wooley, Ph.D., associate professor of psychiatry at the University of Cincinnati Medical College and cofounder, with Susan Wooley, of its eating disorders clinic, the weight dilemma precisely replicates the broader conflicts confronting many of today's women. "The question for women is, how much do they put themselves first, which means striving for success and being like their fathers, as opposed to how much do they want to model themselves on their mothers, which in their interpretation means putting others first?" he says. "From a physical standpoint this translates to, do I want to be in control of my weight, or do I want to let it be controlled by circumstance?" Having a baby can heighten this conflict, he says, for it reduces it to the tangible: Is the woman willing to put the baby's interests before her own and relinquish control over her body?

Weight comes to symbolize the seesaw of identity many women experience. The image of motherhood, on a physical level, is a rounded, nurturant body. But to be successful, women today learn, you're supposed to be thin, have a will fierce enough to control your emotions and appetites, and fit into a man's world, which has come to mean fitting in somatically as well as intellectually. A slim form suggests an ability to "manage," a trait admired in business, whereas excess weight implies emotionalism and a lack of control, traits that are condemned.

Thinness is equated with beauty, health, success, and wealth, while "excess" body weight is linked with ugliness, poverty, and low achievement. For women specifically, body weight is associated not with empowerment—with the life force that maternity represents—but with weakness and passivity. With these as our guidelines, who's going to give up her hold on her body so willingly?

"Women are clinging to androgyny today," says Francine Baras.

> *Part of this reflects the demands of professionalism. But it has more to do with women having a crisis of identity because they lack a clear belief that femininity is okay. The fear is that being a woman, which incorporates all of the physical aspects of womanhood, is simply not okay. The idea is, if I look like an adolescent then I can stay an adolescent and not have to deal with all the complexities of being a woman. In the past women progressed naturally to womanhood and motherhood because that's what was considered successful. Today, what's considered successful involves a completely different model.*

The epidemic of eating disorders among women of our generation suggests an ambivalence toward our own female development. By starving herself, the anorectic is physically doing battle with her femininity. She turns her body into the antithesis of a fertile woman: amenstrual and devoid of womanly curves. She sheds her sexuality, as her form becomes increasingly juvenile. A bulimic "fills herself up" (metaphorically becomes pregnant), then expels what she has taken in, punishing herself for her pleasure while ensuring that she retains her prebinge (androgynous) form. According to Dr. Wooley, at least half of women between twenty-five and thirty-five today have had some symptoms of eating disorders in the past, and at least 20 percent within that age group have them now.

This means that of women on the verge of motherhood today, a substantial percentage are going to confront what they fear (or have feared) most: the loss of control over their weight. The philosophy many women have come to adopt is, if I can control my body, I can control who I am. Giving up control of her body for the sake of the baby, which means allowing the baby to make her temporarily fat, can be unsettling to a woman who has an emotional investment in keeping her weight down. "Women are asking, 'Is it really worth it to get fat?' " observes Baras.

> *For many women, being large with a baby is too close to being large without a baby. They can almost lose sight of the baby in the equation. This comes from a lack of clarity about what having this baby means to them, what being a woman means to them. Often the strongest feelings about the weight gain are not in its connection to having the baby, not in the idea that they're accomplishing something that's important to them as women, but in the idea that they've been ripped off.*

As with many issues of women's identity, feelings about weight often go back to feelings about one's own mother. By being thin, a woman can be other than what her mother was. Most of our mothers were of a generation that wasn't encouraged to be physically active and the majority of them, especially during our childhoods, did not match the slim, androgynous ideal held up to women today. We also may associate our mothers with largeness because, when we were very small, mother seemed large indeed. And she was, of course, physically developed. To gain weight, then, means to become like your mother, which, we've seen, is often translated as *becoming* your mother, or becoming the mother you never wanted to be. We express our ambivalence toward our mothers, and our fears of being like them, through our bodies.

As Kim Chernin has written, food or the control of food is problematic for women because it reminds us of the earliest mother-daughter bond, an emotional tie that continues to haunt us as we grow. But this interplay between mother, daughter, and food seems to be especially tension-filled in our generation. Our mothers were raised at a time when female domesticity was valued; when we grew up it was looked down upon. We sensed the change and expressed our scorn for the domestic at an early age. One of mother's chief domestic roles has always been to feed her children. Her competence as a mother has often been judged by her capacity as a feeder. We learn early on that food is a potent tool in conveying our feelings toward our mothers. When we overeat or refuse food, we reject her and what she represents. We're either saying, "You're not giving me enough, you're not enough for me" or "I don't want to take what you have to give me. I don't want to be what you are."

Girls get the message from their mothers that self-abnegation is appropriate female behavior, Rita Freeman observes in *Beauty Bound.* Girls see their mothers continually denying themselves, serving the best cuts of meat to everybody else, always letting other family members take their portions first. "It really doesn't matter to me," mother claims when challenged. "Why not?" we ask. "Don't *you* matter? I'm supposed to be like you. Don't *I* matter?" The association between female nurturing and hunger is so strong that it's frequently referred to in advertising. The emphasis is usually on food that will "please the family." Attending to their own needs—through food or otherwise—provokes shame as well as pleasure (a feeling exploited in Frusen Gladje's "Enjoy the Guilt" campaign). Feminist scholar Susan Bordo offers as examples commercials for Andes Candies and Mon Cheri (which means "my dear" in French), "where a 'tiny bite' of chocolate, privately savored, is supposed to be ample reward for a day of serving others."[4]

Young women today grow up determined not to be self-sacrificing like their mothers, yet self-denying behavior is deeply ingrained (and, as we've seen, marketed to them). That's why anorexia nervosa, an outright refusal to eat, has its own perverse logic. There is suffering (in the form of hunger pangs), but it's for a higher cause (the pursuit of thinness and beauty), *and* it keeps them from becoming their mothers. Many women with eating disorders are especially concerned about the parts of the body that reflect mature femininity and fertility—the breasts, belly, and hips. As one model and former anorectic wrote in her journal, "If only I could eliminate [my breasts], cut them off if need be."[5] Many anorectics express disgust toward menstruation and are visibly relieved when their dieting efforts put a stop to it.

While we battled our dieting demons, our mothers had their own. When we were children, mother's world was full of food. Food represented home and hearth, a way of life that she had been told was important and suddenly was being told was not. She had been raised to view women in a certain role and now saw that women could go beyond those set limits. Yet she wasn't always in a place where she could take advantage of that herself. So much was happening beyond her grasp that she seized control over the one resource that was ever at her command: food. She struggled to monitor her own intake of food; she would seek to monitor ours. "Eat more," she'd prod us, resentful of our youthful ability to eat without gaining weight. "Eat less," she'd enjoin, perhaps wishing to be vicariously thin through us. We inherited her neuroses about food, as well as her suspicions about her body and its need to be controlled.

We also picked up on her dislike of her own body. If we've earned notoriety as the anorectic generation, our mothers have been described as the Weight Watchers generation.[6] Growing up, I remember my mother resorting to all sorts of chemical formulations in order to pare down. She and her friends would get together at lunchtime and drink chalky milkshakes from cans, glancing at the clock to see how long until the next installment would again partially relieve their hunger. For snacks there would be dry, imported crackers that produced a most impressive crunch. I think the idea was to convince dieters that they were eating something more substantive than they in fact were—twenty-five calories could sound like a stereophonic feast. At an early age I was privy to the miraculous properties of grapefruit and cottage cheese and learned where the cookies were hidden in various neighbors' homes.

When I started shedding weight at age fourteen, for some reason I thought that, by dieting, I was attempting something original. In retrospect, I can see that I was only doing the obvious. Rather than representing a transcendence of the womanhood I knew, as I naively believed, dieting was my initiation into it. What differentiated my experience from that of my mother and her friends, however, was that with me it worked. Planned meals and group weighings proved to be no match for the adolescent will.

"The younger generation saw that their mothers valued thinness but weren't able to achieve it," says Dr. Wooley.

> *They took that as a challenge, adopted the values, and found their own ways of getting thin. Now this younger group began dieting at an early age, and it's easier to diet when younger, in part because of metabolism and in part because it's a time when someone might not have other responsibilities. And to some extent, dieting is a matter of technique. It's easier to learn to diet when young just like it's easier to learn a language. And many in this young group have mastered it.*

Over the last few years I've been struck by how women my mother's age that I know, most of whom are not professionals, react to the presence of food. If someone carts out an attractive dessert, I can feel the collective blood pressure rising. Some seem to take these dangerous goodies as a personal affront, a cruel assault on their self-discipline. "If I eat that, I'll have to diet tomorrow," someone cries out. "Maybe if I sit with my back to the table, I won't be tempted." "Why don't *you* eat that?" someone implores, glaring at me. "The extra calories won't hurt you."

I don't see this kind of social push and pull with food among women my own age. For us dieting is not a group activity. Rather, it's an assertion of self. We worry about staying slim, but to the outside world we must look perfectly cool and under control. For our mothers' generation, the viewpoint seems to be, "I can't control my weight." For us, the feeling is, "I *must* control my weight."

In many ways, this echoes the two generations' respective circumstances in a larger sense. Among those who have not challenged their position, perhaps by establishing a career, the older group feels they have little control over their place as women in a male-dominated society. We feel we do have a place—we work, we support ourselves, etc.—but our grip on it is tenuous. Hence, the emphasis on control over what our bodies look like to the extent that they reflect who and what we are.

Also, in our generation the war against fat has moved to the inner frontier. We believe we should be able to "think ourselves thin." With diet and exercise, we can have a beautiful body if we "really want" one and have "the right attitude." The perfect lean, taut, streamlined figure is so tantalizingly available to us that if we *don't* attain it we must really be losers. According to British writer Rosalind Coward, "this emphasis on the mind controlling the body . . . is in some ways worse than the ideology that preceded it. The old ideas told us our bodies weren't in good shape. But at least we could blame that on nature, if even dieting didn't get rid of 'cellulite jodhpurs.' But now our minds are the problem."[7]

What's most striking about our era is not merely a preference for extreme, even unhealthy thinness, but the fact that we seem to have developed a new way of thinking about the body. In the seventeenth century, the body was imagined as a machine. We've adopted that conceptualization, yet turned it completely around, says Susan Bordo. While the earlier metaphor expressed a *determined* body (we could understand how it worked, but were helpless to alter it), the body today is regarded as a machine with improvable, detachable, replaceable parts. The body is a realm of infinite possibility. "Create a masterpiece, sculpt your body into a work of art," *Fit* magazine tells us. "You visualize what you want to look like, and then you create that form." An ad for Evian spring water proclaims: "The proper diet, the right amount of exercise and you can have, pretty much, any body you desire."[8] The recent growth of the cosmetic surgery industry is bringing Evian's statement closer to the truth.

The media promotes the notion that not only is it possible to control our bodies, it's our right and our duty to do so. How could manufacturers sell so many products if the public didn't buy the idea that we can successfully manipulate our appearance (thicken our hair, trim our hips, alter the color of our eyes)? "Today women are judged by how thin they are," says Baras.

> *On the other hand, you have models going out and getting their breasts enlarged. Five years ago magazines said you had to have small breasts; now you have to have big breasts. So here you can't even hope to keep up with fashion unless you update your body along with your clothes. There's the illusion that we can change anything we don't like about our bodies and that we should do it. There's a weird dictation that echoes down from plastic surgeons, fashion designers, etc., that no one is born with any defects that can't be perfected.*

Pregnancy puts an end to that dream of having a perfect body, a dream that has become a corollary to the American Dream itself. What you gain, where you gain, there's no way to predict how your body will respond. I recently heard of a woman who had had breast-enlargement surgery and then unexpectedly found herself pregnant. It wasn't so much having another child as *carrying* one that devastated her; she was upset that after finally attaining her ideal shape, she was going to lose it again.

Perhaps women have always been somewhat disconcerted when their bodies seemed to run away from them. But today it's often seen as an indignity. In an essay in *Savvy* entitled "Battle of the Bulge: When Pregnancy Feels Like an Enemy Invasion", Elizabeth Stone admits ". . . the truth was I *loathed* it. . . . For me, pregnancy was, to personify it, an adversary, and the disputed territory in question was my body. Pregnancy left me feeling my body was not in the least my own in ways that ranged from irritating to unnerving. It was the unfamiliarity of my body more than the awkwardness that unnerved me." It wasn't until she adjusted to motherhood that her body was returned to her anew, Stone recalls. At that point, she began to lose weight, started reading the fashion pages again, and went back to her makeup regime. "I think now I was reclaiming my physical being with the kind of pleasure and urgency one can feel only when something previously taken for granted has been temporarily lost or threatened," she reflects.[9]

"If a woman gets pregnant today in this health-oriented, body-oriented society, she's going to have some feelings about it," says Francine Baras.

> *There's the feeling, we have to keep ourselves attractive or we'll lose our femininity and allure like our mothers and grandmothers did. On a moderate level, this can be a healthy response. If you decide to go to a prenatal or postpartum exercise class and avoid junk food when you're pregnant and nursing, that's healthy. But further down the road are some so overinvolved with their bodies that they're terrified of being pregnant, terrified of gaining the necessary weight when they're pregnant, and full of self-loathing when they begin accumulating pounds according to doctors' recommendations. The question is: How rigorously does a woman take control over her body? And to what degree is she terrorized by the physical changes?*

One reason these issues come up today is that women are becoming mothers later. By the time we become pregnant, most of us have been actively controlling our bodies for many years. We've dieted and exercised. We know our bodies and our knowledge of them is comforting. Becoming a mother threatens to loosen that control. First there's the pregnancy. Then there's new motherhood, a time when women may lack the time, energy, or inclination to work at staying thin. "I'm afraid my body is going to go berserk on me when I start having children," confides Cathy.

Often, the weight gain—that "enemy invasion"—comes to represent all the other physical changes that may leave one feeling out of control. Exercise, at least, gives a woman a fighting chance to hold onto the body she knows. She can *let* her body fatten or she can *do* something about it. And for today's women, the temptation to *do* generally wins out. In an essay in *Vogue*, for example, a writer explains that during pregnancy, exercise became more important to her than ever. "Mine is by no means a *perfect* body, but it is a *controllable* one. So it alarmed me to find that, as early as the third month of pregnancy, my body began, literally, taking on a life other than its own. . . . But I vowed not to dissolve into milk and blubber, to lose the aerobic fitness I'd worked so hard to attain." She goes on to detail the workout regimen she designed to accommodate her new physical status.[10]

Many women exercise vigorously in anticipation of a pregnancy. There are women today who insist upon continuing their tough workout schedules well into their pregnancies. They want to be in control of their bodies, not have the unborn child control them. It's a widespread belief that practicing athletes have smoother deliveries. While moderate exercise can be beneficial on many levels, when it comes to rigorous training, an easy labor may not be the result of a woman's zenlike mastery over her body, but rather because such babies can be of extremely low birth weight.

Some women are less concerned with an added bulk of pregnancy than with the pounds that may cling afterward. With horror, a woman may envision the maternal version of herself wheeling a cartful of children down the supermarket aisles, the kids reaching left and right to pull fattening items from the shelves. The fear is of somehow being physically thwarted as a mother, of being weighted down by unwanted tasks. "I saw my mother's friends let themselves go. I've seen friends my age let themselves go. It's a bit scary," says Cathy. For many women, pregnancy represents the loss of youthful slimness as, baby or no baby, it becomes harder to manage our weight as the years go by. Corrine, thirty-four, recalls that it took her a couple of years to shed the weight after her son was born. "I never had any trouble with weight before, and now I had to contend with the shift from being a thin person to a not-thin person. It bothered me more than I thought it would."

Women who gain heavily or fail to bounce right back into shape after childbirth often feel disappointed in themselves. A good part of this undoubtedly stems from unrealistic expectations set by the media. One young mother laments: "On TV you see women supposedly about to give birth who barely look pregnant. I was huge. I looked nothing like that. As usual, real women don't measure up." Dr. Striegel-Moore, who was toxemic in her last pregnancy and thus gained a lot of weight through water retention, recalls that in maternity stores a big fuss was made over women who "carried small." "Everyone kept telling these small women how great they looked," she says. "It made me feel I had a second-class pregnancy, like something's wrong with you if you're not still dainty and small."

"Maternal images have changed,"observes market researcher Judith Langer. "Now, they're sexy. Before, new mothers might be a little soft, perhaps loosely dressed. Today, you see pictures of these perfect-figured women pushing a carriage." In many ways this is a welcome shift, allowing that mothers can be sexy. But there's a pressure that goes along with it. Dr. Striegel-Moore notes that when women are pictured with children they're always reed-thin, confirming the message to women that even when they're chasing after a couple of active kids all day they have to look like they just returned from a spa.

Many women complain that they can't escape comments about their figures because once pregnant, your body size becomes open to public debate. (As well as public property: "People in the grocery store would come up to me and want to touch my stomach," Becky recalls.) "When you're pregnant, you lose every bit of privacy," adds Jane. "People would ask, 'How much did you gain this month?' My response was always, 'None of your business.' What I want to do is ask them, 'How much do *you* weigh?' "

Looking at the historical picture, whether female flesh is in or out of fashion has long depended on society's attitudes toward motherhood and fertility. In traditional cultures, a protruding belly was considered a symbol of beauty and vitality, the expanding womb representing a pregnant woman's power. Ancient sculptures and carvings often feature round-tummied women. These pieces foretold good luck, for each new birth meant added security for the group.

A century ago, too, womanly weight was favored. A woman's fleshiness signified her capacity to bear children, which had social and economic value. An ample woman also connoted family wealth. The soft body implied that the woman didn't have to work and that there was no lack of fine, rich food at home. This lent status to the man of the house. Women did narrow their waistlines with corsets, but this was as much to hold up their "frail" female bodies as it was to make them look slimmer.[11] The hourglass figure, which suggests maternal femininity, was admired.

To a greater or lesser degree, slenderness has been preferred since the beginning of the century. One factor has been the development of the fashion industry. The silhouettes dictated from France and the standardized sizing of the ready-to-wear industry created new pressures for women. As Joan Brumberg explains, "In order to be stylish and wear couturier clothes, a woman's body had to conform to the dress rather than the dress to the body, as had been the case when the traditional dressmaker fitted each garment."[12] An androgynous, boyish figure became fashionable in the 1920s. In the postwar era the hourglass figure made a brief comeback with the cinch belt–and–snug sweater look. But this quickly gave way to Twiggy and the worship of thinness, a thinness that, historians inform us, has gotten progressively thinner. Since the 1920s, when the contest began, the waist measurements of Miss America winners—that reliable index of female perfection—have steadily decreased.[13]

The desire to be thin arose in this country just as food ceased to become a scarce commodity. Modern slenderness reflects an active will, rather than a lack of nutrients. When resources are scarce, weight is equated with prosperity. When resources are plentiful, slimness becomes desirable. In terms of weight, status today derives not from the *accumulation* of resources, but rather the *control* of them. The idea is to have so much that you don't need any one thing.

To modern thinking, slimness is associated with women's emancipation: liberation from the obligation to reproduce, the opportunity to be sexual without being reproductive. By choosing to be spare of figure, women were throwing off the corsets and stays that had bound them. By downplaying hips and breasts, they were refuting the sex-segregated Victorian view that polarized men's and women's roles. (Philip Morris's Virginia Slims, the cigarette brand that has made an effort to ally with women's liberation—although no one, of course, can ever be fully liberated from diseased lungs—has tried to capitalize on this theme.) Dieting tactics like calorie counting, enemas, and even bulimia became commonplace as the flapper girls celebrated their emancipation.

One aspect of liberation is that slimness eases the way into male institutions. In the business world, this has certainly been true. A woman who is "full-figured" (as they say) will have a tougher time wearing the straight, tailored styles that have traditionally been the uniform of management. And the more you act, think, and look like a man (camouflage those curves), the better off you'll be. The business world values efficiency, conformity, speed, and economy. These qualities are thought to be embodied by a slim, not a robust, female form.

Through media images of successful women, we get the idea that being thin can bring us power. But to what extent does the slender ideal really empower women? It accepts that the male, straight-lined form is the model, and that a mature female body departs from the norm. It puts us in a position where we have to work ever harder to keep our bodies from becoming themselves. Hence our own body parts become the adversaries that we must fight off: we "attack," "destroy," and "eliminate" bulges, "burn" and "bust" fat.[14] And as we've seen in recent years, the very freedom symbolized by thinness has become imprisoning as the feminine ideal kept getting sparer and sparer, a mere sliver of a shadow of itself.

Since contemporary society has expressed such an ambivalence toward female sexuality, long-held connections between food and sex come into play. The phrase "hearty appetite" is used to describe someone who relishes sex as well as someone who eats with gusto. In Freud's view, the act of eating is a manifestation of the libido. The early advocates of celibacy in the 1800s were also food faddists. Victorian "morality" was served by abstinence in diet as well as in sex. Various foods were thought to have specific sexual powers. Red meat, for example, was said to stimulate lust. Naturally, women were discouraged from eating much of it. Delicate appetites suggested sexual purity. True "ladies," of course, hardly ate a thing (at least in public).

Though we might not consciously make the association, this ethic has persisted to some extent. As Naomi Wolf points out, "[a] sexually unchaste girl was 'fallen'; women 'fall off' their regimes. Women 'cheated' on their husbands; now they 'cheat' on their diets."[15] Still we fear that an unbridled appetite will betray desires unseemly in a woman (for food, sex, power). During a business lunch, how many women would plow through a good-sized rare steak and then follow it up with a slab of pie? How many would do so on a blind date? Despite the fact that our nutritional requirements are not so different from men's, there are masculine foods (steaks, chops, ribs, and the like) and feminine foods (salads, light soups—while not quite the rose petals-and-nectar some nineteenth-century sylphs claimed to survive on, you get the idea). This ethos often gets played out in the eating-disorder drama. The anorectic presents herself as immune to food, immune to sex. In fact, she has transcended food and sex, been freed from them. What higher moral achievement could there be?

There's so much pressure related to food and weight today that sometimes it's a wonder we manage to feed ourselves at all. Part of the issue, for women especially, is a compulsion to control our bodies, which in part stems from our perception that so much is out of control. One way of coping with the overwhelming randomness of our lives is to impose order on one small piece of it: our physical selves. Personal will serves as an internal restraint, while society continues to impose an external one. Thinness gives us the symbolism of liberation while ensuring we stay within the lines drawn by the culture. Society has allotted us a certain amount of space. We are careful not to ask for more.

Pregnancy brings these conflicts to a head. Our desire to control is challenged as we confront the futility of that control. We experience a power in our bodies that is uniquely female. As Sherrie, going into her ninth month, explains it, "Before I got pregnant I was nervous about getting big. But I've been reveling in it. It's a nice feeling. A sense of wonderment. Sometimes I look down and I'm amazed that my body is so big, so contorted. I look at myself and can't believe it." Other women learn to feel good about physical attributes that had previously been a source of misery. "I had always hated my breasts. I was always the smallest one I knew," says Sandy. "Breast-feeding gave me confidence, in that they worked and that I could finally fill a bra."

And to some women, the idea of not being able to control their bodies, and therefore not *having to,* is an attractive aspect of pregnancy. "For once, I won't have to worry about weight and muscle tone," says Gina. "It will be a relief. It's the way I feel about having my period now. If I'm bloated or feel heavy it's not my fault, it's natural, so I don't get myself worked up about it." Julie says, "I see pregnancy as being able to go to hell. Eat whatever I damn want. A total escape."

Food without fear is definitely an appeal to many women. Linda, thirty-nine, mother of three-year-old triplet girls recalls, "I had been looking forward to pregnancy as a time I could eat guilt-free. But the time came and I wasn't hungry. Not for lack of trying, but the problem was that I was really too crowded to be able to eat much. I only gained forty-one pounds. I know of women carrying one child who gained more."

But we're still dealing with a denial model. The issue is still control, whether we choose to assert it or defy it. Even in pregnancy, the ideal is still slender and contained. According to Dr. Striegel-Moore, one reason we lack an alternative model is the discomfort pregnancy provokes in this culture. "There's a resistance to the pregnant body," she says. "You don't see pregnant women in the media. Mothers with young children are fine, but showing fertility is another matter. On television, the actress is only pregnant the last week of the plot. This discomfort then translates to the discomfort women have with their own bodies."

We *will* gain weight during pregnancy, and some of us will gain more than others. This can horrify us, or we can decide that the weight gain will have a different meaning for us. We can recognize the power our bodies represent, rather than diminish it.

Chapter 8

MISCONCEIVED NOTIONS

For me it's been one of those thoughts you have without really thinking about, not quite unconscious but not solidly at the surface either, sort of the internal equivalent of something muttered under one's breath. Every once in a while—not obsessively, only when the subject presented itself—the idea has crossed my mind that I might have trouble conceiving. If I hear of a woman facing the barrage of probes and pokings that is today's response to infertility, I think: "I bet I'll have to go through the same thing." If I learn that an acquaintance is pregnant, I reflect, "That's nice for her . . . but I doubt it would happen to me so quickly." It's not a constant dread but rather an inchoate fear that arises, announces itself quietly, then disappears.

It's also completely irrational. Aside from needing the minor tune-up, my reproductive tract has passed medical inspection year after year. None of my doctors has expressed concern about its functioning. Why should I?

Then, as happens so often to a journalist, about a year or so ago the issue materialized in my work: I found myself interviewing a specialist on the various causes of infertility. There was my fear, just on the other side of my notebook, daring me to confront it. Feeling every last vestige of professionalism wither away, I took each of his clinical comments personally. Alarms kept sounding off ". . . irregular bleeding . . ." [Ding!] ". . . asymptomatic disorders . . ." [Ding!] clamoring so vociferously that at times I didn't even hear what the guy said.

When I got home I threw open my medical references to see whether any of the horrible things he was talking about bore any relation to me. Unfortunately, descriptions of physical symptomatology are a lot like those horoscope capsules you find in the newspaper: they could apply to just about anybody. ("You enjoy people but you also like your privacy . . ." Hey, that's me!) ("Pelvic pain . . . skipped periods . . ." Well, now that you mention it. . . .) Anyway, I did manage to calm down and realize how ridiculous it was to worry.

Up to that point I thought that this was my own little neurosis, that every other woman out there viewed herself as a veritable fount of fertility, ready to burst into life at the first hint of sperm. Then I started explaining the content of my work to women I knew. "He said *what?* At what age should you start to be concerned?" demanded one friend, turning pale, as though somehow I had read her mind. When I mentioned this incident to another friend, she confided to me that in some ways she was glad that she had spared herself that anxiety by having gotten pregnant years ago. "When I had the abortion there was definitely a part of me that said 'This is terrible,' " she recalls. "But there was also a part of me that said, 'I can do it!' And with that came a sense of relief."

That's a comment I began to hear again and again: for many women, an inopportune pregnancy had at least swept away that little question mark lurking in the back of the mind. And then I'd hear the other side: "Unlike most of my friends, I've never had an abortion. It makes me wonder if anything's wrong with me."

"When I was younger, eighteen or nineteen, I certainly wasn't as careful as I've been in recent years," says Cathy. "When I think of all the times I had sex and didn't use my diaphragm, I ask myself: Why didn't I get pregnant? I used to say 'phew,' but now I wonder if something's awry. You get smarter, use contraceptives, and you don't really know if all your parts are working as they should." As we go along, not necessarily planning to have children immediately but hoping to keep the option in reserve, many of us, it appears, are carrying around the vague anxiety that we won't be able to conceive. This fear of infertility might not be universal, but, I soon concluded, I certainly wasn't alone.

Perhaps women have always felt this way. The prevalence of fertility rites throughout history suggests that women who hoped to have children have always looked to hedge their bets. In early modern Europe, brides-to-be would bathe in the "fertile" waters of certain streams or sleep on designated stones.[1] Some American Indian women would stand naked before reflections of the moon, believing that the lunar rays regulated childbirth.[2] Nineteenth-century European brides could expect to be pelted with pomegranates, peas, or even old shoes to ensure a fruitful marriage.[3]

But why the fear today, I continued to wonder? A woman's fertility does begin to drop in her mid-thirties, and more women are delaying childbearing. But perhaps just as important as the percentage point or so dip is that the longer wait to have children creates more time for doubts to creep in. Even so, this would seem the least likely time for women to worry about fertility. Not only are fewer women unable to have children than in previous eras (the result of improved health, education, and nutrition),[4] there are more effective ways of treating infertility.

Also, the social consequences of not bearing children are less dire than was the case in other times. When children were economic assets and marriage was an economic arrangement, a barren wife was thought to have broken her contract. In many cultures, men who suspected their wives were sterile (the fact that they might have been sterile themselves appeared not to have occurred to them) could divorce or take second wives. According to tradition in rural China, a childless wife would not have been allowed to die in the house of her husband.[5] Even today, in India, an infertile woman at a wedding or infant-blessing ceremony is thought to bring bad luck.[6] With childnessness now a socially acceptable option, women who can't have children need not fear being set apart or ostracized.

Certainly there is a rational component to the fear. As mentioned earlier, infertility rates are rising among some age groups (specifically for women in their early to mid-twenties, due to an increase in sexually transmitted diseases and other infections). More is known about medical conditions, such as endometriosis and problems associated with IUDs, that can compromise fertility. Much fuss has been made of baby boomers who put off pregnancy while they concentrate on their careers, only to learn that their biological timepieces have wound down. Then there's the current media panic, the onslaught of press reports on infertile couples and miracle babies, which can lead one to think that to produce a baby at all would take a miracle. Businesses have already begun to prey on this fear: "Life Today Can Make It Harder to Get Pregnant," proclaims an ad for an ovulation-predictor kit that appeared in *Glamour*. "QTest Can Make It Easier."

Media aside, according to the American Fertility Society, actual infertility rates for most age groups (aside from those in their early to mid-twenties) have remained stable for the past twenty years. Particularly since the women I've talked to have no medical justification for concern or have even gotten pregnant in the past, it seems clear that many of us are reacting to more than statistics. The social factors and the numbers surely come into play, but intuitively I felt there was something else—something behind both the fear and the public's prurient interest in infertility—that was harder to grasp and yet truer to our times.

Ironically, it seems that the very forces that have eased the pressure to have children and enhanced our ability to promote fertility have stirred anxieties about our fertility. Our expectations for control are so high that even vast improvements in science's capacity to manipulate fertility can't possibly meet them. Sex and fertility have been so effectively severed (on a conscious level) that (on an unconscious level) we don't trust the two to work together. We conduct our lives so differently from the way our mothers did that we're unsure we can emulate them (bear children like they did) when we want to.

I'm not implying that we should go backward on any of these scores. But we do need to look at how social and medical changes have affected the way we see our bodies and ourselves. Some women's doubts have led them to test out their fertility, sometimes with the result that they launched into pregnancy before they (or their marriages) were ready. What is it about this fear that can provoke responses so intense? And why do we have it?

If I had to chase down my own (as yet proved or disproved) trepidation, I would say it largely derives from the unpredictability of the venture. The terrible truth is, I have little faith in anything I can't control. The prospect of not having control over what happens to our bodies (which is itself a metaphor for losing control over our lives) can be quite threatening to many women. Nearly everything we have (our attractive figures, our skills, our professional standing) results from our discipline and our ability to seize control. Pregnancy happens when it happens. We can't will it to occur at a certain time; unlike school or work, we can't bolster our results by simply working harder. For those of us used to seeking control over our bodies and our lives, this can be a difficult reality to accept.

With fertility specifically, most of us have been controlling it for years. That involves *doing* something. Getting pregnant, then, involves *not* doing (except, of course, for the sex part, which presumably we were doing anyway). How, then, do we make something (conception) happen by *not* doing something? We're in a situation in which we know we can turn it off, but we don't know if we can turn it on.

In our minds we may separate those things we can control (our weight, etc.) from those that we can't (conception). The ability to do something may, in our minds, become tied to the ability to control it: if we can't control it, we can't do it. Sometimes the frustration of not knowing they can get pregnant leads women to conclude that they *can't.* The uncertainty proves so difficult to tolerate that some find it easier to cope with a known—infertility—even if that known is unpleasant.

Lacking control over conception was "one of the scariest things about pregnancy," says Merle, thirty-six, who recently gave birth to a daughter. "There's no immediate gratification. You can't make it happen when you want it to happen. Then when it does happen you have to be pregnant for nine months. That's a very long time. I like to be gratified almost instantly. I'm impatient. If I don't get what I want now, I say I won't get it at all. Or I convince myself that I don't want it anyway."

Merle certainly believed she wasn't going to get what she wanted in this instance; so much so that when the at-home test revealed that she was indeed pregnant, she thought she had used the test incorrectly:

> *The little cardboard stick turned completely blue, which meant it was positive, but I thought it must be a mistake. Did I test the right morning urine? Did I take it too early? Did I take it too late? I even called the company, and they assured me there were no false positives. I had thought I wasn't going to get pregnant. I'd be on the phone with friends and I'd say, "I won't get pregnant." No doctors could have convinced me otherwise. It was probably a defense. I was preparing for a difficult time.*

The more we want something, the more looming the fear that we may not get it. For some women, this fear is so intolerable that they redouble their efforts to boost their chances of getting what they want. Any evidence that the pieces are in place can reassure, while any unanswered questions can torment. I know of a woman who had once been pregnant herself, yet her husband's fertility status remained an unknown. To ease her uncertainty, she urged him to have a semen analysis before they began to try. Another woman admitted that she was relieved to learn that her husband had once gotten another woman pregnant: "I know it sounds terrible, when the two of them had to go through an abortion and all that pain, but my reaction to hearing about this was: at least we know *he* doesn't have a problem."

Then there's the question of sex. Could it be that the separation of sex and fertility, in alienating us to some extent from our sexuality, has also served to alienate us from that hallmark of our femininity, our capacity to bear children? Francine Baras thinks it has. "Because women are sexually active long before they become reproductively active, they tend to regard their female apparatus as merely sexual apparatus," she says. "A woman might think, 'I'm on the pill, so those parts of me are just a part of my sexuality now and have nothing to do with child-bearing.' When it comes to the thought of making babies, she may think to herself, 'Do I have the stuff to do it?' "

In our society, with sex and procreation set apart in experience and in mind, the syllogistic reasoning, "I can make a baby. Sex makes babies. I have sex. Therefore . . ." is incomplete: the "therefore" doesn't happen. Some women stop believing they can have babies at all. At times, the confusion can be strong enough to impel a woman to set the matter straight.

"I think when I got pregnant I almost meant to do it, although not consciously," says Liza, thirty, who had an abortion at twenty-one. "I didn't actually want a baby, but I'd had sex—which is what makes babies—and yet I hadn't made a baby. It sets up a wall of disbelief: this is what you do to get pregnant, but you never do. Getting pregnant breaks down that wall, at least it did for me. The abortion was what reconnected myself to the idea I could do it, that as a woman it was my physical prerogative."

In *Love and Will,* written in 1969, about the time the sexual revolution entered the mainstream, Rollo May touches on this theme. He talks about the conflict between sex and "eros," which he defines as the life-giving force inevitably associated with sex. He refers to "some psychic needs more vital, deeper, and more comprehensive than sex" that are not necessarily satisfied by sheer coupling.[7] He offers case histories, first of a woman, then of a man, who intentionally (he concludes) neglect contraception and initiate pregnancies. He describes a desire "to get some hold on nature, experience a fundamental procreative process, give [oneself] over to some primitive and powerful biological process, partake of some deeper pulsations in the cosmos" as a factor in these instances. A bit florid, perhaps, but he suggests that on a basic level one's procreativity links one to the rhythms of life, a link that's important enough for women (and men) to seek its validation.

If sex can never really be separated from fertility in the unconscious, perhaps in experiencing sex while suppressing our fertility we begin to doubt our ability to reproduce. "With sexual freedom there's often a sense of "fertility macho," a notion that we can control our fertility, a defiance of it," says Dr. Davis. "The fear is of defying it so forcefully that it disappears altogether."

Birth control, then, can "protect" us not only from conscious awareness of our fertility but from our fear of losing it. At the same time, birth control can "turn" us into someone infertile, and thus this idea is incorporated. With the pill, for example, we become "infertile" for the duration of the prescription, and we can begin to see our "immunity" to pregnancy as something inherent in our bodies rather than the medication.

Fertility is connected not only to sexuality but to *identity* as well. Which leads us to another source of infertility concerns: for if sex is presented to us in a somewhat neutral, divorced-from-biology sort of way, how are we taught to deal with our *own* biology as it reflects our gender? Sure, we know we're women, but what is that supposed to mean to us? The world we aspire to is not the traditional world of women, but rather the world of men with an (increasingly) androgynous twist. Where does our "womanness" come in? If it only becomes important when we consider having children, doesn't that involve some kind of psychic leap? Might that not be somewhat disorienting? If we've been actively developing the (supposedly) masculine side of our nature, how, then, do we take the feminine aspects on faith?

One woman (who now has a son) recalls that she had trouble doing so:

> *Deep inside I doubted I was female. I felt there was something wrong with me that kept me from being as complete a female as my mother. I just couldn't believe that I had a uterus, that I had all those parts and they all fit together and worked. As soon as I got pregnant, which I hadn't planned, I never had that lousy feeling again. Until you get your driver's license, you're not going to be confident that you can drive. For me, it was the same way with getting pregnant. I did decide to have an abortion, which was difficult for me, but emotionally the whole thing did have some positive consequences.*

Other women made comments like, "I always felt I was healthy but that my reproductive system was out of whack," or, "I just didn't believe it could happen." Why wouldn't women believe it could happen? They've seen women pregnant. Their own mothers were pregnant with *them.* Could it be that an entire generation of women is unsure about the viability of its own parts?

According to Gordon Deckert, M.D., professor of psychiatry at the Oklahoma State Medical Center, women who work in male-dominated fields in particular may feel a need to affirm their femininity in a way that their jobs and lifestyles fail to. Deckert, who lectures on the medical-school experience, says that he has seen women medical students intentionally get pregnant as a means of experientially confirming their femininity. That observation in itself is noteworthy, as one would expect these, of all women, to be well informed about contraception and to enjoy ready access to it.

"Part of getting pregnant is the question of 'can I?' " he explains. "Since these women often postpone marriage and pregnancy, as do so many others who pursue careers, they may have an ongoing fear that they will not be able to conceive. For some, the fear takes the form of wondering: 'Am I really female?' 'Am I really adequate as a woman?' 'How do I know?' One thing girls hear all their lives is, you have this thing called a uterus. But until you get pregnant, there's no experiential reality to it."

There we go. It's those darn *careers* again, getting in the way of our being women. Maybe we should just scrap the whole thing and go home and wait for some man to provide for us, take care of us, impregnate us. But in Francine Baras's view, the sources of such fears are far more complicated than how or whether we choose to support ourselves; rather, they often evolve out of our family identifications.

"Many women have worked hard throughout their lives to establish identities outside of the mother role," she says. "So when they begin to consider getting pregnant, there's a clash: How can I do what my mother did (make babies) when I've created myself into something completely different? As a result, many women simply cannot envision themselves having babies. So when the desire to do so gets stirred up, they panic and imagine they can't."

The messages women get while growing up convey that it's *not* acceptable to identify with mother, Baras says. Men have power, access, and choice. Father represents the outer world of achievement and success. Mother represents that messy interior world, fraught with confusion and friction. "The question a young girl faces is, 'which is more dangerous, to identify with mother or to identify with father?' " she says. For many girls and (later) women, it's far more dangerous to identify with mother. Many mothers, says Baras, living in a time that doesn't support motherhood or femininity, have simply been unable to give their daughters the inner substance to feel good about womanhood. Either the daughter perceived her mother as deprived, or she saw her mother fulfilled and she felt deprived herself. Either way, those feelings can cause a young woman to be actually repulsed by the notion of becoming a mother.

As a result, Baras says, many women deny that they have reproductive apparatus at all. "The thinking goes, 'If I have this equipment, then I'm like mother,' " she says. "The response then is, 'I don't want to be like mother. I'll be like father. And if I'm like father, then I can't get pregnant.' " In other words, many women see it as "safer" to imagine themselves incapable of conceiving than to picture themselves as being like their mothers. Sometimes, she adds, usually among the younger women of the group, the conviction strikes so deep that they don't bother to use birth control at all.

What often also gets stirred into this psychic mix is a sense of guilt toward one's mother. If a woman feels that she is the cause of her mother's problems, she may be inclined to fear she won't be able to get pregnant.

"A woman's fear of being infertile can reflect an unconscious anxiety that mother is taking revenge on her," says Dr. Williams. Drawing on the theories of Melanie Klein, she explains how very young children, in their attempts to make sense of how babies get born, often fantasize that mother's insides are full of babies waiting to get out. The child may dream of robbing her mother of those babies, as a way of keeping the mother—or of keeping the babies—all to herself. If hostile fantasies toward her mother persist, says Dr. Williams, the woman may fear that her mother wants to take the babies back (leaving her infertile); or, if her mother had suffered miscarriages or had only the one child, the woman may think, "Oh my God, I really did destroy those babies." In any event, the idea is that the mother may choose to deploy whatever power she has over her daughter, and what more trenchant way than over her fertility?

Dr. Williams contends that anger toward one's father can play a similar role. "You can't talk about infertility anxieties without dealing with feelings about sperm or the penis," she says. "Some women feel they can't get pregnant because of ideas they have that sperm and semen are 'bad,' primitive ideas that may have arisen from feelings about their fathers." It's also possible that assumptions about infertility can be rooted in a woman's relationships. The belief (perhaps unconscious) that a romance isn't meant to go anywhere (is sterile) can lead a woman to think she won't be able to conceive with a particular man.

There are women who have dismissed the possibility of pregnancy from their minds and act as though they were physically immune to it; women who would like to think they are fertile yet are plagued by doubts; and, in yet another group, women who may *be* infertile but who ignore their problems because they raise too many troubling issues. The actual fear of infertility seems to intensify with the years—as social, emotional, and physical pressures to have children mount—but women in their early twenties experience it as well. There's a lot of confusion being felt out there. Yet who's talking about it? Beyond the community of therapists, the approach seems to be that women's attitudes toward fertility are the constant and their physical capabilities the variable, when the truth is probably closer to the reverse.

Infertility worries are frequently linked to fears of actually *becoming* pregnant. Regardless of how much a woman may want a baby, ambivalence about motherhood is rife. While this has probably always been the case, the feelings could be aggravated today. "The capacity to have a baby is made so much of now," says Dr. Davis. "There's so much pressure to fulfill the notion that you can have it all, do it all. A woman may feel it's something she has to do even if she doesn't want to and may feel conflicted about that."

If a woman has conflicting emotions about motherhood, it may be easier to deal with these feelings in terms of a fear of infertility. This, says Dr. Davis, may seem to be a more socially acceptable concern, as well as a way of avoiding a painful conflict like rage toward one's mother or toward a husband who wants her to quit her job when they have a family. She may interpret her mixed emotions as "evidence" that she wouldn't make a good mother and go so far as to worry that she may harm her child in some way. She may decide that someone so unsure is "not worthy" of being a mother. Unconsciously, the focus of fear shifts from the ability to mother to the ability to conceive, for a woman who can't conceive doesn't have to fret about being a good mother anyway.

Dr. Davis believes that the fear of infertility and the ambivalence that underlies it is not merely a psychological sidetracking of the issue but is rather "part of the emotional work of pregnancy and preparing for parenthood. A fear of infertility only becomes a problem when women act out on these feelings with panic, making themselves miserable with the anxiety that there's something wrong with them." Instead of trying to pretend away the fear, she suggests, it can be used as a jumping-off point for exploration.

This swirling mass of feelings is so hard to get a grip on because we have no *framework* within which to examine it. We're groomed for many things besides motherhood, yet society expects that when we *do* become mothers we're going to latch onto some mythic role. We learn that following the path of our fathers will bring us the greatest rewards, yet we should be just as happy to accept the fate of our mothers. We're taught to aspire to androgyny (the slender body, not betraying any emotionality at work) but to retain faith in our femininity. Pregnancy may be a step forward for a woman, yet it has also been presented as a topple backward for personhood: a loss of independence, freedom, and control—all a woman may have fought so hard to attain in her life. So who's going to confront pregnancy with a clear head?

One common scenario is that those women who most fear pregnancy are the ones who leap most quickly into it. "It's what we call counter-phobic behavior—that when we're the most afraid of something is when we rush headlong into it," says Dr. Williams. A woman's incessant fear of infertility may mask her strong wish not to be pregnant; by focusing her energies on getting pregnant, she may hope to will her fears of pregnancy away.

Women who feel fairly certain about their desire to have children can also get caught up in the fertility panic. For many women the question is not *should* I have a child, but *when.* Often they're torn between trying to conceive immediately, when they or their partner may not be ready, or waiting, which means running the risk of waiting until it's too late. Because of the agitation surrounding infertility rates (in part stemming from alarmist reports in the media, including a slew of articles in 1982 following a French study, later discredited, claiming that women's chances of getting pregnant plummeted after age thirty), a woman may unhesitatingly say *now* when, in a more realistic state of mind, she may have opted for a bit longer delay.

"I was thirty-three when I got married," says Anita, who recently separated from her husband.

> *I thought ideally it would be better to be married for a while and get comfortable with someone before having a baby, but felt all the advantages paled behind the fear that waiting a year or two might be too long. I got to be quietly panicked about it. I couldn't even look at articles about infertility. I had my husband convinced that it could take a long time. Then he was in total shock when I got pregnant right away. I think he felt manipulated. It wasn't really best for us as a couple to do this before working out our relationship first. I don't think I was listening to him enough. I don't think I was rational about it. I was like a bulldozer.*

Even women who *have* children can feel the fear. Nora wants to wait to have a second child, although her husband wants "a lot of kids" and her parents have made it no secret that they're ready for more grandchildren. "There's the thought that I'll be punished—I'll be thirty-four and won't be able to get pregnant again," she says. "My mother had fibroids. I just had a heavy period and thought, why this bleeding? The little light in your head goes off and you think: that's punishment for not having the child earlier."

Anita, too, says the anxiety failed to dissipate with pregnancy:

> *As it turned out, I did get pregnant easily. But now I hear stories about women who got pregnant the first time, then take five years the second time, and I worry about that. Sometimes I think I shouldn't be greedy. I have one child. But I'm surprised at the intensity I feel. I'm surprised the fear didn't go away. I wish it would. I know I have to relax and get the relationship part of my life in order. If not for my fertility worries, I would be more patient with men. It's definitely had an effect on me.*

Guilt about sexual experience can also come into play. We grew up in a sexually permissive society but one with decidedly Victorian overtones. The "bad" girl always loses out in the end (regardless of how much fun she had in the interim), was the message that lingered. Herpes, AIDS, and the fate of unwed teen mothers only gave the fable a reality base. A century ago, frequent sex (or enjoying the sex you had) was commonly implicated in female infertility. Although today we know that intercourse in itself does not "dry up" women any more than it does men, on some level the connection persists. "When a woman feels ready to have a baby, new feelings come up," says Dr. Davis. "Often these relate to wishes that may have been suppressed before. Women start blaming themselves. All the guilts come up. It's not always rational."

The guilt can surface when the link between sex and fertility is again forged as a woman thinks about having children. Unconsciously, she may separate out the freer "unattached" sex she had in earlier years and almost regard it as something a woman other than herself had done.

"For many women, once you make the decision to get pregnant, your relation to everything changes: to your marriage, your self, your body, your cycle," says Dr. Williams. "Suddenly you see past experiences—like using birth control or taking recreational drugs—in a whole new light: you've tainted the purity of your body. Your body is no longer for casual or hedonistic pursuits, it's a sacred vessel for carrying your child. There can be a fear of retribution. Women who were on the pill, for example, may think: the pill gave me freedom. Infertility will be the revenge of the pill."

The sense of remorse is often experienced in contrast to one's own mother's past. Because her mother's sexual encounters may be associated strictly with procreation, a woman may imagine her mother to be sexually "cleaner" than she is (or was). She might think: "If I am enjoying (or have enjoyed) sex for the sake of sex, maybe I'm not supposed to have babies." If she has ever been involved with a "bad" guy, or has otherwise experimented sexually, this too can contribute to the guilt.

Sometimes there's a degree of truth to qualms about one's sexual past. Clearly, the more unprotected sex you have, the more likely you are to run into a problem. The longer the stretch of time between a woman's intiation into the erotic and her initiation into the maternal, the more opportunities there have been to contract a potentially fertility-impairing infection or to have an abortion.

While most experts contend that a medically performed, complication-free abortion should in no way mar a woman's fertility, the apprehension that it might remains. For some, the fear could be a displacement of other concerns relating to the abortion. A woman who has had one or more abortions may have mentally shut down any thoughts of pregnancy because the experience proved so painful. In such a case, the wish to have children raises some touchy issues. She may feel that she doesn't "deserve" to have a child, that she may be punished for what she had done. "I worry that my abortion may have done something to my body, that I may have to pay for it later by not having the child that I want," confides one woman. The fantasy often assumes a romantic/tragic tone—that the woman gave up "the one baby she could have had."

Even if a woman hasn't suffered any medical repercussions related to sex, she may feel wary. "I hate going to the gynecologist for fear of finding out there's something wrong with me, that something I've done in the past could prevent me from having children when I want to," says Lori, twenty-six. "Whenever I notice the smallest gynecological symptom, I ask my doctor about it," adds Cathy. "The first thing that comes into my mind is that I could have some infertility problem I'm not even aware of."

Unfounded fertility concerns often reflect deeper personal anxieties. We may see our reproductive states (irregular menstrual cyles, PMS, miscarriages) as metaphors for ourselves (that we're chaotic, hysterical, incompetent). We imagine that others have an easier relationship with their bodies. We so fear what our reproductive fate will reveal about us that we imagine that which we fear will happen.

All these doubts may be comfortably hidden, only to surface when some external event triggers the fear. It could be learning of someone else who has a problem. "Just the other day I heard of someone going through an early menopause at age thirty-two. I know it's an unusual case, but it definitely gets you thinking," says Cathy. It could be a birthday (another year gone by and I haven't had a baby yet). Or marriage.

In retrospect, it makes complete sense that my own flirtation with hysteria came a few months before I was due to be married. Suddenly, the ability to make a baby threatened to *mean* something to me. Up until then, as I aged I merely moved my vague timeline along with me. (I'll get married at twenty-five, then have a baby at twenty-eight. No, I guess not. So I'll get married at twenty-nine and have a baby at thirty-two . . .) Now it seemed those numbers and my real life had a chance at converging. The fears about infertility became entwined with the other fears bubbling about: Could I handle marriage? Could I handle motherhood? Just what kind of woman was this nice, trusting man getting anyhow? In what horrible ways might I disappoint him?

Sometimes the fear simply takes root and grows, seemingly of its own accord. "Nobody ever told me that I had a problem, but I had never gotten pregnant and I began to get obsessed with the whole idea," says Marsha.

> *I let myself get sloppier and sloppier about birth control, and sure enough it happened. I think it had a lot to do with being in my thirties with no children yet. I was in my fourth year of medical school at that point, and my career was pretty well set. As for my personal and emotional life, though, it wasn't set at all. I had just broken up with a boyfriend and was having a wild affair. Getting pregnant was a really out-of-control thing for me to do. The last time I had unprotected intercourse was some ten years before. I think at nineteen I may have been pregnant because once my period was very late and then I bled heavily. But I never had a test, so I never knew for sure. My fear was, would I be able to do this thing, this woman thing?*

Oddly, one frequent trigger for infertility fears are physicians. Kristen Luker found in her 1975 study that an astounding *two-thirds* of women interviewed at an abortion clinic reported that they had in some way gotten the impression from their doctors that they could have a fertility problem. What generally happens, Dr. Luker says, is that the doctor inadvertently makes a comment that the patient construes as meaning she'll have trouble conceiving.

"Because of their training, doctors tend to make note of any departure from a statistical norm," she says. "But even if the observation is medically meaningless, the woman who hears it may take it as a pronouncement on her body. Like a 'tipped uterus.' I heard that one so often that I checked with a gynecologist about it. She told me that nearly *everyone's* uterus is tipped either backward or forward at any given time."

A doctor may mumble some comment about irregular periods. But in reality few women ovulate and bleed in time to a set twenty-eight-day rhythm. He or she may mention that taking the pill could cause a delay in ovulation upon cessation. Again, although some studies suggest that it can take a while for ovulation to resume after discontinuing the pill, barring an underlying problem, ovulation should occur naturally within a few months. (According to Kristen Luker, some early studies failed to note whether women found not to be ovulating after using the pill had actually ovulated *prior* to going on the pill. Nevertheless, these studies provoked widespread alarm about the pill's possible effect on fertility.)

Similarly, women with endrometriosis are likely to be told that they could have trouble conceiving later. That is true. Endometriosis *can* be the culprit in infertility—but certainly not in *every* case. Early and mild cases of endometriosis can often be treated to prevent their reaching a more problematic stage. However, lots of women with endometriosis and other progressive hormone-related conditions, like polycystic ovarian disease, are walking around feeling like biological time bombs, left to wonder how long their fertility will serve them. Some of these women may feel compelled (consciously or otherwise) to test out their fertility; others are plagued by the unresolved question.

Heidi, who's twenty-eight and single, learned ten years ago that she had a hormone imbalance (probably polycystic ovarian disease) that had caused her to lose her period, gain weight, and grow body hair. First she was treated with strong steroids; then for years she was on high-dose birth-control pills. She recalls how her condition, and the way physicians handled it, made her doubt not only her fertility but her femininity.

> *No one ever fully explained to me what the ramifications of my condition were. All I knew was what had happened to me. I was terrified of turning into a monster. It really ate into my self-image. I felt dependent on those birth-control pills. I was terrified of even the thought of trying to get pregnant, because that meant going off them and getting all those symptoms again. Doctors never said straight out, I should get pregnant now. They said, ''possibly through pregnancy the condition would correct itself'' and ''possibly the condition could affect fertility.'' I was reacting to this unknown quantity. I would ask about the fertility and they'd say ''wait until it's time.'' It minimized the importance of me as a woman with a healthy body. It's almost as though, when you're ready to have babies, come in and we'll fix you up. Until then, your body's irrelevant.*
>
> *At one point I stopped having my period altogether. I finally realized this was not a good situation. I was feeling alienated from my whole body. I was feeling detached sexually. I felt pressure to find a man, which did my relationships no good. Last year, finally, I went to a woman gynecologist. This doctor really spent time and talked to me. She said if I wanted I could switch to a lower-dose pill or stop them altogether. When I asked about the fertility, she said if I'm ovulating*

I'm okay, and explained about taking my temperature to check. That's so basic, but no one ever told me this before. The first month off the pills I learned I was ovulating. Self-imagewise, this whole thing has affected me a lot. I had felt dried out. Now that I've stopped the medication and am getting my period again, I feel better. I feel more connected to women than I used to. I feel I have my body back again.

It's not that doctors shouldn't inform women when they think there's cause for concern about fertility. Granted, there sometimes are legitimate problems. But the communication can break down as physicians tend to deal in generalities, while women are dealing with specifics: namely, their own bodies. Doctors should realize that their medical statements aren't just going to be filed away until "it's time"; rather, women are going to *live with* them, and seemingly benign remarks can alter how a woman feels about her body.

Too often, says Gary S. Berger, M.D., an infertility specialist in Chapel Hill, North Carolina, "doctors are giving women a double message: that you've got some problem but that you shouldn't worry about it. That's unfair, because it arouses the fear without resolving it. Unfortunately, there's rarely any formal attention paid to this in typical training. It gets left up to the sensitivity of the individual physician."

Women who suffer from any "female" medical disorders may conclude that they may have trouble getting pregnant. Perhaps because of how we learn about the body as children, all of our female parts tend to be lumped together in our minds. Yet doctors, interested strictly in the task at hand and rarely in any possible emotional repercussions, often fail to respond to such fears.

Laura recalls:

I had a fibrous tumor in my breast when I was eighteen. First I panicked that I might die. Then, when I saw that wasn't going to happen, I worried that it might ruin my life as a woman. It made me wonder about my feminine parts as a whole. This was always in the back of my mind. Once I went to a breast cancer specialist and asked in a general way if my body was okay. But I could never articulate the precise fear that I had. And no doctor ever brought it up to me. I think that was part of the reason I was so happy about my pregnancy. Not only did I want the baby, I was relieved that I was able to have one.

Women should try to take it upon themselves to raise the issue with their doctors when statements cast doubt on their fertility. Unfortunately, with our highly technical and specialized medical system and the rushed, impersonal encounters with doctors that often result, this is not always so easy to do.

Sometimes a doctor's observation may be less medical than aesthetic, a remark on our relative size or shape. A friend told me of someone she knew who, at her first visit to the gynecologist, learned that she had a "small" uterus. She was devastated. The notion she carried home from her doctor was that her reproductive parts were not what they should be, in some way stunted in growth and possibly useless. It made her feel less a woman than other women, that her normally proportioned body was hiding this terrible truth about her. But any woman who has never been pregnant will have a "small" uterus. It would only be cause for concern if she has never menstruated and thus may have a physical problem.

Still, our bodies (and body images) remain fair game for the gynecological profession. For some time my sister-in-law Carin and I were going to the same gynecologist. Carin has a strong, solid frame and there is something unmistakably maternal about her in appearance as well as manner. Whenever she went to this doctor, he would tease, "What are you waiting to have children for? You're *made* for having babies." Unsure if she *wanted* to have babies just then, this would shake her up a bit. Whenever I went to the doctor, he would breeze through, literally walking in one door, peering through the speculum, and walking out a second door without breaking stride. He barely glanced at my body. Then he would want to chat with me about the articles I was writing.

In other words, he was treating Carin as a breeder and me as a brain. In biological terms, I am probably no less "made" for having babies than my sister-in-law. But I was apparently *perceived* as less so, at least by this doctor, and thus was treated differently. I can't blame him alone for stirring up doubts about my fertility. Yet it is important to note that how people (and doctors in particular) respond to us regarding our body type can influence our feelings about ourselves as potential mothers.

Some women derive confidence from what doctors say. "When I was nineteen or so, my doctor said that I have wide hips that would be perfect for childbearing, and I've never worried about it since," says Melanie. Others have preconceptions about the ease of conception that are not the result of a doctor's words. "I have one of those large, maternal bodies, you know, like I should be standing out in a pasture for breeding," says Nora, who goes on to say that it never occurred to her she'd have a problem becoming pregnant.

Irrationally, I've always felt that my small size would be an obstacle in childbearing. It wasn't a matter of feeling unfeminine, for I knew petiteness could only be an advantage in boy catching (depending of course on the boy) and fitting into clothes. But as there's clearly less of me than there is of many women, I guess there's been the fantasy that I'm somehow "unfinished" in a fundamental way. At the same time, very large women may imagine themselves infertile because they may feel their bodies are too masculine. Yet, aside from extreme underweight or obesity (which can be a problem), how large or small you are or how broad your hips are has little bearing on how easy it will be for you to get pregnant or give birth. The shape of your build on the *out*side does not necessarily reflect your shape *in*side.

To ease our concerns or to maintain control, we often look to our doctors to reassure us about our ability to conceive—or to hasten the process if a delay makes us doubt it. We don't know where else to turn. We don't put much stock in moonbeams, nor in the natural rhythms they represent. So rather than questioning where our fears stem from in the first place, we get caught up in the medical community's vision of fertility, which, as we'll see, often creates more anxiety than it resolves.

Chapter 9

THE FERTILITY INDUSTRY

A medical-student friend told me about a doctor she knows who seems to have the whole baby thing figured out. She is thirty-eight, married, and doesn't feel she wants a baby just yet. But someday she might. So she's freezing her eggs.

I'm not sure exactly how it works, but in theory, when she decides to have a baby she can take one of the ova out of cold storage to be fertilized (maybe her husband has already put sperm on ice for the occasion), and then she'll have herself a pregnancy. And why not? Who says we should be constrained by the conventional limits of the body? Why should we submit to the movement of chronological time when we can figure out a way to arrest it?

It is a pretty wild thought: all those tiny spheres, glistening with condensate in their frosty beds, waiting patiently to fulfill their reproductive destiny. Well, we're getting there. Last year physicians at the University of Southern California reported a study in which four of seven postmenopausal women aged forty to forty-four became pregnant and gave birth to healthy babies using donated eggs. Dr. Marcia Angell, an editor at the *New England Journal of Medicine,* wrote in comment, "The limits on childbearing years are now anybody's guess; perhaps they will have more to do with the stamina required for labor and 2 A.M. feedings than with reproductive function."[1]

The process of baby making has worked reasonably well for the species up to now, but what's to stop us from finding a way to perfect it? Maybe eggs themselves will soon be obsolete. In the not-so-distant future we may simple preserve our genetic material in microscopic capsules that we'll cache away in airtight cubicles, like safe deposit boxes, until we're inspired to reproduce.

Granted, such scenarios are a bit farfetched. At this point we still have to depend on our bodies to some extent, and few of us would be willing to entrust our childbearing to the biomedical fringe. And who knows what will happen with this unusually venturesome doctor? I think it not unlikely that when she turns forty or so, she'll decide it's time and try to have a baby the regular way.

It seems clear that we've entered a new era of baby making. Today's women, having controlled their fertility with contraception for so many years, regard *conception* as something that should be controllable as well. Medical technology is forging ahead at a fast, often dizzying, pace. Our hormones, our genes, our very parts are ripe for manipulation. Science's capacity to control our functions means we're increasingly apt to ask for that control. With scientific advancement comes added knowledge; we're conscious of every aspect of the process, from conception to birth. Knowing what we know, our bodies are more *observed* than bodies have ever been before.

This lucid childbearing we now engage in is bound to change the way we experience making babies, bound to change our expectations for ourselves and for the children we bear. Whether or not we employ technology in our own quest to become mothers, how we approach and how we perceive baby making can't help but be affected. We can't just choose to do things the "natural" way; our childbearing is, by definition, contrived. In many ways, for a mother in the 1990s, the newborn child is the point at which the natural and the unnatural meet. Somehow, the more we know about what our bodies do, the less we trust them to do it on their own.

The basic dilemma here is on a biblical scale: How do you "uneat" the apple? How do you unlearn something you know? If you know that you increase your odds of conceiving by having sex on a certain day, how can your conception be completely spontaneous? If you know taking your temperature to time ovulation will boost your chances yet further, why wouldn't you do it? If you have any question about your cycle and taking a pill will trigger ovulation for certain, how could you resist? There are certainly many couples, particularly younger ones who might not feel in a hurry, who do "let nature take its course." But many of us are applying more of a problem-solving approach to conception—despite the fact there might not *be* a problem—and leaving less and less to chance. Indeed, it makes that time, not so long ago, when a couple just made love and let the baby come when it chose, seem like some lost, innocent age.

Instead, the impression we get is that conception requires effort. The verb we use to describe our commitment to starting a family is "to try." Once conception has been defined as a goal to be achieved, one feels compelled to summon any resources that can aid in its achievement. Some women chart their cycles on computers. An electronic calendar offers a pregnancy and lactation software card. There are apparently skin-sensitive devices women can wear around their wrists to tell when they're ovulating. One such watch also advises which day to try for a boy or a girl.[2]

"Our lives are medicalized," says Cathy. "Even when rationally you know it should happen on its own, you do what you can to make sure it does. You get a clean bill of health from your doctor, take your temperature, and have sex every other night because that way men are more potent than if you do it every night. Even in small ways, you adapt your behavior based on what we know of the technology."

The magic has disappeared. What we have instead is *measure*. Who can think about romance and passion when we're contending with mucus elasticity and sperm count? We plan our conception, decide when it should take place, then court it. We try to outsmart those eggs and sperm who may have had it in mind to take a bit longer to pair off. Why? Are we in that much of a rush? Perhaps sometimes we are. Will we somehow get better results, an easier pregnancy, or a better baby? There's no reason to think yes or no. I think it's more of a matter of being unable to justify *not* using something that's available to us. Having grown up in a technological society, we feel a moral obligation to take advantage of whatever resources we can. We would see the question more along the lines of: Why be an amateur in this game when we can be a professional?

"The fact that so much of the birth process has been technologized makes it very difficult to approach childbearing in any other way," says Dr. Williams.

> *Our culture teaches us that there is a technological answer for everything. With conception, there's the fantasy that there should be such an answer, and many women go out looking for it. It can start turning into a delusion. A woman feels that if she does everything right and*

conceives tomorrow, as opposed to letting it happen and perhaps conceiving three or four months later, it's going to provide her with much greater happiness. The belief is that having mastery over the process is going to make you happier.

In earlier, simpler times, the language of birth was the language of poetry. Today, it's the language of science. The child is seen less as the fruit of lovers' ardor than as the issue of proper medical management and good sperm motility. In describing a desire to bring life into the world, couples talk of "opportunities" and "maximizing their chances."

Increasingly for us, the model is the machine. We think in terms of efficiency; the thought of "wasting" sperm or allowing an entire cycle to go by without an attempt at pregnancy is abhorrent. The baby becomes the product. Once set on the production mode, our bodies should, then, produce. If nothing is produced, that represents a failure on the part of the equipment. The body didn't *function* properly in that case. The act of sex, once far removed from procreation, becomes a means to an end: Making love is what switches the reproductive machinery on.

Having bought into the technology myth, we feel entitled to the perquisites of industry: predictability, expedience, and, as far as the results are concerned, a conformity to regulation standards. Not getting what we want, then, means double the blow. "Oh no," a woman laments, upon noting the familiar spot of menstrual blood. "It didn't *work.*" Sue, thirty-one, who has one child but is having difficulty conceiving a second, says, "Sometimes I don't know whether it's not having another child that's so difficult or the idea that I've failed."

Nearly every culture has had some notions of how the qualities of the conception can determine the fate of the child. For centuries in Europe, it was believed that women in love conceived readily while those forced to have sex wouldn't get pregnant. Illegitimate children, begotten in the passion of an extramarital affair, were thought to be unusually robust.[3] Feminist reformers in the nineteenth century based their pleas for women's rights to refuse intercourse on the argument that children conceived during desired sex would be smarter and healthier, while those born from *un*wanted sex were likely to turn into criminals, beggars, or fools. The belief remains that there's a way to get the best possible baby out of you. Today the formula seems to be to work harder at it.

In the past, after conception occurred it was accepted that couples had to sit back and wait for the baby to arrive. Today, however, the work has only begun. The modern-day embryo has to pass as many tests to get born as students do to get into college. Couples seek to reassure themselves with prenatal testing, not always considering the risks posed by the tests themselves or the fact that such tests do not detect all that can go wrong. The tests also start couples thinking about the "quality" of the child before the child is even there, and this sets up expectations of perfection and perfectibility. Once their unborn child has made it through the screening processes, a couple may feel that a perfect, problem-free child is their due. Weren't they told as much?

What odd frontier has science led us to? Is this where we want to be? Do we want to live by a standard set by industry? Ironically, back in the days when frozen eggs and embryos were but a gelid gleam in some futurist's eye, women looked to reproductive technology as a means of freeing women. Shulamith Firestone, the radical feminist author of *The Dialect of Sex* (1970), called for technical alternatives to conception and birth. She railed against what she called the "reproduction of the species by one sex."[4] Artificial reproduction, she felt, was imperative if women were to escape obligatory reproductive service and achieve equality with men. But while feminists of the sixties and seventies looked to technology to liberate women from restrictive roles, today we look to technology to liberate us from anxieties—anxieties that technology itself has at least in part caused.

But who's going to liberate us from the technology? Perhaps this is the essence of our ambivalence: We've positioned ourselves to have control of a situation (having children) that ultimately one can't control. But at the same time, we can't just leave things to chance because we've got all these tools around us begging to be used. Every step we take is chosen and thus conscious. Every move we make is serious, heavy with responsibility. With everything we do we must test and retest our convictions. If we're going to take positive action, we'd better be positive about what we want.

Perhaps the "old" way made more sense psychologically in one respect: If we accept a certain lack of control over the outcome, we can allow for a lack of control over our feelings and motivations. In other words, when we're less sure when and if pregnancy will happen, we might be better able to tolerate ambivalent feelings about it. Living with an entire set of unknowns requires a certain degree of fatalism. And if we allow a little fatalism about when a pregnancy will occur, we're more apt to be somewhat fatalistic about the outcome, about accepting and coping with the consequences.

With our self-conscious baby making, however, we can't *afford* any ambivalence. Going for it inevitably means going all out. We can't "try" for something we're not clear about. Unfortunately, what can happen when couples are immersed in the effort is that they simply suspend their ambivalences rather than resolve them. Often there's an element of superstition: if I *question* my wish, it's not going to come true. Although in abeyance, those feelings are still there. There have been cases of couples undergoing extensive infertility workups only to request an abortion when the pregnancy finally occurs. The "project," it seemed, was all that had been sustaining them.

According to Dr. Williams, one reason women hold onto the technological answers is that they provide armor against one's own confusion:

> *The terror of uncertainty is really the terror of the unconscious. There's the idea that technology obliterates the unconscious—that now we never have to worry about all the things we don't know about ourselves and others. It gives people the illusion that they can master all these terrifying unknowns. Doing everything they can to get pregnant and learning everything they can about pregnancy makes women feel they're more in charge of the process than they in fact are.*

The questions we have regarding our fertility are connected to many fears we have about ourselves, fears we may have been able to avoid facing up to now. The predictability of, say, the pill may have hidden from us the fact that our bodies are unpredictable and out of our conscious control. Going off the pill (or other birth control) pits us against our bodily chaos—as well as what that may represent to us. The anxieties that surface may cause enough discomfort that we again seek refuge in technology.

The sense of control technology offers also creates an enormous sense of arrogance. We should be masters of our bodies rather than letting our bodies master us. Some women announce precisely, nearly down to the month, when, due to the exigencies of their schedules, they "must" have a baby. When conception doesn't occur on cue, they feel not only disappointment but *annoyance*. Many couples plot out a rigid timeline for themselves and then panic when life doesn't follow suit. The fantasy is that once the pregnancy has proven to be out of our control, our entire world will disintegrate. The elusive conception calls into question more than our specific plans; it challenges the way we approach our lives.

But now that we have this technology and the consciousness that goes with it, we can't turn our backs on it. We negotiate the technology, integrating it into our plans and our lovemaking.

I've long had the fantasy that I would turn thirty (or thirty-one or thirty-two . . .) and officially throw my birth-control pills out the window. It would be a fantastically liberating act, sort of the biochemical equivalent of letting down my hair. Good-bye little plastic purse-pack, good-bye chemicals, good-bye menstrual periods so meager that the entire monthly yield would fit in an eyedropper. I would simply sit back and let my body do its thing.

But then I realize I'd have to wait several months before conceiving anyway, because there's a potential risk of birth defects associated with the pill. I'd also have to be sure I was ovulating as there can be delays after stopping (my doctor, however, has assured me I can take other pills if I seem to be running slow). And waiting until my cycle regulates will help my doctor "date" the pregnancy.

So much for my natural ideas.

The paradox is that our pressures stem from the very thing that was supposed to relieve our pressure: the expansion of our choices. Both social and technological developments have contributed to our broadened options. Many of these choices have enhanced women's lives tremendously, such as the right to abortion and the right to seek treatment for reproductive problems. But the question is, how does the spectrum of choice play out in women's experience of motherhood?

One scholar who has probed this question is Barbara Katz Rothman, author of *Recreating Motherhood* and *The Tentative Pregnancy*. She makes the point that adding technological choices often limits other choices, noting the "silent closing of the door" that we may not even detect. Once the "horseless carriage" was invented, we no longer had the choice to travel by horse, she offers as an analogy. Nor did we have the choice but to live with the pollution and danger that the automobile brought. If technology can "improve" our baby making, do we really have a choice but to use it?[5]

Ruth Hubbard, who writes on reproductive issues and the law, argues that "as 'choices' become available, they all too rapidly become compulsions to 'choose' the socially endorsed alternative."[6] If a woman has the choice of limiting her fertility, does she also have the choice *not* to limit her fertility? Might not a woman be pressured not to have a sixth child if abortion is available to her? If a woman has the option of pursuing infertility treatment, does she also have the option *not* to? Granting that she can choose to forego treatment, might she not *feel* obliged to seek it? Let's say a pregnant woman is offered amniocentesis and she declines the exam. If the baby turns out to have a chromosomal abnormality, who's "fault" is it? How will other parents, many of whom did seek testing, regard her situation? Can she ever feel confident that she has done the right thing? As Rothman says of prenatal testing, "In gaining the choice to control the quality of our children, we may rapidly lose the choice not to control the quality, of simply accepting them as they are."[7]

Feminists argue that no reproductive choices are truly free choices because they take place within a particular social structure and are thus affected by ideologies promoted by society. Can a woman freely choose to have a third child at a time when having any child is such an expensive proposition? Can a woman freely decide not to undergo painful infertility procedures in a society that still ties women's worth to their reproductive capacity? Can a woman freely choose to continue carrying a Down's syndrome child in a society not fully committed to caring for its disabled?

Some women do rebel against the high-initiative approach to getting pregnant. "I went off the pill," says Melissa. "I'll use something else for a few months, then I'll wait and see what happens. Really it's a stressless plan. I feel that baby making should be a fun thing. I really can't look at it scientifically. The process is important to me. I have this romantic notion that a baby should be a kind of a gift."

In talking to Melissa longer, however, it appeared that her formula for the stressless plan involved keeping the stakes artificially low in her mind: "We don't want to make any special deal about it. I don't want to go through all the hassles infertile couples go through, and I certainly wouldn't want everybody to know the trouble we were having. If it's going to happen it will happen. We're not in a hurry at this point, but maybe later we will be. If I do get my hopes up now, it would be upsetting if I didn't get pregnant. If I downplay it now, it will be a neat surprise."

Anita also avoided the technology trap, but for different reasons. "I paid attention to when I was fertile, but I did no temperature taking or planning beyond that," she says. "I was afraid of the technology itself. I thought it would be bad for the relationship. If my husband was ambivalent about having a baby to begin with, what if we really had to work at it? Actually, I did stay in bed with my legs up after intercourse, which is supposed to help, but I never told him about it."

Where all the technology and efforts to control really come to the fore is in the treatment of infertility. Indeed, infertility is the menace in the back of many women's (and men's) minds as they edge, in small ways, toward using technology: they don't want to find themselves in *that* position. So what seems to be going on is that we start attempting to control conception to avoid being in a situation where we *have* to apply control. Somehow, the infertile couple has become some sort of generational standard, with all couples desiring children hedging their bets against that specific scenario.

Combatting infertility has become an industry in itself, with well over $1 billion spent annually in this country by couples trying to conceive. The 8 to 15 percent of couples estimated to suffer from infertility (defined as failing to achieve a pregnancy after a full year of unprotected intercourse) are being aggressively pursued by the medical and business communities. Major teaching hospitals and treatment centers are advertising heavily and offering free lectures and seminars to lure patients. Informational literature includes endorsements from "satisfied customers" like slick marketing brochures.

Private clinics are promoting "twenty-first-century medicine," often using their fancy trademark treatments before low-tech measures (such as determining the man's sperm count) have even been tried. Highly touted specialists assume as high a profile as any corporate CEO. When New York Hospital-Cornell Medical Center hired Zev Rosenwaks, a noted "in vitro guru" in 1988, the chief of obstetrics and gynecology told *Manhattan, inc.*, "He'll attract not only people but money. . . . I think he'll be a fantastic investment."[8]

For couples who find themselves shopping around for specialists and procedures, it can take a lot of money to make a baby. An initial couple workup can run $3,000 and *each* in vitro embryo transfer costs up to $7,000. With only a 20 percent conception rate, the treatment may need to be repeated several times. Insurance may not cover reproductive technologies, and there's no guarantee any efforts will work. But once someone has spent so much to get so far, what's one more cycle? The price is not only financial, but emotional. As one mother-hopeful told *New York Woman*, "People think infertility is a passive state—that it's something that *doesn't* happen. But it's an immensely active condition. Being infertile is a full-time job. There's always something to keep you busy."[9]

Doctors and investors are salivating over America's infertile couples, not necessarily because the number of infertile couples is so much higher than in the past (statistics show it isn't), but because they are such an attractive *market*. Women and men who chose not to spend their twenties making babies were often making money instead. While years ago a childless couple tended to accept fate, many of today's couples believe they have the financial and technological wherewithal to *surmount* that fate and are more than willing to apply it. It's hard to give up the idea that boosting the investment will boost the odds. American "can-do" celebrates overcoming obstacles, not accepting one's limitations. As one sign in an in vitro clinic's waiting room claims: "You never fail until you stop trying."[10]

Many of the new infertility entrepreneurs are appealing to the modern couple's guilt. The bulk of this is centered on women, as the contemporary myth holds that most infertility is due to the fact that a woman opted to start her career before her family. Had she just gone out and gotten pregnant at twenty-two as she was supposed to, the rationale goes, she wouldn't have the problem in the first place. The guilt that results propels couples to pound on the doctor's door, insisting that science produce the longed-for child. They've postponed parenthood in the name of economic advancement and self-sufficiency—goals society promotes. Doesn't society owe them a baby when they want one? Undoubtedly, many women are frantically seeking a pregnancy not merely because they want one, which they well might, but to redeem themselves from not having one when they (supposedly) could have.

Beyond the pulling of these sensitive strings, other dubious aspects to some of the promotion techniques emerge. There are reputable clinics, but as you move down the list you can find yourself among the 1990s equivalents of snake-oil salesmen. Clinics boast fantastic success rates without defining success. Getting egg to meet sperm is one thing; getting that meeting to produce a live infant nine months later is another, especially with the high miscarriage rates associated with high-tech procedures. Barbara Katz Rothman recalls visiting an in vitro clinic and being impressed by the wall full of baby photos near the entrance, only to realize that it was the *same* baby being photographed in several different poses.[11]

The field is also unregulated at this date, leaving it wide open for any physician of an entrepreneurial bent to claim to be an infertility specialist. (In fact, there are fewer than 500 doctors nationwide who are board-certified in the gynecological subspecialty of reproductive endocrinology.) The authors of *Tomorrow's Child* point out the questionable ethics of large corporations funding the research and development of new techniques, even noting some instances in which doctors themselves have become involved in launching and promoting companies. What will be the bottom line in these places? What about the doctor charged with using his own sperm for in vitro fertilization at his clinic?

The availability of infertility treatments has been a blessing for countless couples: well over half who seek help for infertility do ultimately bring home a child. How many would have had children *without* treatment can't be guessed. A friend told me of a woman who got fed up with taking Clomid (which induces ovulation) and went off the drug. The month *after* she stopped she got pregnant. Infertility literature is full of anecdotes of couples who conceive immediately upon adopting a child. Often there doesn't seem to be any explanation as to why things do or don't happen, a situation that ever confounds those—couples and doctors alike—who are looking to find some order in the process.

It can be argued that the new approach has actually exacerbated the pain of infertile couples. The fact that infertility is seen as a medical problem thrusts the couple into the patient role. As a patient, one is expected to defer to the physician and to do everything possible to "get better."[12] Some couples, experts contend, might be better served by learning to adapt to their situation. Many find ways other than parenthood to seek value in their lives and contribute to the future. Others pursue adoption, although that can take years. But this can seem a less-than-satisfying solution in a society that defines *biological* parenthood as normal.

The illusion of control and our worship of technology also adds a sting because there's the implication that if you're not getting pregnant, you're not doing enough. "You don't have to be childless," claims an article in *Parade*. "It's all a question of how much a couple really want a baby; of how much they will pay, how far they will go. Science does have the answers."[13] Since there's always one new tactic to try, and one newer yet on the medical horizon, a couple may have a hard time calling it quits. They may stress their relationship beyond salvation because they feel they have to keep doing.

In our technologized culture, we can accept something not working because we assume it can be fixed. But something that defies fixing is beyond us: this can't be. We refuse to admit that something *not* working means that it *can't* work. Since we believe that technology provides a certain standard, we can only conclude that the fault lies in ourselves—even when the numbers aren't so promising to begin with. The medical community can feed into this tendency to blame oneself. Barbara Katz Rothman describes how IVF clinics' practice of terming a chemical pregnancy (when the pregnancy test registers positive even if there's a miscarriage soon after) a success can be a way of shifting blame: The suggestion is that the clinic got the woman pregnant, but *she* lost the pregnancy.[14]

And today everything is public. With "how long have you been trying?" a frequent conversation-opener, it's hard to keep any problem to yourself. "After a point I didn't want to tell anyone about it, even—or maybe especially—my parents," says Sally, who conceived after several cycles of fertility drugs. "I didn't want to be asked for a report every month."

Since everybody who follows the news or reads magazines today is an infertility expert, the infertile couple's choices are constantly called into question: Why didn't you go to this doctor instead of that one? Have you had this test yet? After expressing their ration of sympathy, other people are likely to think, "What's *wrong* with them anyway? With all of these miracle procedures out there, shouldn't *something* work?"

Often there's an element of blaming the victim. I recently heard a friend describing her sister-in-law's fertility-drug treatment: "She's so uptight about it. If she'd just relax, she'd get pregnant without a problem." This assumption remains common, although there is no scientific evidence that psychological factors cause infertility. Theoretically, there is some justification, since emotional stress can affect menstruation and hormone production, but wouldn't "relaxing" be easier if a woman were not apt to feel judged for not getting pregnant?

Though knowledge about fertility and conception is extremely sophisticated today, that knowledge didn't come to us until recently. Many early cultures believed that women became pregnant by touching a particular object or by eating a certain food. Others attributed pregnancy to acts of the spirits or the whims of the planets. From the time of the Greeks onward, it was believed that both men and women made semen. According to Hippocrates, the woman's role was to nurture the seed while the man contributed genetic characteristics and the basic spark of life.[15] Aristotle added the notion that "menstrual residue," which contained the egg, would mix with the semen to cause conception. One seventh-century thinker contended that, upon mixing, male and female sperm battled to create a child. Depending on which parent's semen was more "potent," the newborn would resemble either the father or the mother.[16]

Infertility had numerous explanations. Some believed it resulted from a "bad fit" between partners or from awkward coital rhythm. The woman's orgasm was considered necessary because it allegedly prompted the womb to close itself off and seal in the vital fluids. Soranus, an influential physician in the second century, reflected on the importance of desire: "Food eaten when one has no appetite is not properly digested, and seed received by a woman when she has no sexual urge is not retained."[17]

A womb that was either too dry or overmoist was said to be an inhibiting factor, as was insufficient or excessive "heat": A certain level of warmth had to be achieved in intercourse to generate life, but if a woman became too feverish, it could "burn up" the seed.[18] If extreme heat was the culprit, cooling medications were in order. If heat was lacking, the fires were stoked with "lascivious words mixed with lascivious kisses."[19]

The Renaissance saw great advances in our knowledge of anatomy and reproduction. As this knowledge was interpreted, however, the man played a much larger role in procreation than the woman. When the Dutch scientist Leeuwenhoek examined a semen specimen under his newly devised microscope in 1677, he was able to observe spermatozoa. He concluded that these were in fact miniature human beings (actually they were called "homunculi," from the Latin for "little men"), which would grow into regular human babies after incubating in the mother. And when the ovum was identified in the nineteenth century, scientists believed that it was an inactive body until male semen transformed it into a living being.[20]

In order to make conception happen, preindustrial societies had an arsenal of fertility rites, prayers, amulets, and herbal concoctions that were supposed to ensure impregnation. Since doing nothing often remedies infertility, enough births probably followed to "prove" the viability of such efforts.[21] When the usual conception strategies proved fruitless, more urgent measures were taken. In some societies, the barren wife was to sleep with other men, often relatives of the husband, in hopes of producing a child. (That was one early acknowledgment that the man might play a role in infertility.)

For the most part, until quite recently the best-known cure for infertility was adoption. In cultures where blood ties are secondary to social relationships, adopted children were undifferentiated from biological offspring. In some traditional societies, more than half of all families have adopted children. Among certain groups, a childless couple can simply request that a family member give them one of theirs.[22]

Advice for the childless in the nineteenth century might have involved a change of air, sea bathing, sexual abstinence, and rest. Poor alignment of the uterus might have been implicated, with the possibility of surgical treatment. Lydia Pinkham's Vegetable Compound, a popular patent medicine, was marketed as a cure for infertility (and everything else, from irregularity to headaches to nervous prostration). One ad made the claim "there's a baby in every bottle."[23]

Effective means of enhancing fertility were lacking, in part because of widespread misinformation on the subject. Women were once thought to be most fertile around the time of their menstrual periods. Women desiring children were told to have intercourse then, and those wishing to curb their fertility were instructed to wait until midcycle, when they were "safe." In other words, women were using the rhythm method, except that they were decidedly off the beat.

The timing of ovulation was scientifically determined in the mid-1900s, but widespread confusion about a woman's "safe period" persisted until well into this century. One popular marriage manual warned that women could conceive at any time in the month because with the excitement of coitus, "an ovum may slip from its moorings."[24]

In the absence of physiological clarity, women themselves were singled out as the problem. In 1883 a physician raised the question of whether efforts should be made to treat infertile women since they "were clearly genetically inferior and should therefore not be encouraged to propagate." Another doctor blamed "poor hygiene" among adolescents, which by his definition included young women leaving their beds during menstrual periods.[25] Some psychoanalytic thinkers, such as Therese Benedek, linked infertility to a resistance to the female role.

One reason infertile women have endured such disdain is that barrenness has often been associated with sin, specifically sexual sin. This isn't always completely off the mark, as promiscuity increases one's likelihood of contracting a fertility-compromising disease. Among the Chippewa and other Indian societies, infertility was considered proof of infidelity and previous abortions. The Japanese had a saying that sensual women were often sterile.[26] In the Victorian age, the sins that could cause infertility were expanded to include having "too much" sex, enjoying sex, and masturbating. A doctor early in this century warned women against postponing childbearing, cautioning that when she did want to become pregnant, a woman might find she had "sinned away her day of grace."[27]

Such reflections on sin and blame bring up a major theme in discussions of infertility: In most instances, infertility is assumed to be the woman's fault. This is ironic considering the minimal role women historically have been thought to play in the actual process. In retrospect, it seems that all failures of reproduction were actually considered to be merely failures of incubation, since that was allegedly all women were needed for; the viability of the man's "seed" was rarely in doubt.

Although today we know that 40 percent of infertility cases are due to factors in the male (40 percent are due to factors in the female and 20 percent result from a combination of factors), this assumption persists. One infertility specialist told me about a robust Texan, who, when told that it was his low sperm count and not his wife's physiological shortcomings that caused their problem, was so incensed that he punched the doctor in the jaw. (This attitude is referred to in the field as "The Henry VIII Syndrome," recalling the king who divorced two wives and beheaded two others when they failed to provide an heir.) It's changing to some extent, but the woman in an infertile pair is still burdened by the guilt that she waited too long, slept around too much, or otherwise erred.

Infertility has been viewed as a woman's problem chiefly because women have tended to be seen in terms of their potential fertility. If a couple has, even unconsciously, divided up their responsibilities so that the woman's are domestic and the man's professional, infertility difficulties are going to seem to be *her* responsibility, even if his low sperm count is found to be the cause. In such a case the woman may still feel that it's her fault, that if she were *really* fertile she could somehow compensate for his lack and give him the child he deserves.

And once the couple starts talking to doctors, the woman is most likely to be treated, regardless of the biological realities. She's certainly more likely to be tested. One trouble is a basic asymmetry within medicine: while women see gynecologists, there's no corresponding specialty for the male reproductive system. (Urologists generally see male infertility patients.) Even so, considering how easy it is to do a semen analysis—a man masturbates into a jar and the specimen is then inspected under a microscope—it's remarkable that some physicians still regard examining the man as close to a *last resort.* Frequently the man isn't even brought into the picture until the woman has had several tests and been on fertility drugs for some months.

It's as though the medical community regards the man's ejaculating on demand to provide a specimen more traumatic than the woman's undergoing expensive and often painful tests. As Barbara Katz Rothman says, the establishment seeks to protect men from having their "manliness" questioned: "The man in the infertile couple is treated as fertile until proven otherwise, while for the female, infertility is assumed and implied."[28]

In a patriarchal society, Rothman writes, the treatment of infertility has one basic goal: "to get George's baby growing in Martha's body." As a result, women are the ones treated for male infertility. A woman whose husband is infertile may attempt IVF, which involves hormonal treatments, surgery, and frequent testing, as a way of ensuring his genetic contribution, even when there's little likelihood of success. (Artificial insemination by donor would be a method with a much higher success rate, but then the husband wouldn't be the biological parent.) Hers is the body that's medicated; hers is the body watched. Rothman writes: "[I]f a man has a high sperm count, the infertility problem is treated entirely as the woman's, whereas if the man has a low sperm count, the problem is *still* treated largely as the woman's," and adds that often women undergoing treatment for male infertility are told about "some little thing wrong" in themselves as well.[29]

We protect men. We protect men in all sorts of ways, and protecting them from possible infertility problems is only one of them. We take our bodies to gynecologists all the time, so what's the difference, we reason. We know that if they feel "blamed," their "manhood" will suffer. Well, what about our womanhood? That's where medical technology has taken a positive role, Cathy suggests. "Women have always been blamed for infertility. Now, with improved testing, we can point the finger elsewhere. However," she concedes, "I would bet that a lot of women may lie to the rest of the world and let people think it was her problem instead of her husband's anyway."

Many women do feel that an infertility impairment would lessen their value as women. "One of my friends recently found out that she couldn't have children," says Carolyn. "I think in some respects that would be a relief to know, as it's no longer uncertain. My concern, though, is that this will make her less marketable to men. That's *my* fear. Not that being infertile would mean a great sacrifice on my part, but that it might cut down my chances of finding a man."

For the ten or so years she thought she couldn't have children, that fear was a very real one for Holly:

> *The guy I've been seeing had married very young and now has a son in his teens. He says he's looking forward to being a grandfather, but he doesn't seem interested in going through it again himself. Once I thought about it, I wondered if he was attracted to me because there was the possibility that I couldn't get pregnant. At the same time, maybe I was attracted to him because he already has a family. This way I have the security of knowing that if I can't get pregnant, I won't disappoint him.*

Sally describes the inadequacy she felt during her years of treatment. "In our case, it was my infertility problem. I simply didn't ovulate," she recalls.

> *What really bothered me was knowing that if Jerry had married anyone else, he would have had a family. That was an obsession on my part, the unfairness that he was stuck with me. We looked into adoption, but we were told it could take years. Jerry kept saying, "We're a family. That's enough." I didn't believe him. Being infertile made me feel ugly, worthless, unfeminine. Totally invalid as a woman. Basically not a woman. I used to joke with Jerry about who the man of the house was.*

In part because women feel they need to conceive to prove they're women and in part because of widespread anxiety about conceiving in general, women who do know they're fertile often take great pride in the fact. "It's almost this competitive thing," says Anita. "When you know you can get pregnant easily, you feel you have this special thing about you, better inner workings. It's not something you brag about but something you know. It's a big topic of conversation among women, how long did it take. It's a subtle form of competition, although no one would admit to it."

According to Dr. Davis, the feelings aroused by such jousting are very similar to those of sibling rivalry. "The woman compares herself with her 'sisters,' " she explains. "It becomes a way of asserting competence. Once a woman decides she's going to do it—get pregnant—she wants to do it well." Dr. Davis adds that the bravado may in part serve as a defense against the ambivalence a woman might feel about motherhood. "She decides to highlight the more positive aspects of reproductive functioning," she says. "The response is, 'I'm good at this. I like this game,' or 'I'm still in control.' "

Women do want to know they can reproduce when they want to, but at the same time there can be a discomfort with fertility. In *Sex and Destiny,* Germaine Greer points out that class biases have tended to color attitudes toward fertility. The assumption is that lower-class (or non-white) women breed like rabbits, whereas refined women are more "moderate" in their reproductive habits. Society as a whole has been reluctant to associate middle- and upper-class women with the body, or lower- and working-class women with the mind. Greer laments that women in the third world often don't get treated for infertility, in part because of these prejudices, despite the fact that in certain societies being childless causes great personal hardship.

In *Sacred Bond: The Legacy of Baby M,* Phyllis Chesler suggests that preconceptions of class played a large role in the furor over the famous case in which a surrogate mother, Mary Beth Whitehead, was ultimately unwilling to give up the child she had "contracted" to turn over to Bill and Betsy Stern. The public and the media, she writes, were "biased in favor of the educated middle class and had more sympathy for the problem of middle-class sterility than for the problem of either working-class fertility or sterility."[30]

Chesler argues that the Baby M case symbolizes the ambivalence today's women have toward their own fertility:

> *Many women, including feminists, seem to dislike the way Mary Beth romanticizes her "instinctive" or natural bodily functions. They are disgusted by the way she relies on her fertility instead of seeking her identity in a career. Who does she think she is? Mother Nature? Is*

> *she actually proud to be so out-of-control, so fecund? . . . What if we don't happen to share Mary Beth's reproductive frenzy? Does this mean we're "unnatural" women? . . . Shouldn't we (the Betsy Sterns of this world) actually be* rewarded *for not giving in to our base animal instincts?*[31]

If women are feeling a mind/body split, fertility is likely to be a key point of division—understandably, since mind and maternity have long been seen as mutually exclusive.

Perhaps this particular ambivalence plays a role in our eagerness to use technology to conceive. Perhaps the idea that we can control the event tempers the awkwardness we have with our own "naturalness." "Biology is frightening to us," says Dr. Williams. "It represents all that is dark and primordial in ourselves. Medical technology brings it to us in a way that's palatable. It keeps it at a distance. Like these new devices to detect ovulation—heaven forbid you should notice a discharge, or on your own know your body well enough to know when you're ovulating." We look to medicine and technology to save us from our physicality, as well as the inherent unpredictability of our reproductive natures.

Once we attempt to gain control over reproduction through technology, our experience of our fertility will be mediated through the technology. And as some critics have noted, by seeking alternative conception strategies, women are in fact *giving up* power to those who control the technology—at this point mostly men. The ability to bear children is something only women possess. But in the reproductive near-future, anyone with a degree of lab expertise will be able to "make" a baby.

Feminist scholar Paula A. Treichler observes how women are literally erased from childbearing in medical textbooks, as the process is described as the physician acting on the infant. "[S]uch erasure is quite possible through the development of in vitro fertrilization, alternative 'growing mediums' (now 'surrogate mothers,' tomorrow artificial wombs), and procedures for cloning human beings. From the [feminist] perspective . . . , this is not science fiction but a genuinely feasible version of the alchemists' old dream of reproducing the seed of The Father with no help from females."[32]

Doctors already choose who is eligible for infertility treatments. What criteria should they (and do they) use? Class? Race? Sexual orientation?

Ability to pay? Will doctors be deciding how many children are "enough" for a family? Reproductive technologies raise many social, legal, and moral issues. Use of these technologies poses a great benefit to society, but we must continue to assess how their very presence affects women's childbearing experience. How do we retain the integrity of our experience in a time of rapid technological change? How can women's knowledge and power remain central in reproductive decision making without women again being reduced to their reproductive capacity? What is the price of predictability and control? These are questions we need to keep asking as the emphasis shifts from the body to the machine.

Chapter 10

AND DOCTOR MAKES THREE

"1:00 P.M. I have come here to die. Why else would I be in a hospital?"

From the January 5, 1978, entry in Phyllis Chesler's
With Child: A Diary of Motherhood

During the women's health movement, women started asking some difficult questions about how their babies were being born: If giving birth is a woman's crowning achievement, why are we made to feel irrelevant to the process? Why are we automatically "put out," as though it's assumed we don't want to be there for the event? Although we do the hours and hours of laboring, why is it said that the *doctor* delivers the child?

Many activists have worked toward rehumanizing—or rather *rewomanizing*—the experience of pregnancy and childbirth. Writers like Adrienne Rich, childbirth educators like Doris Haire, and Sheila Kitzinger in England, groups like the Boston Women's Health Collective (of *Our Bodies, Ourselves* fame) and C/Sec (a cesarean education and support group that advocates vaginal birth after cesarean) have done much to bring control of pregnancy and childbirth back to the woman. Autonomy in birthing was also linked to women's liberation in a larger sense: As a uniquely female endeavor, childbirth should be directed and shared by women, not managed by men. The naturalness of the process and the healthfulness of the woman should be emphasized, instead of approaching every pregnancy as though it were a medical crisis.

Because of these efforts, women today can have the father present for the delivery (in the past fathers-to-be were looked upon as a source of contagion rather than a source of support). We no longer have to face the indignity of "prepping" (the shaving of pubic hair) or enemas when we arrive at the hospital. (These once-common practices were found not to aid in either the safety or ease of childbirth, as had been believed.) Even with surgical deliveries, we can in most cases be awake for the baby's arrival. We now have more say in decisions throughout the process.

And yet, there seems to be an eerie silence about these matters today. The movement for humane and natural childbirth is by no means defunct; training programs can't turn out enough midwives to keep up with the demand. But strong feelings about childbirth today are often put on hold. One gets the sense of a collective shrug of the shoulders, an attitude of "You do what you have to do."

It's not a matter of indifference, nor a lack of knowledge about pregnancy and birth. We seize all the information we can; we take classes, ask questions, read books. Rather, any misgivings are overshadowed by an intense desire to "do the right thing." Most women today are interpreting doing the right thing to mean listening to our doctors. And whatever we are seeking in the experience of childbirth and pregnancy, whether it's a "natural" delivery or a feeling of bonding with the child, we view it through the medical matrix.

Brin, twenty-nine, who gave birth to her daughter by cesarean, describes how she planned her delivery:

> *I wanted to deliver naturally, but have medicine as a backup. The midwife idea sounded interesting, more personal and connected, but I never really looked into it. I felt maybe I wasn't hip, but I had to admit I did feel more comfortable with the hospital situation. The doctor was a doctor—talked like a doctor and everything else—but that was okay. It felt weird that this man knew more about what was happening with my body than I did, but in truth I found it comforting. He was open to questions, but I wasn't too concerned with the specific answers he gave because I had already decided to trust him. You do get to feeling whatever he says is right.*

A deference to doctors has generally been the rule since doctors staked out their turf in obstetrics. The difference is that today women *perceive* themselves as having more control over childbearing—even as childbearing is getting more and more medicalized. In conversations, women often say that they've discussed the options with their physicians and plan to have a "natural childbirth." But what *is* a natural childbirth? Depending on whom you talk to, natural childbirth can mean anything from a midwife-attended home birth with no medication to a hospital birth accessorized by a fetal monitor, an IV, and an arsenal of pain medication—anything on the interventionist scale up to a cesarean, basically. It's easy to appreciate such confusion, because the word "natural" is bandied about by hospitals like any other marketing talisman. "Give birth in a natural environment," a maternity center's brochure may beckon. But what does this mean—that there's a tree-filled courtyard in view, or that exempting medical emergencies, birthing mothers are spared the heavy artillery?

These are crucial distinctions to make. But, regrettably, they're distinctions that have become blurred. As a result of the women's health movement and increased knowledge about health in general, women today do have a sense that maintaining a degree of naturalness in pregnancy and childbirth is important to them as new mothers. But we've let the *medical establishment* define what natural is. We focus on the concessions the hospitals have granted us—such as fathers in the delivery room and rooming-in after the birth—and fail to question all the other medical interventions, the little extras like fetal monitoring, tests throughout pregnancy, etc. On some level, we accept this as the price we pay for the "naturalness" we've been given. We take the goodies such interventions afford (reassurance about the fetus, the doctor's unquestioned support) and leave it at that.

"One thing that was important to me was to be in an alternative birthing room," says Brin.

> *It's private, more homey, and you can labor, deliver, and recover there. My doctor had some pull and made sure I got the room, but then I needed a cesarean and had to go to a regular hospital room anyway. The birthing room was a little tacky—pictures of waterfalls and all—but if you're someone who wants the security of the machines but wants a bit of pleasantness too, it is a compromise. Maybe I was conned by the idea, but it worked for me.*

Whatever it has taken to get the child out of her body, the new mother's response will invariably be, "The baby's okay, and that's the most important thing." Yes, the baby's welfare should be the priority. But why is there the assumption that all of medicine's magical tricks are needed for the baby to be okay?

I'm not antidoctor. Doctors, too, more than anything else, are concerned with doing the right thing. With the threat of malpractice ever in mind, doctors nowadays admittedly feel under pressure to perform more procedures than they might otherwise choose. The march of technology seems an unstoppable force, with patients, doctors, and hospitals alike swept along in its momentum. For many women technology begins to encroach on motherhood as early as conception. In all aspects, there appears to be a progressive eclipse of the human by the mechanical.

It seems to have become a pattern in reproductive medicine: A treatment or procedure is used under certain situations, then it becomes widespread, then it becomes regarded as *essential* before either its safety or even its *usefulness* has been firmly established. (Think of fetal monitors, sonograms, episiotomies, etc.) The mere existence of a technological option seems to speak louder than any concerns about its actual value. The operating view behind many procedures and tests becomes, "It can't hurt, so why not?" (That's what they thought about diethylstilbestrol [DES], a drug used to prevent miscarriage in the fifties and sixties, which was later found to present a risk of certain cancers to those exposed *in utero*.) Because all these procedures that can't hurt do add up, the typical birth today involves far more technology than the kind of birth feminists were criticizing nearly a generation ago. What's disturbing is that many of us fail to recognize the trend.

I'm also disturbed by this personally, by the fact that I'm not sure I can act on what I know. Despite all my beliefs, despite everything I've read on the subject, I know I'll have to fight myself *not* to simply turn my body over to the pros. I still see doctors as the pros. I can't help it. Compared to the unruly ordeal of labor, a cesarean seems blissfully predictable—even though I know it's *abdominal surgery* we're talking about, not a neat trick like pulling a rabbit out of a hat. Intellectually I know that, as a woman, I already possess the physical resources needed to bear a child. I believe that the fewer drugs and tests the fetus is subjected to the better and that, on a psychological level, the experience of giving birth can enhance the bonding process. But when actually confronted with all the fears and uncertainties that are sure to plague me, stacked up against all the shortcuts and sneak previews medicine can provide, I'm afraid I'll suffer a failure of nerve. Who am I, I'd ask myself, to question all the accumulated knowledge of obstetrics embodied in this chosen doctor?

I've grown up believing in medicine. My father is a doctor. My father always knew the answers to things. Whenever I had a question, my mother, less sure of her answers, would urge me to ask him instead. I believed, by inference, that his doctoring had something to do with his knowing. Being a doctor meant you took care of serious and important matters. My father would get phone calls in the evening. Without explanation, he'd reach for the pen in his pocket and walk off to his "office," a spare bedroom cluttered with file folders and incomprehensible jottings. When he left the dinner table, the mood of the entire house would shift.

I learned that doctors could fix things. My father had a black bag that contained pills for stomachaches, strong-smelling lotions for burns, a stethoscope to listen to your insides. If I cut myself, my mother could clean it and put on a Band-Aid too, but when my father looked at it he'd use big doctor words and that's how I'd know I was really okay.

Something about the calmness, the knowingness of doctors has always been soothing to me. Yet I recognize that it can be patronizing. If a doctor tells me a pill will make me better, I believe it. I make a decision to believe it. I know that the pill is often prescribed just to please me—that it really doesn't do anything—but I take it anyway. In my mind, I'm still the child and the doctor is the grown-up who knows things. I've had trouble getting over that. I've demanded that doctors fix things that didn't need fixing, or fix things faster that were fixing themselves on their own. I've trusted medicine more than I've trusted time.

These feelings are bound to be roused in pregnancy, and perhaps most keenly in labor, which presents what science is most adept at fixing: pain. The pain of labor is a prospect terrifying in its magnitude, something larger than any unknown I've met. I've had my share of pains, but I don't know *pain.* What is its scale, its pitch? How will I know what I can take? I know that one can experience the pain in different ways, that one can choose to do so. One can approach the building waves of contractions with a desire to overcome, to *prevail,* or with a desire to be saved from them. I've spent much of my life looking for people to save me. When faced with the unyielding wall of pain that is second stage labor, would I find the strength in myself to traverse it?

As I've grown up in a medical family, these issues hit home in a powerful way. But I think many women struggle with similar questions.

The medical community dangles before us an appealing package of information, reassurances, and near-guarantees. It's an offer that's hard to turn away. I don't think medicine is lying to women, or necessarily exploiting us. I think what's happening is more along the lines of a *seduction.* The goods the doctors hold out to us tap into certain needs we have—needs that may be heightened during pregnancy and labor. In order to understand our decisions, and to find that fine line between temptation and necessity, it's important to explore just how we're being (and allowing ourselves to be) enticed.

The wish to trust a doctor can play directly into a woman's emotional needs during pregnancy. For many women, the awareness of having to take care of an infant stirs up old feelings of wanting to be taken care of ourselves. "A woman wants to care for the baby and be in control, yet another part of her wants to be cared for and protected," says Dr. Davis. "Whether real or in fantasy, medicine provides the structure for these dual needs. When anxieties seep in, a woman can look to her doctor and imagine that she's safe."

One particularly vulnerable spot medicine touches is our distrust of our own bodies. Just like conception, pregnancy and labor can seem a test of our feminine stuff. As discussed in other chapters, women today do have a greater familiarity with their bodies than women of some earlier eras had. But the understanding we have of our bodies is largely a *medical* understanding as opposed to a spiritual one or an appreciation of our female capabilities. We know what our heart rate should be when we run. We know how many calories we can consume and not gain weight. Regarding the reproductive aspects of our bodies, we know how to look for *symptoms,* which secretions or sensations require a call to the gynecologist. We're trained to be medical consumers. We know how to *manage* our bodies without necessarily being in touch with them.

Until a woman begins to grapple with the physical realities of a pregnancy, her body's potential has yet to be explored. By this time, she may be most comfortable relating to her body through the medical model. According to Dr. Williams, to a certain extent this ignorance is willful. "I think people have always wanted to keep themselves ignorant of their anatomy because of their discomfort with it," she says. "It's extraordinary how many of us know more about our cars' inner workings than our own. The more ignorant we are about our own anatomy, the greater our idealization of the medical community, and the more we imbue our physicians with omniscience."

Women who come to childbearing after having postponed it for several years can feel especially burdened with doubts about their bodies. "There's the question: Will my body really work on its own?" says Dr. Davis. "Women bring this uncertainty into their pregnancies, and then they want to have the big, godlike doctor come in and reassure them that their body is indeed adequate."

The generalized doubts and fears women experience are often centered on the body. During pregnancy, this can become especially acute as the body is the focus of so much change. "A woman's mistrust of her body may be connected to her not trusting her desire to have a child or her competence as a mother," says Dr. Davis. "She takes all these doubts and wants to give them over to the strong hands of medicine. 'You take care of my body and all of my fears,' she's saying. 'You do it—despite how I feel about what's happening to me.' It can be a very strong pull for women." The doctor promises relief not only from the physical burdens of pregnancy and birth, but the emotional ones as well. The certainty that the doctor represents can subsume the uncertainty a woman feels, "cure" her of it, in a sense.

Another reason we're ripe for medicine's enticements is that we're comfortable with medicine in other ways. We live in an increasingly medicalized society. To us the language of medicine is reassuring without being intimidating. We can become semiexperts in health matters by reading magazines, or even the daily newspaper. We have all the terms at our disposal. With more women doctors today (about half of ob/gyns in training today are women), many women are no longer suspicious of medicine as an exclusively male preserve. A doctor can be "one of us" now.

Ours is also a statistics-oriented culture, and we appreciate exactness. And if nothing else, modern medicine is an exercise in precision. For Sherrie, this proved a more meaningful approach than the support-oriented, woman-centered alternative. "The first time I was pregnant I went with midwives until I had a miscarriage, and the second time I went with a doctor," she recalls. "The midwife I found more annoying, her always trying to pat me, comfort me. I'm a person who likes to seek information. I'm able to deal with negative information. I had chosen women caretakers on purpose, because I thought there'd be real advantages. But they've tended to stress comfort over facts."

All of these needs—the desire for information and a wish to be reassured about our fitness for motherhood—can play out in the issue of prenatal testing. There are several prenatal tests in use today, but I'll focus mainly on amniocentesis. This is a test performed at about sixteen weeks to detect certain birth defects. It also reveals the fetus's sex. In the test, a needle, inserted through the mother's abdomen, extracts fetal cells from the amniotic fluid. It's most commonly used to check for Down's syndrome, a chromosomal abnormality characterized by mental retardation, distinct facial features, and possibly vision and heart disorders. The risk of Down's syndrome increases with the mother's age. Age thirty-five has been regarded as the dividing line: A woman younger than thirty-five faces a greater risk of miscarriage resulting from the procedure than she risks carrying a child with Down's syndrome. Beyond thirty-five, the chances of the defect are considered greater.

On the surface, amniocentesis is appealing. Should the fetus have Down's syndrome or certain detectable spinal defects, the couple is alerted. They can then decide if raising a child with that birth defect is something they can handle, or if this is unacceptable to them. The test is presented as a means of minimizing risk. If a problem is found, the fetus can be aborted. The vast majority of the time, however, the parents are assured that their developing baby has been spared these defects. The desire to hear the reassuring news, and be able to complete the pregnancy with renewed confidence, can be a powerful draw.

But as Barbara Katz Rothman points out in *The Tentative Pregnancy: Prenatal Diagnosis and the Future of Motherhood,* amniocentesis represents more than one added needle in a nine-month gestation; it threatens to change the meaning of pregnancy. As she explains it, chance (which is what pregnancy has always entailed) is replaced by choice. Rather than a steadily evolving relationship between a mother and her growing child, pregnancy becomes a weeding-out process, with amniocentesis the decisive cut. She describes how pregnancy becomes tentative, with the mother reluctant to feel too bonded with the fetus before she's sure it's "normal." Almost by necessity there's a suspension of commitment, a sense that it's not "safe" to connect with the fetus, or even to acknowledge feeling its movements. Amniocentesis raises the spector of a deformed fetus in a palpable way. Once the test has been scheduled, the focus shifts from the healthy pregnancy to the potential abnormality.

Women have always worried that something may be wrong with their unborn babies. These fears are real. Women who have seen problems occur in families close to them, or who have suffered infertility problems or miscarriages, may feel particularly vulnerable. Such fears may be connected to other feelings and fantasies that can arise during pregnancy. A woman may still have trouble believing she is going to have a baby, so she imagines the baby isn't really a complete baby. She may fear giving in too fully to her attachment to the baby; the fantasized abnormality, then, keeps her at a distance. There may be an unconscious wish to rid herself of the fetus and the responsibility it represents. Rather than suggesting that a woman is unfit to mother, Dr. Davis says, such fantasies, though uncomfortable, are part of the normal working through of ambivalence. Prenatal testing can be seductive to women because it absolves them of their "dangerous" feelings and imaginings.

"We project all sorts of fears onto the fetus," she says. "Amniocentesis can seem a convenient way to deal with them. The woman learns: everything is fine. My projections onto the fetus aren't going to prove real. My fears about my own capabilities as a mother aren't real." But rather than urge her to confront her own feelings, the tests lead the woman to conclude that medicine can take care of them. "She sees the doctor's omnipotence in the form of the test and seeks to tap into that omnipotence," says Davis.

Amniocentesis is not a bad test. But there are concerns about how it's being used. For one thing, the ages for which it's deemed essential are creeping downward. Some physicians order the test automatically—regardless of the mother's age. It can be presented as an added frill in the treatment: I can tell you your baby's fine. Or even, I can tell you whether you're having a boy or a girl so you can go ahead and decorate the room.[1]

Once a procedure becomes entrenched among physicians—and expected by the public—as is beginning to happen with amniocentesis, questions about risks versus payoff become harder to raise. Rather than regarding a procedure as useful only under certain conditions, it becomes used *except* under certain conditions. So instead of being used "only when," it's always used "unless." One has to make a case *not* to use it. Some nonmedical firms are now marketing prenatal pictures through ultrasound. ("See the miracle of your pregnancy. . . . Prenatal portraits and *videotape* of your baby *before birth!*") As fetal snapshots start getting handed around like party favors or holiday cards, will we forget to question the safety of sonography?

Many women describe feeling pressured into taking tests. "The doctor makes it seem like everybody's doing it so it's not a big deal," says Erica, twenty-nine, recalling her feelings after taking the alpha fetaprotein test, a blood test performed early in pregnancy that would be followed up with amniocentesis if blood levels were higher or lower than usual.

> *You're given a release form, which means you can say no, but it almost seems easier to just go along with it. I was very troubled by the whole thing. I asked the doctor what the test involved. I wanted to know if I would need an amnio if anything showed up and if I would have the option to abort. He said I could abort if it was found not to be a viable fetus. I still didn't know what he meant by a viable fetus, and I didn't necessarily want that choice. For me, my religion would kick in and I'd have to decide what was right according to my beliefs. I was committed to having this baby. I didn't want to think about all this. But the doctor suggested it, and you do get to believing what the doctor says.*

Even when a woman is aware of the issues raised by testing, it can be hard to refuse an opportunity to be reassured. "I really struggled with the idea of amniocentesis and only decided to have it because I'm forty," says Sara, a nurse-midwife about to give birth to her first child. "I kept thinking, if only I was really attuned to my body, I wouldn't need this. After years of the work I do I thought I would have an intuitive, spiritual connection with the baby, that somehow I would *know* that everything was fine. But I have to admit that I'm not there. To this day I don't know if he's fine. I kept thinking, if only I had an amnio, if only I had a sonogram, then I'd believe it."

As with conception, we're faced with the irresistibility of technological advances. We do have the choice not to use the technology offered to us, but it means stemming the tide. With amniocentesis, the choice is in part between doing and not doing something, but it's also between having and not having information. In our society, information is perceived to have value in itself. The prevailing belief is that the more information you have the better, in all situations. Information about the pregnancy is a resource, and the more resources you have at your disposal the better for you and for the child. In order to be responsible one is obliged to seek it. To society's way of thinking, the advantages of information tend to outweigh the disadvantages, as well as any risk getting that information might entail.

Some women find they feel compelled to accept information they simply don't want. With amniocentesis women can choose whether or not they want to know the sex of their baby. Sandra said that she originally wanted *not* to know the sex so as to preserve the mystery. "It seems so much a part of the whole experience, that moment when they say 'it's a boy!' or 'it's a girl!' " she explained. But when she had amniocentesis the information was suddenly *there,* and she decided: "If the doctor knows, then I want to know." The thought of walking around with a question mark in her belly when the doctor had the answer on file was anathema to her. And by that point, the notion of "mystery" seemed little more than a contrivance.

Also, the information gleaned through amniocentesis is presented as a black-and-white issue: the diagnosis is either negative or positive, okay or not okay. The impression is of a clean assay, a yes or a no, which appeals to the rational in us. But the information only goes so far. Information can give us facts, but it does not necessarily provide the answer we might want.

For example, Down's syndrome is not a precise disorder but a *range* of disorders. Depending on the degree of impairment, a person with Down's syndrome can require constant care or live independently and hold down a job. Amniocentesis only tells you that the general disorder exists. Other chromosomal abnormalities that can be detected, such as sex-linked disorders like Turner's syndrome and Klinefelter's syndrome, may or may not cause certain problems. Is knowing that the child *might* have learning disabilities or *will probably* be sterile sufficient reason to abort? What are the psychological implications of knowing you're carrying a chromosomally abnormal fetus, even if the disorder might hardly interfere with a normal life?

There are also plenty of birth defects that amniocentesis doesn't catch. Many couples, however, concentrate all their anxieties about the fetus on this one test. Once the baby "passes" the test they believe everything is fine, mistakenly viewing the test as a guarantee of a perfect child. The belief is that nothing else *can* be wrong. It gives one an illusory sense of control and predictability.

If the choice to procure information seems weighed, how about the choice of what to *do* with that information? No one is going to tell a woman to abort if the fetus is found to have a serious defect. But merely having that information makes the choice a burdensome one. The "unviability" of the fetus is expressed as an irrefutable clinical fact. If you have the test so you can take care of a problem if it occurs, and that problem occurs, shouldn't you take care of it? If you ask science for an answer and science gives it to you, shouldn't you act on it? Science is giving you an opportunity to be spared the pain of one of nature's cruelest tricks, in fact, to transcend nature. Shouldn't you go the way of progress? The problem is that while the diagnostics are medical, the issues they raise cannot necessarily be handled "scientifically."

Our ability to procure information prenatally has outpaced our capacity to deal with that information. And sometimes such information can push us into a corner. *The New York Times* interviewed women who learned late in their pregnancies that their fetuses were severely deformed. Their doctors suggested abortion, but none would perform the procedure (only a few physicians perform third-trimester abortions). "The point is, the technology has gotten to the point where you can find out about your fetus," one woman lamented. "But the doctors say, 'Sorry, we'll tell you what's going to happen but that's it.' To me, it's almost unconscionable."[2]

Having this kind of information puts the couple in the position of playing God. Many women feel that they could accept a child, say, with Down's syndrome, but there's a difference between accepting the hand fate's dealt you and *actively* inviting that fate. And the question of what the couple must deal with extends beyond the boundaries of family. Who's going to sympathize with a couple if they've decided to continue such a pregnancy? Why should society provide services for children with problems if the parents have willingly taken on a problem that could have been "solved"?

Choosing to bear a child who requires special care means taking on a great responsibility. Choosing not to know whether the fetus you're carrying has a defect means taking on a great responsibility. But medical practice today is organized around the idea of shifting the responsibility elsewhere. A woman places herself in a doctor's care, assuming to a large extent that he or she will take responsibility for her welfare. The doctor asks her to sign a release form to be exonerated of responsibility if a problem occurs in treatment. Many tests and procedures are done so doctors can keep themselves in the clear. Unfortunately, the fear of litigation requires doctors to act this way.

The litigiousness of our society has led us all to think in terms of assigning blame. We're accustomed to having recourse. We assume it is our right. If a purchase doesn't please us, we feel entitled to take it back. We see it as a breach of trust on the part of the seller rather than our mistake. The money we spent and wish we hadn't is the store's responsibility, not ours.

We bring this cosseted attitude into our childbearing. "If I have reason to feel anything's wrong, I definitely want to have amnio," says Melissa. "A friend of mine, after ten years of trying to conceive, had a low-tech pregnancy, with no tests. The baby was fine. I held my breath for her. How neat to be so trusting, I thought. But I think there's something about us today where we want to have the option of 'blaming' the doctor if something goes wrong. We want to feel someone will either fix the problem or pay for it."

The history of childbirth in this country has been marked by a clash between the technological and the natural. In large part, the story of technological additions to childbirth has been the story of the medical profession's consolidation of power in obstetrics. While it is tempting to look at this trend as physicians seizing control of births from women, the issue is a great deal more complex, with current fashion and social beliefs affecting women's perceptions of appropriate pregnancy care. In some periods woman attendants were subjected to a merciless usurpation of their traditional role in healing and childbirth. (In the colonial era, for instance, practicing midwives risked prosecution as witches.) But for the most part, the changes occurring over three centuries can be more appropriately characterized as a negotiating process, a continual give and take between medical practitioner and patient.

Early in this nation's history, midwives tended the vast majority of laboring women. According to Richard W. Wertz and Dorothy C. Wertz, authors of *Lying-In: A History of Childbirth in America,* this was a reflection less of basic philosophy than of social exigency: there were simply very few trained physicians in the colonies. The inhabitants of young America generally adhered to a pattern established in Europe—childbirth was a female affair, except for emergency situations. These rescue missions, however, were usually served by surgeons, who were tradesmen regarded as a lower form of doctor at a time when even doctors were held in low regard.

Though perilous by modern standards, by contemporary standards midwife-attended births in America were quite successful. It has been suggested that the relatively low mortality rate during the colonial era was a testament to the physical robustness of American women, those who survived the initial trip to get here. They enjoyed better nutrition than their European counterparts, got more exercise, and were spared the squalor of the Continent's urban industrial centers. But since difficult births did frequently lead to fatalities, the prospect of labor still filled many women with dread.

As the 1700s gave way to the 1800s, physicians attended an increasing percentage of births. The initial forays of "male midwives" into infant delivery were none too promising: the incidence of puerperal fever, literally a wound infection following childbirth, skyrocketed. Doctors who treated other pregnant women, not to mention operating on ill patients and performing autopsies, were more likely to spread infection than were midwives who stayed with one woman throughout her labor. Scarcely more than a century ago, in 1883, one-fifth of the patients in one Boston hospital perished of the fever.[3] Some women would flee rather than allow themselves to be brought to the ward for their lying-in. The problem persisted until late in the century, long after Pasteur made the link between bacteria and disease and sterilization measures were instituted to combat it; most physicians were reluctant to implicate themselves in the epidemic and so denied there was a connection at all.

Other hazards of medical intervention were those associated with surgical tools: the forceps, hooks, and knives used in stubborn deliveries—crude, unwieldy instruments. Practitioners were often poorly trained in their use, frequently causing lacerations, infections, and bruises. The epidemic of "women's problems" in the Victorian age was no doubt partially due to fallout from poor obstetrical techniques. Babies delivered surgically often fared worse, and many died from crushed crania or hemorrhage. Contributing to the danger was the fact that much treatment was conducted blindly—literally. Doctors performed pelvic examinations and even deliveries on their middle-class patients strictly by feel, since it was considered improper for a male physician to look at a woman's body. Textbooks, in fact, maintained that it was best for the doctor even to avoid eye contact with his patient.

But numbers cannot bear out women's *perceptions* of doctor- versus midwife-assisted birth, for women increasingly began to favor physicians for their deliveries. In hiring a physician, many women were seeking not only safety but status—doing something that allied them with the wealthier classes. The medical alternative was also seen as a way of preserving femininity in a time of physical stress; practically minded midwives were probably not keen to attempt their tasks through several layers of petticoat. The inclination also reflects a growing trust in science and the belief that science could—and should—be employed to improve on nature.

Another significant factor in the turn toward physicians was the medical community's active campaign to sell its obstetric services to female patients. Nineteenth-century medicine was something of a free-for-all, with specialists trained in European methods (termed the "regulars"), faddists, and borderline quacks all competing for customers. With the cult of female invalidism among the middle and upper classes, a coterie of well-off women clients could keep a doctor's business hopping. Obstetrics was a good place to launch a medical career, as it meant steady work and the promise of loyal patrons.[4]

A key part of this marketing effort was the discrediting of midwives. Midwives were accused of being filthy, culturally backward, incompetent, and, inescapably, female. With the medical community's conviction that women were physically and emotionally incapacitated during menstruation, the fear was raised that even the most able female attendant could be nonfunctional nearly one-fourth of the time. Midwives were barred from using the latest obstetrical tools, which, no doubt, few could have afforded anyway. If a woman wanted the security of having the instruments accessible, she had no choice but to opt for a doctor.

Merely having doctors present increased the chances of those instruments being used: While midwives were trained in the art of normal deliveries, physicians still saw their role as heroes in an emergency. Consequently, more births were *treated* as emergencies. Doctors, in trying to affirm their position, often felt the need to justify themselves by using the tools they had advertised. Getting the baby born wasn't enough; many doctors felt a responsibility to satisfy an audience. (Indeed, the site of operating has traditionally been called the surgical "theater.") And once it was observed that tools could shorten the length of labor, shortening the length of labor became a goal in itself. Some attendants were apt to rush the birth so they could get on to the next delivery. Training in medical schools perpetuated the bias toward speed and technology.

These trends were only accentuated by the movement of birth to the hospitals. The early part of this century saw a massive migration of deliveries to the hospital, a place that in the past had been reserved for poor, homeless, or "fallen" women in need. But women welcomed the switch in locale because of the centralization of expertise, the availability of emergency measures, and, not insignificantly, the promise of better hygiene. America at this time was extremely conscious of germs, and the average home was thought to be reeking of festering, disease-bearing agents. Besides, the hospital was seen as the modern place to give birth, an architectural emblem of progress and efficiency.

Accompanying the change in approach and location was a change in the basic philosophy of obstetrical practice: childbirth was defined as a pathological event. In part, this evolved as pregnancy was being viewed from a male doctor's vantage point. According to medical wisdom, the male body was accepted as the norm, and anything that deviated was deemed abnormal. If women's general health—including puberty and menstruation—was seen as problematical (as it was in the nineteenth century), pregnancy became viewed as a crisis of dire proportions. Since the potential problems, rather than the probable normality, of births were stressed, doctors placed an emphasis on the *control* of all births. In order to account for deliveries taking place in a hospital and physicians routinely attending pregnancies, pregnancy itself became classified as a "disease."

Feminist scholars have suggested that the increased medicalization of childbirth reflected the predominantly male profession's discomfort with female power. "Civilized" childbirth, as it was accepted, was essentially enforced female passivity: the woman lay down with her feet in stirrups, discouraged from moving about or making any noise. The ostensible goal was to provide women with a "ladylike" delivery, but such physical limitations invariably led to increased intervention—in other words, to an increased dependence on the *doctor's* power.

Many thinkers have linked men's incursion into obstetrics to men's fears of women, fears of mortality, and feelings of exclusion from the birth process. By appropriating the tools of childbirth, the medical establishment has kept it—and whatever natural and female forces it represents—under male control. One writer connects the rise of medical intervention with scientific discoveries in the late nineteenth century that proved the male not to be the sole life giver in conception: "As male illusions of procreative power were destroyed . . . men's dominant role in childbearing was re-established through obstetrics and gynecology."[5]

But as the twentieth century wore on, few doctors ended their dominion at childbirth. Medical expertise in managing female pathology was further confirmed as women's *psychological* states became its purview as well. This had certainly been the case in the nineteenth century, when obstetricians would attempt to cure their patients of personality disorders—such as "unruly behavior" or "erotic tendencies"—with operations like ovariotomies and clitoridectomies. Psychoanalysis and the discovery of hormones contributed to the belief in the connection between body and mind, which, as it was generally interpreted, broadened medicine's role yet further. Apart from this, in keeping with the increased secularization of society, physicians had replaced the clergy as the arbiters of reproductive, sexual, and emotional matters. In the past, the question of import was what behavior was correct in a moral sense. With doctors doing the judging, the question became what was *normal.* As the official guardians of normality, doctors tightened their grip on women patients: no one wished to be found neurotic, hostile, or rejecting. Of course, women who challenged the medical model of childbearing (including those in the 1940s who expressed a desire for natural childbirth) were seen as among the sickest of all.

What women of a given period expect from doctors and from themselves in childbirth is to a great extent determined by social attitude. One example of how this plays out centers on the experience of pain. At various points, much attention was paid to the birthing habits of peasant and native women, who, it was reported, casually delivered their babies during breaks in their chores. Experts then concluded that "real," or natural women wouldn't find labor painful. On the other hand, it was widely thought that the suffering was "purposeful," indeed, that the agony of labor was the very benchmark of femininity.[6] Depending on the period, a woman who experiences minimal pain or one who suffers greatly might be deemed "unfeminine."

The midcentury authors of *Modern Woman* assert that childbirth pain is greatly exaggerated as a "new and powerful means of control over the male."[7] Focusing on the discomforts, they contend, betrayed a rejection of the feminine role. Such assumptions have subverted women's autonomy by placing value judgments on subjective experience and invalidating the experiences of many. This bound women to their doctors yet more, because the implication was that by "submitting" to medicine in an archetypically feminine way, women could be "saved" from their shortcomings by their doctors.

Childbirth pain has continued to have varied meanings. In the late nineteenth and early twentieth centuries, women viewed relief from pain in liberating terms. Feminists advocated the use of painkillers in childbirth. Queen Victoria's taking chloroform during her seventh delivery has been described as the monarch's single true radical act.[8] But in the context of highly medicalized births, since the 1940s many women have protested against the use of anesthesia. The "numbing" effect served to deprive women of the intensity of the experience, which was frequently described in ecstatic terms. It also prevents the laboring woman's ability to push, often necessitating the use of forceps.

Which brings us to where we are today. Women of recent decades have been able to focus on experiencing the naturalness of childbirth because medical advances have minimized many of its real dangers. As a result, women have become concerned about naturalness at a point when our dependence on doctors is at its pinnacle. Once it is accepted that doctors possess tools and knowledge essential to safe deliveries, women can hardly afford to reject or disobey them. So we're still carrying around two contradictory goals: an increase in naturalness and an increase in control. We're still making concessions to medical wisdom, even as we feel our doctors are making concessions to us. We still bow to the shifts in fashion, in everything from weight gain during pregnancy to delivery style to breast-feeding.

In an effort to be freed from previous controls on labor, we impose controls on ourselves: minimizing our own outbursts and expressions of pain through prepared childbirth and controlled breathing. This, while seeming to empower us, may be another form of silencing.[9] In consequence, we're often plagued by confusion and self-blame—a feeling of not being able to live up to the prevailing standard—which leads us to depend on our doctors still more to assume responsibility for the risks and to reassure us.

One recent medical trend affecting women's experience is the separation of the pregnant woman into two distinct entities. The fetus has come into its own and is now accorded patient status and rights. The more doctors have been able to learn about the fetus—through listening to the fetal heart, watching it through X-rays and, more recently, sonography, and determining its chemical makeup through tests—the more *real* the fetus has become, and thus more important in a medical sense. In the past, the mother's health was of greatest concern. Early in the century, women were advised to keep their weight low during pregnancy because small babies were easier and safer to deliver.[10] It was believed that whatever was good for the mother would be good for the child.

All this has changed. Fetal medicine is now one of the great frontiers of medicine, with surgery sometimes performed before birth. While this is an area of tremendous promise, the new emphasis on the fetus has altered the nature of pregnancy. The feeling is that the fetus may be *in* the woman but is not necessarily a *part* of her. "There's this new terror of the fetus trapped, locked in our bodies with the worry of how we're going to mess them up," says Barbara Katz Rothman.

One technology that contributes to this separation is sonography, which allows us to "see" the fetus. But what we see is the fetus detached from the maternal setting (the doctor turns away from the woman to look at the screen).[11] Sonography allows us to "bond" with the fetus, but we experience it as distinct from us. The fetus exists in its own realm (at least visually), creating the illusion that it is its own, self-sufficient being. Feminist scholar Rosalind Pollack Petchesky points out that antiabortion activists have exploited sonography as a way of convincing people that the fetus is a "person." Prolifers have actually sought to impose sonograms on pregnant women in the hope that women who bond with their fetuses will choose not to abort them.[12]

The mother and fetus as a complementary and inseparable unit is an image from the past; today the two are often seen to have different, even conflicting, needs. The fetus is viewed as being *at the mercy* of its carrier and dependent on doctors to act as its advocate. Public cases involving what have been called "the pregnancy police," in which women have been forced to undergo cesareans or face charges for drug use, have heightened the anxiety surrounding the issue.[13] Doctors aren't trusting women; women aren't trusting themselves. "Medically, doctors are skipping the woman and going directly to the fetus," says Dr. Rothman. "What counts is what can be seen on the screen, not what the woman herself is experiencing." It's an approach that only serves to alienate the woman from her body—and from the life she's carrying—even more.

"I was confident I could take care of myself fine, that I was a healthy person who exercised and ate well, but I didn't know how to be healthy for the fetus," Brin recalls.

> *I felt good, but I'd ask: should I be walking on the beach instead of the street? I'd see signs everywhere: "could cause birth defects." The alcohol ones are easy: you just don't drink. But once I saw a sign at a car repair shop and I got panicked, even though I was on the other*

> *side of the lot. Then I was torturing myself over asthma medication I really needed to take, until the doctor pleaded with me not to worry. Society makes you paranoid, and the message is that whatever happens is your fault. I had the feeling that if they could have put the baby in a plastic bottle instead of my belly, she would have been better off.*

In a lecture, Joan Raphael-Leff, a British psychoanalyst, talked about what she terms the "placental paradigm," the unique way in which a mother relates to her unborn child, whom she is both connected to—and separated from—at the placenta. The paradigm assumes one of four configurations: good-good (meaning the mother is good and the child is good); good-bad; bad-bad; and bad-good. The pattern can affect how a mother perceives the discomforts of pregnancy. For example, nausea can be experienced as a positive sign of pregnancy, or a threat to her well-being, or a punishment upon herself, depending on how she has constructed the pregnancy emotionally. The patterns generally reflect vacillating states of mind, but often one of them dominates. The ideal state would be good-good, achieved after the mother's ambivalences, surfacing as "badness," are worked through, a sense that both beings are "real" and valid.

What is of concern here is not that a woman may feel she or the fetus she carries is "bad," since such feelings are inevitable during the overwhelming physical and emotional changes that pregnancy represents, but how we experience pregnancy on the psychological level. Let's say a woman is thinking about her upcoming amniocentesis. Since the test focuses on the potential "badness" of the fetus, might she not be prone to experience the pregnancy as good-bad? If a woman is made conscious of all the dangerous things she might be doing to the fetus (like breathing the wrong air), instead of the nurturing she's already doing for it, isn't it likely she'd feel more along the lines of bad-good?

"One problem is that women wait for the technology to determine the goodness or badness of the fetus, rather than work these matters out themselves," says Dr. Williams. This can then lead women to turn to technology even more. According to Dr. Raphael-Leff, women whose pregnancies are characterized by patterns other than good-good are more likely to seek technical assistance in birth. Medicine's control is counted on to ease the threat of the possible badness involved.

Once the technology is employed, however, it becomes harder to trust the validity of our own experience. Many women feel they know when they got pregnant, or have their own sense of the progression of their pregnancies through their symptoms and sensations. But tests like sonograms are used to date the pregnancy precisely. Such tests, anthropologist Rayna Rapp suggests, bypass—and subsequently replace—women's immediate experience: "[W]hen pregnancies are medically managed, most women learn to redescribe their bodily changes through the language of technology, rather than dating their pregnancies experientially."[14] It's only through the technology that we can claim the pregnancy.

When does information help us, and when might it interfere? Do we want our pregnancies to be fact-finding missions? Is this what's best for us and our children? But what is the alternative when the facts are *there?* Do we have to have a see-no-evil, hear-no-evil kind of pregnancy to let the story tell itself on its own? For at this point, we're constantly sneaking a glance at the end of the chapter (with the pages turned for us, daring us to peek). The technology employed today presents the answers before the reality, fracturing the narrative: the slow, natural unfolding of new life. Our bellies full of potential answers, we forget our questions. But the one question we should be asking ourselves is: as we come to term, on *whose* terms is it?

Chapter 11

PARENTAL PARTNERS

While rummaging through the twenty-five-cent bin in the local public library, I came upon an intriguing cultural artifact: an issue of *Life* magazine, vintage 1972, chronicling "The Marriage Experiments." The lead article describes a New York City couple who are trying for a fifty-fifty marriage and have drawn up a contract to ensure they stick to their pledge. The accompanying photo shows the pair engaged in the rapt teamwork of making a bed (as the husband continues to smoke a cigar, should anyone start to wonder who's who). Pictures of the woman writing at a desk and the man pouring cereal for the kids merit prominent shots. A companion piece reveals how a California couple sought therapy to save their marriage after the woman took a part-time job and asked her husband to help with the housework. Yet another item closes the geographical gap by telling of an "unconventional" Nevada couple who have decided to enhance their marriage by running their ranch and hunting camp together. "I've never wanted to have my own career, heaven's sakes no," Joy Potts tells the reporter. "I enjoy working with Stan and get lonesome when he's gone."[1]

It's astounding to me to think that, if transported back twenty years, my own marriage might have been viewed as a radical social statement. Our domestic routines which, in practice, are not terribly interesting, may have been fodder for contemporary debate. The fact that our roles around the house are for the most part blurred might have heralded the dawn of a new era of equality to some and the demise of civilization to others. I can just envision the cameras zeroing in on the moment when I sign a paycheck over to Tony so he can buy us groceries, or a newspaper feature writer marveling over Tony's ability to whip up a stunning meal on a half hour's notice. But in the context of the 1990s, not only are we not revolutionary, we're probably—shudder—rather normal.

Equality has not exactly descended upon the American marriage like a mantle of enlightenment. Research that breaks down spouses' actual contribution to the household have effectively cured us of that illusion. In her 1989 book, *The Second Shift,* sociologist Arlie Hochschild estimated that women worked an average of fifteen hours a week more than men once paid employment, housework, and child care were figured in. Other studies have shown that the amount of time—"quality" or otherwise—the typical father spends with his child per day can be measured on a stopwatch.[2] One reason these reports spark such interest is that they belie the quantum leap in the male species we've been told to expect: the arrival of the New Liberated Man and his subspecies, the New Active Father (the latter having been announced with great fanfare by celebrities like Bill Cosby and movies like *Three Men and a Baby* and *Parenthood*).

But the fact that the job isn't finished doesn't mean the work hasn't begun. The extent to which the changes and questioning of roles *have* occurred is pretty remarkable, especially considering how recently it was that gender roles seemed set by holy decree. (Masculinity was deemed so fragile that doing "women's work" like laundry could threaten it.) The average dish may still be washed by a woman and the average dollar brought home by a man, but it does appear that today more dishes are washed by men and more dollars brought home by women than ever before.

The marital task studies might not tell the full story because the greatest shift is likely to have taken place among younger men and women, those newest to marriage, who might not yet be listed among the statistics. Men now in their twenties and thirties grew up alongside the women's movement and are more likely to be aware, as a result of osmosis if not conscious commitment, of women's needs and rights. Unlike generations before them, today's younger men have coexisted as peers with their female counterparts, from grade school to college to career. With such shared experience, men are less prone to regard women as their opposites. Men's empathy for women has further been enhanced by two decades of men being told to *emulate* women, the idea being that "female" qualities like sensitivity and nurturing do not erode a man's masculinity but rather make him "whole." Then there are the practical aspects. If a woman's professional demands consistently delay her return home from the office, a hungry husband might be inspired to learn how to cook. And if he has lived on his own before his marriage, he may already know how to cook—and even to iron his shirts.

While in reality there may not yet be a revolution of marital roles, there has at least been a revision of *intentions.* Today's men expect to marry women with careers. They expect to share tasks around the house and to participate more in child rearing than their own fathers did. Women expect their husbands to respect their needs for independence and professional growth. Both men and women embark on their marriages with the assumption that their experience within the union will be more alike than not.

Up to a certain point, these expectations can be met. In many contemporary couples, for example, both the wife and the husband cook. In other cases, neither cooks and a stack of takeout menus serves as their nutritional lifeline. But whatever the arrangement, it gets tricky when the couple become parents. For all the measuring of who does what, all the liberationist posturing on both men's and women's parts, a basic truth seems to be obscured: It is difficult to retain egalitarian roles in a marriage after having a child. Compromise—the hallmark of the 1990s marriage—still goes on, but once an infant arrives, a larger share of compromising seems to take place along traditional lines. Many couples who go into marriage with the idea that everything will be fifty-fifty find those nice even numbers jumbled up. "One thing I didn't think about when I got married was how children change the relationship," says Dale, thirty-two, a first-time father. "I always focused on the equality we had—on how we both worked and both took care of the house—not on how we were going to be as parents."

Or, it comes out that their respective visions of marriage had diverged all along. According to one study, nearly nine out of ten men agreed that fathers were just as essential to child rearing as mothers, but three in five still believed mothers of young children shouldn't work outside the house.[3]

The discrepancy in expectations might not have surfaced before, but when a pair becomes parents and priorities demand to be sorted out, the tensions come to a head. Dale concedes: "I always talked about equal roles. But it's been a shock to realize that my thoughts were really traditional all along. It was always my idea that when the kid came along, I was going to work full-time. My wife could work or stay home.

She had an option. I never allowed myself that option. If she wanted to work, we would need day care and have to deal with that."

The experience of Suzanne, the mother of a three-year-old, shows how making even one basic decision, like deciding to breast-feed, can put the marriage on a different path. "I had to get up at night, alter my work schedule, etc., while he pretty much went on as before," she explains. "We would try to even it out by having him 'participate' and bring the baby to me during the night, but that didn't really pan out. He'd roll over and say, 'I have a meeting at seven in the morning. You can nap tomorrow. I can't.' Within a year or so we were exactly where we said we'd never be."

What we're seeing is a situation in which two groups of marriages seem to be changing in two directions concurrently, each nodding respectfully at the other as their paths intersect. Recently formed, childless marriages are heading toward increased equality (as women gain economic parity, as other couples provide egalitarian models, etc.) at the same time that other, newly childed marriages are retreating into more traditional roles. The latter movement is a silent one, for, despite our talk of revolutionizing roles, a woman changing a diaper (or ten diapers, or twenty) is scarcely surprising news.

On an individual level, however, the shift can be cataclysmic. Our generation has been sold on the idea that marriage as an institution is moving in an evolutionary manner to a higher, more equitable state. Images of a new breed of fathers are so rampant in the media (if not in reality) that we've begun to accept this as the norm. So couples who experience a pull toward traditional roles may feel themselves throwbacks to a less advanced age, and, as a result, may be reluctant to admit that it's happening at all. For a combination of reasons, traditional roles do seem to reassert themselves once "couple" becomes "family." But because we haven't acknowledged this tendency, or examined it in the context of egalitarian expectations in marriage, lots of new parents are confused by the change and lack any framework within which to work things out.

In watching friends sprout offspring, I've noticed that those who appear to ease most smoothly into parenthood are those with the most traditional arrangements. Often it's a subtle thing, that over the years they start staying in evenings and the woman does more of the cooking, or that they both continue to work but her ambition shows signs of wear. Just as such couples often have the foresight to land housing with room for a nursery, there seems to be a corresponding space in their marriage where a baby would fit right in. I've envied them their clarity, their apparent ability to traverse effortlessly into the realm of Mothers and Fathers. At the same time, I've been somewhat taken aback. This new family motif seemed unreal, even surreal, given the way our adult lives had begun. How did this happen? I'd wonder.

My suspicion is that for me (and my yet-unsuspecting husband) the inevitable change in roles promises to be far more jarring. Again, the structural metaphor seems apt: In the same way that, as perpetual sub-letters, it's difficult for the two of us to preserve a physical space for a new baby, I'm not sure where the "room" for one would be in our marriage. As it is now, economics and time demands would not fall neatly into line.

I basically knew what I was in for when I got involved with Tony. Although I didn't realize that having drinks on our first date meant his breaking the last twenty-dollar bill he had to his name, I quickly got the idea that life with him would not include having my way paid. I got plenty of other things, however, and after accepting that my parents (particularly my security-minded father) might not immediately approve of a struggling fiction writer holding down part-time jobs while he finished a first book of stories, I decided not to let the imbalance stand in my way.

On another level, I would have to admit that this situation worked for me. In a certain way it brought me forward. In other relationships, more conventional ones, I was this young thing and I had my writing, which was some sort of accessory to me, an endearing little hobby. With Tony, I was forced to take myself and my career seriously. Although I might have complained to girlfriends, for the most part I felt comfortable in this position. Aside from giving me a sense of importance, it also relieved the pressure to take on the traditional female role—which my mother had performed so well but I was never quite at peace with.

But lately I've been having other feelings, feelings quite new to me. The small flickers of dissatisfaction suggest an end to my little romance with the kind of life my husband and I have built. It's not the marriage itself I question—I think he and I are happily stuck with each other for the duration—but in certain respects its form. As I've been writing this book and thinking through my feelings about motherhood (and maybe here's where that nursery is making a space for itself in my mind), the game I've played with my writing feels less right. I no longer need to see myself riding through the skies on my sleek laptop, generating copy at the speed of sound. The fantasy bores me. I still want to write and contribute, but I've grown tired of being consumed by the process. There's something else, feelings inside me hint, that I want to experience in myself.

Tess, a sales executive who is married to a graduate student, says that since she started planning a family, she has resented being locked in her "egalitarian" situation:

> *My baby's due in a few months, and, to be honest, I would like not to be worrying about my job right now. But my job is it for us. Part of me is very supportive of what Neil's doing, but another part is saying, Why couldn't he have started his degree a few years earlier? These feelings surprise me because I made this decision knowingly. But I look around and see my friends switching to part-time, taking time off, working because they want to, and I'm envious. No one's lifting any pressure from me. It's not that I want to be waited on, but I'd like to have some choice.*

The prospect of children can prompt a realignment of roles, as well as a reassessment of ourselves. We may begin to feel protective of that psychic space in which our maternal self will evolve. "I've always been more comfortable with the aggessive, professional side of myself but I can feel that other side is stirring," says Tess. "At this point I feel I can't get there, can't fully relax into myself and into this experience. I'm resentful that it has to be suppressed, in part because I have to play the provider. I wonder, is that other side still there? Is that really a part of me?"

I, too, started to begrudge my husband's very unconventionality. His love and understanding had given me the emotional wherewithal to get to the point where I was open to new feelings, yet I felt unable to express them because of the demands placed on me. I've taken it as a stroke of psychological brilliance on my part that I did not marry a clone of my father, but I began to demand that Tony act more like my father in specific ways: *Tell* me you'll get a job sometime. *Reassure* me that we'll have enough money when we want a family. *Let me believe* you'll take care of us.

What exactly is going on with this gender-role two-step many of us seem to have choreographed for ourselves, however unwittingly? Does this mean that we're less liberated than we thought we were, or that we've adopted our parents' values to a greater degree than intended? Could this be a belated sign of maturity, or realism? And, in revising our expectations for men, how fair are we being? Just as we have set impossible standards for ourselves as women, are we doing the same to our men (i.e., demanding that they be better than our breadwinning fathers but be the same)?

It's hard even to read our own reactions because we're responding not only to emotion but to blunt reality. The fantasy of marrying the good provider (or having our men suddenly *become* good providers) may not be just a flight into female dependency but instead may reflect a straightforward desire for a viable family life. True equality is difficult to achieve in a society stingy with paternal leave and uncomfortable with women who defer domestic responsibilities to men. To a certain extent we can carve out roles in the relationship, but this takes place within the larger asymmetry that is married family life in this culture. Our needs and expectations for each other as parental partners are bound to differ from those of soulmate and playmate.

What I find interesting is that all this shifting and adjustment often eludes our attention altogether. We might move from a gender-blind arrangement to an at-times awkward transition to some new blend of egalitarian and traditional roles without so much as commenting on the fact. We might abide tensions without ever understanding where they came from. I can't yet picture how my own marriage will arrange itself in the context of family. I don't expect it will ever be a traditional one—still harboring our ambivalences, still wrestling with the example of our parents, we're each too invested in avoiding that—but I'm sure things will be different from when we launched our life as a couple, and certainly from what we envisioned they would be.

For many of us, expectations of equality in marriage have set us up to believe that things would be otherwise. We may, in our preparent configuration, underestimate how differently the sexes respond to the onset of parenthood, or, perhaps more significantly, deny the differences. We may ignore the invisible pull that our own backgrounds provide. Our own family models can emerge seemingly out of nowhere. From the moment one couple I knew brought their first child home, the man started harping on his wife about housework, insisting the apartment wasn't clean enough. This is new, she thought, until she realized it was actually very old: Her husband was beginning to treat her the way his father had treated his mother. Her liberated husband, she saw, had just set the clock back.

Similarly, we may not be prepared for the external pressures to assume more traditional roles. Other people are bound to treat us differently once we have children, and that can't help but intrude on how we see ourselves. Women who have kept their names often take on their husband's names when they have children so as not to have to continually explain their relationship to the child. Society makes a big fuss about getting men more involved in child rearing, but few companies have made paternal leave a real choice. For all the rhetoric, most men get the message that corporate America is not truly ready to embrace fatherhood. "Gary had said he wanted to make a statement by taking the baby to evening meetings or classes," says Tina, twenty-nine. "But now he's reluctant to do that. I think it's not the image he wants to present. He sees it as too risky."

The problem is that what we are led to expect and what we are encouraged to do will not always jibe. And as we haven't really grappled with this discrepancy, for some couples the marital reality of parenthood comes as an emotional shock: it wasn't supposed to be this way. On a personal level, both partners may feel tremendous disappointment. Because she is counting on a more helpful spouse, a wife may feel let down when her husband chooses to work late rather than relieve her of cleanup duty. Because he thought parenthood was something they were doing "together," a husband may feel rejected when his wife seems more attuned to the infant than to him.

From a more intellectual standpoint, both partners may feel defeated. They had established their marriage along the ideals of equality, and they aren't living up to that vow. A woman may feel that by being subsumed by motherhood she has betrayed the vision of equality she has lived by all these years—or that her husband is being a traitor to those ideals. "I was furious the other day when Gary went out and played squash when he had a break in his day," recalls Tina.

> *He justified it by saying that it was an hour when he would normally be at work, and that he has cut down on a lot of his appointments, but my view is that when he has a free hour he should be spending it with me and the baby. Whenever he leaves me with the baby like*

> *that, I get this subtle fear that he's acting just like a man. It's such a macho thing, leaving the woman alone, such a classic situation. I feel angry and ask myself, "Where's my egalitarian husband?"*

Some men may feel threatened when their wives, allegedly progressive and assertive to the core, start acting more like "traditional" mothers. They may want their wives to have the opportunities their own mothers were denied. "My husband wanted me to go back to work," says Aimee. "He was afraid I was going to turn into a Junior League, stereotypical Mom. He liked the fact I was a lawyer. He didn't quite know how to deal with it when I wanted to stay home and be with the child."

Similarly, a man who has consciously set out to be more involved than his own father may fear being more like Dad than he had hoped. "It's always been important to me to be more emotionally present to my kids than my father was to me," says Dale. "That's easy now that my son's ten weeks old. I get bored easily when I play with my nephews. I'm afraid the same emotional block will come back to me with my own kid."

In other cases, women whose husbands do assume a prominent role in child rearing may be unnerved by the ambivalence this stirs in them. In her journal *With Child,* Phyllis Chesler expresses this confusion: "Your father leaps up at your slightest cry. He makes me feel useless, incompetent. He says I'm not as good with you as he is. He tells other people so . . . Is this how 'fathers' are traditionally made to feel by 'mothers'? Well-meaning, but only suited for paying the bills. 'Fathers': thrown over for an infant. Ariel: What guilt, what rage I feel about not being your most preferred parent."[4]

Most marriages, and perhaps today's more than ever, need to go through a renegotiating process once a child arrives. But the important question is: What beliefs are informing our negotiations? In the 1990s, gender roles are imbued with such psychological and ideological significance that we may be hard-pressed to know what we're actually feeling. On one level there's the basic narrative (the woman gets pregnant, the baby is born, the couple has to figure out who does what), but beneath that there are any number of subtexts (what he claimed he would do, how she expected she'd feel) bumping up against one another, affecting our feelings about our relationships and ourselves.

But maybe *equality* isn't even the right word. Perhaps the egalitarian/

traditional continuum isn't the most appropriate measure, for this model doesn't account for the emotional changes of parenthood, which cannot be reduced to a matter of civil rights. If we've been able to achieve equality within our marriages (respecting each other's needs and abilities), then we should be able to accept some differences without shaking basic egalitarian beliefs.

And how can we appreciate the meaning of "equal roles" when we don't really understand the roles being equalized? At this point the idea of "motherness" has been saturated with fantasy and dogma, and "fatherness" has been studied hardly at all. Only when we address the way parenthood may draw us to different roles will we be able to distinguish between the role shifts that enhance us and those that are inflicted upon us.

One problem may be that we're imposing political ideas (equality) on what is an overwhelmingly emotional transition (becoming a parent), as well as a biological one. "We can deny the differences between men and women longer than other generations have been able to, but parenthood is ushered in through biology, and you have to deal with the differential," says Dr. Williams. "When she gets pregnant, nearly every woman starts thinking: I have to do all this? I have to do all of this *alone?* There's the powerful recognition that carrying this child is something *only she* can do." As Tess reflects, the distinctions between a woman and her mate are thrown into sharp relief: "It's strange, when you're pregnant for the first time and feeling things in your body you never felt before. As in touch as he is, he can't feel all that. It doesn't matter what he puts in his mouth, it matters what I put in my mouth. Sometimes I wonder, 'How come he's not more sensitive?' Other times I think, 'How *could* he be?' "

This basic recognition sets off a chain of emotional reactions. "What happens when a woman, committed to equality and independence, for the first time wants to be protected by her husband?" Dr. Williams poses. "She can feel shame, or self-condemnation, thinking 'This is stupid' or 'I'm being old-fashioned.' But pregnancy is above all a physical state, and a vulnerable one at that. You want to be protected. If someone runs after you, it's going to take longer to get away. This kind of awareness transcends the political, the ideas you thought you were going to have."

This sense of the woman's physical vulnerability prompts corresponding feelings in the father, she contends. "As she gets bigger, he may feel less inclined to go off on a business trip, to leave her alone. To some extent, the woman becomes identified with the baby she's carrying. He sees in her the vulnerability he imagines in the child. At the same time, the woman has a new power, which can evoke awe in the man."

If women become increasingly identified with their babies, men seem to grow increasingly identified with their work. "No matter how hip or untraditional he may be, I've yet to see a man who does not start worrying about supporting a family when his wife gets pregnant," says psychologist Barbara Counter. "Something about having a baby sets a certain psychobiology into motion. The man is thinking, 'I've got to get out in the world and set things up out there.' He wants to provide a financially secure nest, get a house, etc."

Clyde, thirty, a new father, says he has felt inklings of a "provider instinct" in himself:

There's the real base notion that this baby would die without us. Before he was born, if anything happened to me, Angie would survive. Here there's a qualitative change. There's this obligation to provide for the next eighteen years. It's mind-boggling. I'm looking into life insurance, something I wouldn't have thought of before. Before we had the baby, we thought I would work out a four-day-a-week arrangement. But with Angie working part-time, it seems more important for me to get my full salary. I'd love to stay home. It's not called "work" for nothing.

Such differences can provoke conflict when couples believe they shouldn't exist. "Women might get angry when their husbands don't fit into their notions of equality or if there's not a one-to-one split in what they do," says Dr. Counter. "The new father's response may be, 'I don't want to stay in the house. I want to have two jobs.' He may feel guilty about this, believing that he 'should' want to be with the baby every minute like his wife does. She might think he's not being a good father."

Having made a commitment to shared roles, we may resist the idea that our emotional experiences might differ. Says Tina:

Neither of us wants to think that we relate differently to the baby. We want to think that it's equal. But I don't feel it's equal now after what I went through for several months and in labor. I don't know

> *exactly what my husband feels. I don't know if he has the same deep dread about the baby's safety. Just today we took Johnny to the pediatrician for his first booster shot. I cried. Gary didn't. I wondered, Did he want to cry and couldn't because he saw I was crying? Or did he just not feel it as intensely as I did?*

With our generation's shuffling of gender roles, we seem to have gotten the idea (or wished) that female and male parents are interchangeable, that the mother can be the father and the father can be the mother. Dr. Counter recalls a case in which the father tried to launch a new business soon after the birth of his child:

> *He spent time with the baby, but the mother wanted him there when she wanted him there. It caused tremendous tension. She didn't understand that he had different needs. Basically, this woman was asking her husband not just to be involved but to bolster the mothering. She had had a terrible mother herself and was anxious about her own mothering. She didn't want to see that he couldn't truly fill that role and didn't really want to.*

In truth—with my own love/hate relationship with traditional roles—I've indulged in that same fantasy myself. When I think about having children, often I dwell on certain of Tony's qualities—his generosity, his patience, his ability to stay calm in a crisis—qualities that I would associate with good mothering. I concentrate on this vision of my husband, I think, because I so doubt my own capacity to mother. If I do turn out to be a complete maternal disaster (as I fear), I can be comforted by the notion, real or otherwise, that *he* can be the mother, that he can save me from my failings.

In part, I think this sameness idea comes from women's ambivalence about our traditional role in motherhood: about whether we want this role and whether we believe we can succeed in it. But I also think it stems from a lack of consensus on what the *male's* role in child rearing should be. Without a clear vision of what fatherhood means in our time, the prototype, by default, becomes that of *motherhood*. Hence our disappointment. "The model of parenthood remains the mother, so when we compare men to that they inevitably fall short," says Dr. Counter. "I don't think we have enough appreciation of the differences, and not enough respect for men."

One widely quoted study concluded that men can satisfactorily fill the role of primary caretaker and that such fathers do achieve a "biorhythmic synchrony," reminiscent of the maternal bond, with their infants.[5] Other research has suggested that a father's interaction with his children differs qualitatively from that of the mother and that it plays a key role in development.[6] There have been other related studies, but far more research is needed for us to get a clearer sense of the father's role. And if material on the effects of paternal participation on children has been scant, works that explore the effects on the fathers themselves have been even scanter. Professionals in the field lament this dearth. Psychiatrist John Munder Ross, Ph.D., writes: "[T]he parental ambitions of the boy and man, their urges to create life, have generally remained linked to maternal, womanly ambitions and prerogatives. . . . It is almost, one senses, as if to be a parent one must be a woman."[7]

It's ironic that the new man/new father—the sensitive guy who can cook gourmet meals when his wife works late and give a baby his bottle without a fuss—has become something of a cultural icon without our really knowing who he is. With many women moving out of the nursery, there's been an expectation that men would be moving in. But no one has articulated what we want them to do there. I think there's been a reluctance to explore this issue because both the notions of sameness and of difference between the sexes are threatening. Men and women committed to egalitarian roles are afraid to learn where they might diverge. At the same time, men (including male theorists) and women who have a stake in preserving women's traditional roles are loath to accept the androgynous aspects of child rearing.

But I also think the notion of sameness has another draw. I think it's an attempt to solve "the man problem": what to do with masculinity. Writers on men's issues, most publicly the poet Robert Bly, have asked the question: What does "manhood" mean in a postindustrial setting when man as worker, lover, and leader has essentially been domesticated? Society's answer (which, according to Bly, in *Iron John,* does not solve but rather skirts the problem) has been to "retrain" men to be more like women. In the 1970s men learned how to cry. Today there's an obsession with fatherhood, a new and improved kind of fatherhood where he's just like a mother except that he's a man.

Part of the challenge of finding a satisfying family role for men is that in contrast to motherhood, which is an overtly physical matter, the meaning of fatherhood has always been somewhat vague. The male contribution to reproduction is so ephemeral, so *meager* compared to the woman's physical and emotional investment. I don't want to overstate the case, nor suggest that men's new interest in babies and children can be reduced to a genderwide case of wish fulfillment, because I think the "man problem" vis-à-vis fatherhood is more a social than a biological issue. But men's relative distance from childbirth—and theorized displeasure over the fact—has a rich literature of its own. For more than a century, men's thwarted desire to bear children has been blamed for everything from impotence to misogyny to nuclear war.

In the 1920s Karen Horney stunned the psychoanalytic community with her suggestion that most males suffered from "womb envy," that they are awed by women's capacity to give birth and nurture young. So intense is a boy's disappointment at learning he cannot make babies like mother that he represses this envy and compensates for his inability by glorifying the male genitals and seeking power over women. The envy as postulated could, however, prove a constructive force, as its sublimation has led men to build great cities and produce great art: "Is not the tremendous strength in men of the impulse to creative work in every field precisely due to their feeling of playing a relatively small part in the creation of living beings, which constantly impels them to an overcompensation in achievement?"[8]

In *The Politics of Reproduction,* British writer Mary O'Brien overlays this psychoanalytical interpretation with Marxist exegesis. The defining characteristics of patriarchal Western culture—competition, autocracy, domination of women and children—have arisen from men's alienation from the birth process, she argues. At the very moment man is most connected to his genetic continuity—at conception—his seed is, literally, alienated from his body, no longer a part of himself. It was men's consciousness of paternity that led to the institutions of monogamy and marriage, she says. Men as a group have colluded to erect societal structures to affirm their control. Never able to be quite sure whether a particular woman's children are his, a man can nonetheless secure legal claim to her sexuality and offspring.

The male longing to give birth has been explored in anthropology (male initiation rites in which the penis is cut in imitation of female genitalia) as well as psychoanalysis (fantasies of bearing children). It has also been the rationale for *couvade,* men's mimicking of women in childbirth. (The term stems from the French word meaning "to hatch.") Here the man's efforts to join in the process are accomplished not surgically, but *dramatically:* he acts as though he's pregnant too. In certain traditional cultures, the father-to-be writhes in pain on the ground as his wife calmly goes through labor in a nearby hut. In the contemporary version, the man suffers the aches and pains of pregnancy along with his expectant spouse. It is estimated that between one-fourth and one-half of fathers-to-be get pregnancy symptoms like weight gain or nausea, sometimes to the point of needing medical care themselves.[9] It's common for today's couples, ever fans of the idea of partnership, to say "we" are pregnant. With *couvade,* there sometimes seems to be an element of competition, as if the man were saying: "You think *you're* pregnant . . ."

But to get a clearer sense of why we are where we are today, and to see how the idea of sameness in parental roles has arisen, we need to look at how men's place in the family has evolved in contemporary culture. Historically, participatory fatherhood has gone in and out of vogue. In Western patriarchal societies, the father was a dominant yet distant figure, exerting his influence over family discipline and moral values much the way a priest or pastor held authority in a village or town. After the Industrial Revolution, men left the home each day to produce in the factories, and children became defined as women's domain. The father's presence, once constant, now became occasional. Because he was the family's social and economic connection to the outside world, the father's importance in the family grew. Yet much of what he was encouraged to express in his work life—competition, ambition, pursuit of wealth—was in direct opposition to the mores of domestic life. While woman's daily existence was increasingly circumscribed, that of man was split in two.

As the economy changed from industrialism to a capitalism marked by corporate consolidation and consumerism, work was—in a literal sense—taken from men's hands. The physical component of labor diminished as work itself became abstracted: the Gray Flannel man of the 1950s seemingly disappeared into a hole for forty hours a week, and an impersonal institution would reward him with a paycheck. Barbara Ehrenreich notes in *The Hearts of Men* that "masculinity" had come to be defined by the breadwinning role. Winning bread, however, required that a man curb his masculine, and often even human, instincts. The American male ideal of the rugged individualist was still celebrated in myth, but it was the noncombative, nonquestioning *conformist* who edged up the managerial ranks. The military metaphors of the business world—"big guns," "corporate sharpshooters," and "doing battle with competitors"—masked the truth that men's economic life was only becoming more passive and tame.

As the *reality* of middle-class male life gravitated toward androgyny, society's vision of what manhood meant was enlarged upon significantly. In *Him/Her Self,* Peter Filene contends that in past eras, the opposite of "manliness" was "childishness." Beginning in the Victorian age, however, *femininity* was seen as the antithesis. To maintain gender integrity, men needed to keep their characters free of the taint of the feminine. The notion of masculinity that emerged with the new century was inherently contradictory: it was seen as a vital, often uncontrollable force, yet it could be easily upset. Women were called on to protect their husbands' masculinity by taking care of household tasks and child rearing and by not usurping the man's position as family head and provider.

How did fatherhood fit into this precariously balanced family structure? As Elisabeth Badinter points out in *Mother Love: Myth and Reality,* father's traditional role in education and discipline had been largely assumed by the modern state. Mother, left to create her own miniature kingdom within the home, had taken on everything else. No one was quite sure where father belonged.

After World War II men returned to find that not only had women gained work experience and economic power, but that their families had gotten along fine without them. Fathers shuffled about the house, buried their heads in newspapers, and busied themselves with chores like lawn care and barbecuing that basically kept them out of the way. The domesticated Dad as depicted in mass culture was, like Dagwood Bumstead, his prototype, a buffoon. Men in cartoons were generally shorter than the women, and they cowered at the sight of their wives.[10] Fathers were then brought back into the fold when it was decided that mothers had gotten *too* powerful in the home, dominating husbands and children alike.

Once the dangers of maternal overprotection were discovered, the haunting specter of "Mom" always gave father a role to play.[11] In the fifties, Dad's task was to keep Mom sexually fulfilled to ensure that she'd be a good mother. The idea was that unless two parents loved each other, they could never really love their children. This was also a protective measure—an attempt to siphon off some of mother's energy in order to keep her from overpowering and infantilizing the kids out of frustration. A decade later research on gender identification concluded that sex roles had to be taught. It was Dad's job to make sure Junior was playing with the right toys and didn't let Mom turn him into a sissy. As a writer in *Better Homes and Gardens* asked men in 1950, "Are we staking our future on a crop of sissies? . . . You have a horror of seeing your son a pantywaist, but he won't get red blood and self-reliance if you leave the job of making a he-man of him to his mother."[12]

The form that fatherhood was supposed to take at any given time generally fit in with the ideals of that era. In the fifties, for example, just as "team-playing" and "cooperation" were buzzwords in the office, "togetherness" was urged upon men at home. In Peter Filene's words, "[D]ecisions were to be made jointly, disagreements were to be resolved by consensus, and household chores were to be distributed among everyone."[13] Men started attending classes on marriage and the family, while popular magazines published articles like "Families That Play Together Stay Together" and "Men Make Wonderful Mothers." With Dad the expert on "group management," the family should function like a benignly democratic corporation.

The sixties' counterculture rejected the prevailing standard of fatherhood and masculinity but did not offer a viable model to replace it. On the surface, rebellious youth with their long hair, beads, and unisex jeans did dispense with accepted gender definitions. But a closer look at hippiedom reveals that it was still the women who baked the bread and washed the diapers while their men discussed philosophy or smoked dope long into the night. Ultimately, the youth culture simply allowed men to postpone fatherhood, and possibly adulthood, altogether.

To some degree, the human potential movement of the 1970s eased the dilemma, assuring men that expressing emotion was okay as long as it aided the realization of their inner selves. To many men, fatherhood was one route to getting in touch with the playful, loving souls buried within them. But rather than truly exploring what participation in child rearing meant to men and to families, it was presented as a "fun" thing. Appearing within the context of the self-help and men's liberation movements, active fatherhood was seen as an antidote to traditional male responsibilities instead of a deepening of them. Also, the focus remained on the thwarted child within the man rather than the grown-up father within the man. Lip service was also given to the *woman* within the man. Men were invited to discover their feminine and nurturing aspect, but rather than integrating this into their identity, the emphasis was more on adding to one's behavioral repertoire.

Certain other trends, however, have led to men's rethinking their roles as fathers. Ironically, the high incidence of divorce is one. Many men, abruptly dismissed from family life, long for their children with a surprising intensity. Some realize that their emotional distance was instrumental in the decay of their marriages and seek to close the gap with their children before they, too, are lost to them. In one study, Anthony Astrachan reports in *How Men Feel*, 20 percent of men said their relationships with their children had improved after a divorce.[14] Considering the number of couples who divorce every year, even that is a significant number of men awakened to active fatherhood. And many marital refugees are starting new families, vowing not to make the same mistakes they made first time around.

Similarly, men and women alike have reacted against the excesses of the 1980s. Weary of taking on the world with their credit cards, couples have returned to the physical and psychic comforts of home. And what could be "homier" than to start a family? Many men have seen their job demands getting out of hand and have decided their careers were giving neither the security nor satisfaction they had promised. Some, in what *New York* magazine has dubbed "The Daddy Track," have begun to shift their energies toward family as a way of seeking fulfillment.[15] Often, a man's reconsidering of fatherhood is a variation on the male midlife crisis so touted two decades back. With couples starting families later in life, many men are becoming fathers as they approach this midlife phase. Greater participation in child rearing may be a man's way of improving himself or starting anew.

Another factor is that just as young women today are reacting against their mothers, young men have been reacting against their *fathers*. In the business world of the 1980s, we've seen this generation of men recoil against their gray flannel fathers by placing a new stress on entrepreneurship. Correspondingly, young men are reacting against emotionally absent fathers. Dale recalls: "Once I said to my father, 'I think it really hurt me that you were out of town so much. If you had known how much it hurt, would you have done it?' He said, 'Yes. It was that important to me.' I was shocked. My strongest commitment as a parent is not to be like that."

Arguably, among certain groups of men there has been a resurgence of interest in fathering. This is certainly the case in the media. The popular press portrays father love as the greatest new thing for man since the disposable razor. But for every attentive father pushing a baby carriage on a Saturday morning, there are a dozen mothers doing the same during the week—who don't get the same applause. What does the current fascination with fatherhood reveal about the state of equality in marriage today? And, more specifically, what does it say about the role of father?

Some critics have suggested that the "new fatherhood" is yet another attempt at denigrating motherhood. In a sense, it trivializes parenthood. It emphasizes the "cute" parts of parenting, the recreational or sentimental aspects, rather than the infuriating disarray that can be daily life with a child. Since our society still believes that the mother is ultimately answerable for a child's well-being, fathering can be portrayed with greater levity. It can be endearing when Dad makes a mess in the kitchen with the kids because it's assumed that Mom can always clean it up.

The entertainment industry, it seems, has caught on to this. In a *New York Times* piece, writer Joy Horowitz notes that mothers have virtually disappeared from situation comedies. Rather, the story line of choice these days features men contending with children on their own:

> *The current rash of shows without mothers can be traced to a confluence of psychological, sociological and economic factors, including the exploitation of every working mother's most basic guilt about deserting her children and the flip side of that—a child's fear of abandonment caused by women's changing roles in society. . . . [T]he message is hardly subliminal: if Mom's not going to stick around the kitchen, then—poof—let's dump her.*[16]

In Dr. Davis's view, fatherhood's ascendance in popular lore suggests anger directed not only toward mother but toward father himself. "In America, we've never really had enough of Dad, never really experienced him enough," she says. "This new image is partly a way of deflecting the anger we may have toward him by saying, 'Gee I can have father after all.' "

In many ways, she says, the new fatherhood represents a *reluctance* to challenge the role of men in society. "The heroes are still the men, even when the 'feminine' in them wins out," she observes. "At bottom this is not 'new.' It's a way of keeping them in a place of power in the family and the culture. Father remains an idealized object. It's a way of balancing the scale: If women are going to go out into the workplace, men need to find new ways to be important."

Also, the images of active fatherhood are often presented in the context of consumerism. Advertisers have seized on the new father as a fresh way to market products: A picture of a father holding a child grabs attention. A woman with a child is a less striking image. Companies that use such marketing can count on being seen as more thoughtful and sensitive and thus gain public relations points. In recent campaigns, The Gap (for the GapKids line), Tyson Chicken, and Van Heusen shirts have all played up fatherhood. These images perpetuate the vision of fatherhood men want to see—and thus invite men to buy more products—without challenging the status quo.

There are reasons to be optimistic about men assuming more responsibility in child rearing. Perhaps the most positive sign is men's increased participation in birth. When we were born, it was a rare father who saw the inside of the delivery room. Today, perhaps the majority of new fathers don surgical gowns for the event.[17] Men who witness the birth and are involved in early care experience a greater bond with their children and are therefore more likely to feel a strong commitment to them. Also, more men are asking their employers to respond to paternal needs. For example, while Clyde opted not to push for part-time work as he had originally intended, he did stay home for five weeks after the birth. "It made me more comfortable with being a father and helped me feel more included," he says. "The birth meant a significant disruption in my life as well, a period of time that was different from any other time."

But the dialogue on the meaning of fatherhood—both on the societal level and that of the individual couple—is not yet complete. In her critique "A Feminist's View of the New Man," Barbara Ehrenreich argues that the so-called new sensitive male is a deceptive character in that his "newness" is limited to his receptiveness to the feminizing aspects of consumerism. Women, including feminists, have allowed this to happen, she claims, by not demanding a deeper exploration of roles. She writes:

> *My generation of feminists insisted that men change, but we were not always directive—or patient—enough to say how. We applauded every sign of male sensitivity or growth as if it were an evolutionary advance. We even welcomed the feminization of male tastes, expecting that the man who was a good cook and a tasteful decorator at twenty-five would be a devoted father and partner in midlife. . . . Up until*

> *now, we have been content to ask them to become more like women—less aggressive, more emotionally connected with themselves and others. That message, which we once thought revolutionary, has gotten lost in the androgynous drift of the consumer culture.*[18]

Are we extending this into the realm of parenthood by asking men to be mothers? Are we creating a situation in which the more a man is like a woman in behavior, the heartier our approval of him is? Rather than actively working through the meaning of gender roles, are we suggesting that men pursue an image of fatherhood as presented in advertisements, where the idea being sold is that playing Daddy is as fun as drinking beer? In *Mothers on Trial,* Phyllis Chesler contends that men who seek custody usually get it because mothers are judged according to a higher standard. Parenting behavior that would be criticized in women can be praised in men. In such cases, our reluctance to define fathers' roles—and our haste to regard every man who so much as smiles at a child as some kind of saint—can have devastating effects.[19]

By allowing the consumer culture to define who the new father is, we are letting men off easy, but we're also doing a disservice to them—and to ourselves. The new active father—like Ehrenreich's new man—is, on the surface, an attractive figure. But he remains an elusive one, part repository for ambivalence toward mothers and part decoy, distracting us from the vigorous reckoning of family roles we need to do. Within our own relationships, we need to be open to the possibility that equality as parents might be different from equality as nonparents, open to being surprised.

Chapter 12

THE LEVERAGED CHILD

▣

> *"[I]n a world of silicon chips and hard-nosed nursery school admission committees, who can afford to take chances? The Age of Spock is over: nature is no longer enough. You've got to play to win, and you've got to start early. Suddenly it seems almost criminally negligent to raise a child in the old-fashioned way."*
>
> From "Goodbye, Dr. Spock" by James Traub,
> *Harper's*, March 1986

Near the southern California coast where I live right now (I move around a lot) you see them everywhere. Babies: lifted in and out of the car on errand runs; gurgling approval at the day's warmth; being led down to the beach for a salty first meeting with the sea. Tony and I had been seeking good weather, novelty, and proximity to his parents, but it was a fluke of real estate that landed us in this sunny paradise at what must be the country's most extravagant edge. In tune with the spirit of the place, these babies—many of whom were not yet born when I arrived here six months ago—are getting an early induction into the pleasures of aerobic exercise. Strapped in pouches and special seats, they're party to their parents' jogging, cycling, and fitness walking. Transporting an infant seems not so much an expression of love as an added element in a workout, like hand-weights.

The babies are also getting used to the vehicular culture, growing accustomed to its speed. The "center" of my neighborhood here is a long sidewalk that runs between the coastal road and the beach. This strip acts like a concrete conveyor belt abutting the shore; the locals gather here not to meet but to move. At crowded times, like late afternoon when professionals return from work and the surfers change shifts,

I think of it as a miniature version of the freeway. You have to time your entry onto the walk, as from a merge lane. People move along, pass each other, make way. There's a hierarchy of pace: bicyclists, runners, roller skaters, adult strollers on foot, baby strollers on wheels.

If southern California is, as I have come to believe, a caricature of the rest of the country, this beach scene is in many ways a microcosm of modern life. The continual movement, the undercurrent of competition (who's faster, who's better sculpted, who has the coolest car), the emphasis on the visual. The point of being here, after all, is to perform, not to interact. The momentum is fierce, like the tide it counterpoints, and all-encompassing. Inevitably, these children so new to the world are being absorbed into it. Already they're moving, being planned for, being bought for, for now on their parents' power. And the pressure mothers feel to move, to plan, to purchase, is palpable. All of us, privileged to have the ocean lull us to sleep at night, know we have it good in this town. But there's a tension hounding new mothers, although not generally articulated in such blunt terms: How can I live in such a perfect place (or a place so invested in presenting perfection) and not be perfect myself *and* have a perfect child?

"It's really getting out of control," says Brin, one beach-dwelling mother.

> *It's the in thing to have a baby now, but it has to be the perfect pregnancy, the perfect birth, and the perfect child. Everyone is conscious of her child's social development, analyzing every stage. You can almost forget these are human beings we're talking about, children we love. The attitude is: my child is going to be smart and beautiful, an Olympic star, and a brilliant lawyer. We laugh about Superwoman, but here we are trying to raise a Superchild.*

You would think that living in an affluent community that is fairly safe, has good schools, and is drenched in natural beauty would offer parents some peace of mind. But it seems no one, no matter how well situated or well off, is immune to anxiety about doing right by their children. As the nation is finally coming to recognize how poorly our less-fortunate children are being cared for, professional and middle-class parents are worrying whether their children will have the means to survive and succeed. Richard Louv, a *San Diego Union* columnist and author of *Childhood's Future,* calls it "The Bogeyman Syndrome": a vague sense of perpetual threat, intensified by the fact that crime and other dangers are brought into the home each night on television. The pitch and the focus may vary as the child grows, but the anxiety pervades. And with it, the competition.

Says Brin:

> *In northern California, among a more intellectual pool of people I know, the competition centers on which school your child goes to. I know of children under three going to three different schools in a week. I think that's a lot for a young child to adjust to. I know one woman who felt her four-year-old wasn't doing enough artwork. So she hired an art specialist to tutor her. Around here what seems to matter is how pretty your child is. There are people here who will spend $1,500 on an outfit for a kid who will wear it once, or give their girls perms. This to me is ridiculous, but the more you see others do, the more you wonder if you're doing enough. My little girl is often mistaken for a boy. Sometimes I think, Is there something wrong? Is she not pretty enough?*

In *The Hurried Child,* David Elkind, a professor of child study at Tufts University, reported observing stress symptoms, including headaches, stomachaches, and lack of motivation, among young children. He attributes this to the pressure on children today to grow up quickly: to take on adult responsibilities when both parents work, to carry extra emotional burdens after a separation or divorce, to meet adults' standards of achievement. Throughout the last decade child development experts have warned that pushing children faster and farther can only cause problems. They've urged that such children get the idea that they merit love only when they succeed. They've noted that unstructured time for fantasy and play is ultimately more important for the child's well-being than an added skill, no matter how pertinent or impressive.

Despite this caution, many children today maintain daily schedules that would weary a jet-setting executive. Tales abound of mothers planning toddlers' play hours weeks in advance. The battles to get children into the "right" kindergarten—which can involve coaching, bribing, and hard-core résumé-building—have become the stuff of urban lore. Present-day parents, it seems, have been unable to resist any opportunity to boost Junior's development, whether through specialized classes, learning videos and computer software, or, for those loath to waste those idle months of gestation, prenatal curricula in which you can "talk" to the fetus through tape recorders and speaking devices. Companies that sell toys and educational material for infants and young children sport names like "Right Start" and "One Step Ahead," giving the impression that childhood is not a stage so much as a race.

Observers have commented on how baby boomers have brought their competitive values to child rearing: Those who live in quest of the consummate vintage and the top-performing car are bound to want, as *People* magazine labeled them, "gourmet children."[1] These new-breed parents are rapaciously grabbing kudos for their kids with the same enterprise applied to creating fortunes on Wall Street. But I think it's too easy to dismiss this get-ahead mania among parents as one more yuppie fad, for this belies the confusion and apprehension most new parents today feel. There have always been status symbols and those who chase them. The six-figure parent who feeds his toddler brie and communicates with her through flash cards is but a parody. Most parents are not interested in raising a four-star palate or a fact-retrieving machine, but rather in giving their children the tools to make it in the world.

Underneath all the boasting and gadgetry, the basic problem today's parents face is: How do you do well by your child in an age of uncertainty and diminishing expectations? We're painfully aware that in terms of the economy, the country's international standing, and the environment, the world has gotten meaner in our lifetimes. Even during the eighties boom, when things seemed to be getting nicer for many of us, we saw the nastiness creep ever closer, as homelessness and random violence crossed neighborhood lines.

"What I fear is, what if one day my child asks me if we're going to get blown up by nuclear weapons?" asks Melanie. "What would I say?" Though we don't dwell on these matters every day—we'd go mad if we did—on some level the insecurities are with us. We're highly conscious of economic slippage and may feel we're barely hanging on to our station. We still look to economic, political, and psychological experts yet have grown too cynical to be fully reassured by them. In other eras, such as the beginning of the century and the fifties (the bomb notwithstanding), childbearing was imbued with tremendous optimism. The future promised technological advances and greater prosperity, all of which our children—more open and better equipped to reap the benefits of modernity—would inherit. Today, we want to protect our children from the future we fear is theirs.

"In my parents' day, the fundamental concerns were that the child be healthy and well educated," says Donna, thirty, whose daughter has just entered preschool. "Today, the child has to be healthy, well educated, well adjusted, self-confident, independent, and assertive—all this so they're ready to cope with the world. I think it's that we're pretty pessimistic about things. We're preparing them for a struggle. Do you think we'd be worried about all this stuff if we had any faith in the future?"

What we have today is *defensive* parenting. We're raising our children with worst-case scenarios in mind. We want our children to be *so* rich in skills that no employer could afford to let them go, *so* academically prepared that no college would dare turn them down. If it comes down to brute survival of the fittest, we want to make our children know how to wind up on top. With uncertainty all around us, we want to provide our children with every certainty we can—and backups, just in case.

We want to give our children every advantage we can, in the hope that they can save us. We may not have the same optimistic atmosphere our parents raised us in, but if we work extra hard we can put our children in a good position and maybe even do our parents one better. "I saw a '20/20' episode on development, with kids on accelerated learning programs," Clyde reflects. "I couldn't help but think, What would I have been like if I had had that opportunity? Would I have been happier? It does raise a question mark when you have children."

Not surprisingly, since we live in recessionary times, many couples express this anxiety financially. True, the cost of living has been climbing steadily, but it seems our need for security—at least when it comes to children—may have risen even faster. Says Brin:

> *I hear all the time people saying that financially it's not the right time to have kids—when they're making lots of money. When is the right time? It's never enough. In my case, the baby came sooner than expected. We had only just applied for insurance. I cried when I learned I was pregnant. I didn't think we could handle it, but my doctor assured me we could. I felt so dumb—I was saying I didn't think we were ready. I was putting a price on my baby. Here I thought I was being responsible about it. It took someone to say it to me before I saw what I was doing. The idea is that we should have a million dollars for the baby before we even think of getting pregnant.*

And the ante keeps getting raised. If we build a golden stage around our child, we can't help but expect a performance worthy of the setting and props we provide. With the admirable intention of shielding the youngster from the vagaries of modern life, we can fall into the trap of measuring and comparing and setting goals more appropriate to a full-grown adult than a gurgling tot. The objective is to assuage our own anxieties about what we can offer the child, but the too-common result is to pawn those anxieties onto him or her.

The perfect-child syndrome as it afflicts parents today also seems to evolve naturally out of the contemporary approach to reproductive medicine. The recent tendency has been to invite medical controls and technology ever earlier into the process. Asserting such controls frequently leaves parents with the belief that the outcome can be controlled, and the constant checks along the way only confirm that. There's the impression that you can—and should—"know" what you're getting, in everything from the timing of conception to the "normality" of the fetus, and with that comes the idea that you should get what you want. It gives parents a sense of omnipotence regarding the child.

Rather than a mysterious life taking form somewhere beyond the realm of the parents' eye, the child becomes observable. Once observable, the child is—at least in fantasy—subject to the parents' desires and will. Ultrasound technology, originally developed in the form of sonar detectors for submarine warfare, has been applied to obstetrics—for "surveillance missions" in the womb—since the 1960s. What we have now, says feminist scholar Rosalind Petchesky, "is a kind of *panoptics of the womb,* whose aim [in the words of a prominent pregnancy specialist] is 'to establish normative behavior for the fetus at various gestational stages.' "[2] Expectations for the child are set earlier and in more concrete form. Parents prone to worrying about whether their children walk or form sentences at the "developmentally appropriate" time may soon be advised by doctors when their fetuses fail to turn around or flex limbs on schedule.

The stepped-up efforts to explore the "fetal environment" create more opportunities to observe and manage the pregnancy.[3] We get used to looking to numbers and comparisons (the *language* of medical management) to ease our anxieties about the child's well-being and retain that tendency long after the child is born. We may not consider the range of normality in children—the fact that children are going to grow, learn, and speak at varying rates. We become dependent on medically derived norms and accept them as gospel—in part because that's how they're presented to us. We panic if our child slips on the charts and believe that we should *do* something about it.

As historians Wertz and Wertz point out, the emphasis in reproductive medicine has shifted from providing a humane childbirth to producing the "perfect" child.[4] The notion of the fetus as patient, the idea of the prospective parent as medical consumer, and a broad trust in medicine's capabilities have given doctors the mandate to ensure the "quality" of our children. Celebrated cases of life created in test tubes and petri dishes have given us the impression that you can create the perfect child almost the way you can create the perfect meal, by following the recipe and using only the best (from a genetic standpoint) ingredients.

Over the last decade there has been a great deal of debate over the high number of unnecessary cesareans performed in this country. The soaring cesarean rates—more than 50 percent in some hospitals—is cause for concern, and the number can be significantly reduced, particularly by eliminating automatic repeat cesareans, which account for more than a third of all surgical deliveries. But it has been argued that physicians are only responding to women's demands. Women expect their doctors to do everything possible to ensure a "perfect" child. The more a woman has invested in having the child, from infertility treatments to medical controls during pregnancy, the higher her expectations from medicine are likely to be. Physicians are well apprised that failing to live up to patients' expectations can prompt a lawsuit. They're also keenly aware that for older first-time mothers, those in their late thirties and early forties, this baby may represent their "only chance" at motherhood and approach the pregnancy and delivery accordingly, employing every diagnostic and surgical defense available. Certainly each medical intervention makes it more likely that subsequent intervention will be used.

The fact that we're having children later in our adult lives plays into this in other ways. Because our children are longer awaited than those of other eras, we have more time to build up expectations for them. As the delay often reflects our ambivalences, in order to ease our doubts we may—perhaps unconsciously—make "deals" with ourselves: I'll have a child as long as (as though this could be negotiated) it's the kind of child I want. The fantasized child, rather than putting a drain on the parents' prosperity and degree of control, will promote it.

The stress on the genetic over the social contribution in parenthood (which underscores the discussion of surrogacy and other legal cases in which men who have donated sperm have asserted their "parental" rights) has also enhanced the child's value to the parents as an expression of their genetic potential and thus further boosted the stakes. Recent scientific studies have affirmed the role of genetics in everything from intelligence to shyness to resistance to disease. This has made adoption less attractive to many people as well as made it all the more important to have one's *own* child. In an essay in *New York Woman,* an adoptive mother describes a waiting room in an in vitro clinic where many of the women seeking treatment had already adopted children—and several had brought them along. Concerned about the effect the in vitro process might have on such families, the writer wonders why these adopted children weren't enough. "A biological child is my only link to immortality," one woman explained to her, even as her young daughter sat on her lap. For many today, viewing a child as an extension of one's self is less a sign of egotism than an acceptance of scientific fact.[5]

The same ambivalences (toward our bodies, our mothers, motherhood itself, etc.) that breed anxieties about our fertility and our capacity to carry and deliver a baby can also be a factor once that child is a reality. Unless we've worked through those feelings, they're bound to be with us still. As we might have done throughout conception, pregnancy, and birth, we continually seek ways of keeping that ambivalence, and any damage it might cause, under control. We project the idea of perfection onto the child because that reassures us that we have not harmed the child through our unconscious feelings.

"Once you have a perfectly coiffed, perfectly dressed, perfectly schooled child, you can completely split off all of your anxiety about damage," says Dr. Williams. "That's how we compensate for all the unconscious hostility and fear that we might have about motherhood and about the child." The constant checks of the child's appearance, behavior, and performance allow us to sigh with relief: "Thank God my child's not damaged."

For some new mothers, the ambivalence deepens after the child is born, as they might not have been prepared for the changes motherhood would entail. They may feel anger at the child because they underestimated the magnitude of his demands or underestimated the force of their own attachment. They may have planned to leap right back into work only to find themselves torn about the choice. In their jobs, in their marriages, in their feelings about themselves, they simply can't live their lives exactly as they did before. The conflict between wanting to be with the child and wanting to be freed from him often results in tremendous guilt.

According to Calvin Colarusso, M.D., a psychiatrist in La Jolla, California, this guilt in turn adds to our perfectionist expectations:

> *The baby becomes the premium out of the conflict that arises between trying to raise the child and trying to maintain a profession. The mother is thinking: I feel guilty because I know I should be spending more time with the child. So I have to look for every possible indication that the child is okay. It's a reaction formation to the underlying ambivalence, resulting in the idea that "I'd better be super and the kid better be super."*

Mothers who don't work may, in contrast, feel pressure to generate perfection in order to justify the decision to stay home. They may imagine that their lack of career (even a temporary lack) has diminished their own value, so that value must be instilled in the child. With all the controversy surrounding child-care options, many mothers feel they're always under the magnifying glass and must "prove"—to others and to themselves—that their choice is the correct one.

Guilt about our ambivalence, guilt about the limits of our time and energy, guilt about the lack of control we ultimately have over the child's future. Guilt has come to be the normative state of motherhood. Parenting magazines write about women feeling guilty about feeling guilty. We may yet see articles on guilt about *not* feeling guilty, although at this point it's not clear who would admit to such a lack. Guilt is so accepted that marketers are openly exploiting it as a means of selling products. A *New York Times* article on children's cosmetics and personal care items explained that new companies "are hoping to capitalize on . . . the guilty consciences of working parents."[6] The publisher of a magazine geared to young mothers put it bluntly: "Expectant parents have a guilt complex you can cut with a knife."[7]

Companies who are marketing to our guilt inevitably start marketing the guilt itself in order to keep us shopping. This toy will help your child develop motor skills (implicit message: his motor skills will suffer without it). This line of clothing is made of the softest cotton (implicit message: other, less expensive fabrics may be abrasive). Because the messages hit so close to home, we can get caught up in a buying spree.

We so much want to do the right thing. Unsure of what that is, it's often easier to do the obvious thing: buy what we're told to buy.

"It's impossible to avoid the pressure to buy," says Donna.

> *Take "Sesame Street." There's not much bad you can say about it. But now they've got this whole line of products and your child wants them all. On the one hand, you think, the right thing is to resist the pressure and stick to products you think you really need. On the other hand, you worry that you're depriving them. Unfortunately, most mothers just don't have time to evaluate all these things. It's easier to go along.*

Children have always formed attachments to fantasy characters, whether based on storybook heroes or favorite dolls. Today, the figures children are encouraged to identify with are advertising vehicles.

The word "no" doesn't exactly spread harmony and good will through the home, so parents are often reluctant to buck the forces of commerce. "It's an immediate-gratification thing," says Melissa, who, as an elementary school teacher, deals directly with parents' concerns.

> *Time is short. No one wants to spend the time to work things out. Parents would rather buy something to put the kids in a good mood so the time they do spend with them is pleasant. What we're all doing is treating the symptom but not the cause. We're so invested in everything going smoothly in the short time we're with the children. Everything should go well, and if it doesn't, it should be immediately fixable.*

What particularly troubles Melissa is how this approach has made its way into the schools:

> *Teachers find they can keep peace in the classroom with prizes, so now kids expect a prize for doing anything. Kids used to be satisfied with a star on their papers. Now you have to go out and buy scratch-and-sniff stickers. Or toys. Or food. There are kids so overweight they don't take gym class, and teachers are giving them candy. Now there's graduation from kindergarten, as though nothing counts unless there's a ceremony and an award. All over you see bumper stickers that say: "My child was citizen of the month at. . . ." I wonder, is that for the child, or is it PR so the parent will feel good about the school? Before, it was only when you* weren't *a "good citizen" that people knew about it.*

The bumper-sticker phenomenon—parents broadcasting their children's laurels—has led many to lament the narcissism of today's parent. But according to Dr. Colarusso, it's not quite as simple as that. "Some narcissism is quite normal and healthy in parenthood," he says.

> *As a mother, you revel in your child. Your child is an extension of you. You have created life. Your body works. It's an important element in allowing you to tolerate the needs of the child. In this society, the notion of gratifying yourself as a mother through this emotional connection has been shunted aside. Instead, the superficial aspects of narcissism are stressed. Society is telling women that it's okay to indulge in the child's appearance, development, and success, but not in the other, deeper, connection. The idea is, you should give the child everything—except yourself.*

This surface narcissism—with its twin poles of indulgence and denial—is also revealed in what seems to be a growing tendency to treat children as little adults. Critics have noted how children in many films and television series are uncannily precocious and grown-up (shows like "Doogie Howser, M.D." and "Baby Talk," movies like *Look Who's Talking*). Nowadays children often have great autonomy around the home, preparing meals and sometimes buying groceries for the entire family. Today's children, who may talk like experts on everything from sex to the ozone hole by spouting back what they've heard on television, can seem remarkably sophisticated. But this suface "grown-upness" of children is often taken as actual maturity.

"Many parents today are less willing to be parental and to take authority," says Dr. Williams. "People are more interested in saying 'I'm equal with my child' than in disciplining or making unpopular decisions. It's the democratic idea gone wild. The belief seems to be, I buy my own clothes or wear makeup or whatever, why shouldn't my child? It's almost as though parents don't realize that children have different needs and might only be ready for certain things."

Dr. Williams notes that businesses have seized on this: "Today there's a child's corollary for everything. There's babyGap, GapKids, designer fashions for kids, even a kid-sized Mercedes-Benz—at the very same showroom where they sell the big ones. Whatever the parent has the child should have." In an essay in the *New Yorker*, fashion critic Holly Brubach observes that this trend has brought fur coats, tuxedos, and leather bomber jackets to children's clothing racks. She quotes a spokesman for the Ralph Lauren Polo for Boys collection as saying its ideal customer is "an up-and-coming yuppie family that has young children and disposable income to spend, and wants the son to look like the father."[8]

The tendency to see the child as a little adult—in other words, like the self—often comes from a strong wish for the child to *be* a little adult and therefore to diminish the enormous responsibility we feel. Says Dr. Williams:

> *Raising a child is the most demanding job there is. There's simply no vacation from parenthood. It's unrelenting. Parents feel incredibly burdened. Yet we somehow got the idea that life should be easier. The message from the eighties was that everything should be fun. There are all kinds of ways of getting around the burden, and one is to make the child an adult in your own mind. Pretend the child needs less—less of your guidance, less of your emotional presence.*

The precocious development we demand from our children—and that our models of childhood (film characters, tennis stars negotiating million-dollar deals at fifteen) exhibit—is a way of circumventing childhood itself. Childhood is associated with feelings of vulnerability, dependence, and helplessness, the very feelings that becoming a parent stirs up in us. We want to avoid seeing these qualities in ourselves, and we don't want to see them in our children. In order to protect ourselves from the need to protect our children (as overwhelming as it is), we pretend they don't need us.

This blurring of the line between childhood and adulthood—if it is indeed occurring—is an interesting historical twist, as the *idea* of childhood has up to now been gaining strength in our era. Although the notion of childhood as a unique phase of life seems axiomatic to us, historians point out that it is a relatively new one in Western civilization. According to Philippe Ariès, the French author of *Centuries of Childhood,* the art of the period suggests that children were not differentiated in medieval times; in both dress and physiology they were depicted as miniature adults. Parents not only didn't know the ages of their children, they might not even have distinguished them by name: frequently, for simplicity's sake, all siblings might be given the same moniker. Children were in no way protected from the realities of adult life. They were sent to labor or apprenticeship at an early age, they enjoyed the same games and diversions as adults, and were exposed to the jokes, gestures, and activities of adult sexuality, which often included sexual play between adults and the children themselves.

Childhood began to assert itself during the Renaissance. Only at that point, according to Ariès, did people begin to regard the death of children as a significant loss. (At least it seemed to become significant, as evidenced by representations in art and the official documents available to historians; privately a child's death might have had a very different meaning.) The first books on childhood diseases and child care appeared at this time. In art, children were now featured prominently in family portraits, and by the seventeenth century they even assumed the central place. Instead of moving directly from swaddling blankets into adult clothing as they had done, children were given their own clothes. While children of the past were expected to perform whatever adult duties they could, becoming educated and literate was now seen as the task of youth.

A number of factors led to this shift. One, Ariès contends, is the fact that more children lived. Because the risk of losing a child in the Middle Ages was so high, parents were reluctant to grow attached to each one individually. Intellectual developments contributed as well. Scientific advances enhanced scholars' understanding of nature and human anatomy, which led to avid inquiry into human nature and the stages of life. With the rise in humanism came a decrease in fatalism: There was a new belief that one could change things, and the child became symbolic of man's capacity to change. In the seventeenth century John Locke portrayed children as eminently impressionable, largely formed by the ideas they absorbed. In the eighteenth, Jean Jacques Rousseau saw the child as a "noble savage" who should be reared in a way that preserves his innocence. Both arguments figured prominently in debates on how children would become a part of the world they lived in. Once the child's upbringing and edification became seen as important, it became the job of adults to train and teach them, creating a clear separation between children and adults.

The changing perception of a child's "value" has also helped to shape the idea of childhood. Up through this country's colonial period, children served as laborers in home and agricultural production. They were valued, therefore, more in the aggregate than as individuals. By the nineteenth century middle- and upper-class children were seen less as laborers than as the *beneficiaries* of adult labor. Their value took on a sentimental, rather than economic, bent. With less need for large numbers of children, family size shrank. The fewer the children, the more they were valued individually. Labor (which the children had previously represented) is replaceable; an object of affection (which the children had become) is not. As children grew in emotional significance, mothers' responsibility for raising them rose in tandem. Mothers' role was to instill—and sustain—moral values in their children.

Also in the nineteenth century, advances in science provided intellectual grounding for child-rearing beliefs. Throughout much of this era, medicine was basically considered a do-it-yourself affair; books carefully outlined cures (leeches, blisters, purgatives, and the like) for childhood ills, since mothers were expected to attend to them. But as more was learned about physiology and medicine, mothers' reliance on doctors grew. Children's physical well-being was increasingly put in the hands of physicians, while maternal participation in children's emotional and intellectual development was encouraged. With the ever-expanding stores of information on the subject, however, expert advice was needed to tell mothers how to go about their newly defined child-rearing duties.

One popular movement around the turn of the century was "scientific motherhood," led by psychologist G. Stanley Hall. With the widespread "child study groups" that met at this time, children became the object of scrutiny, and mothers became the scientists. As Ehrenreich and English put it, "[I]n Hall's view, the truly scientific mother did not simply raise her child, she studied it, making notes which could serve as field data for the male academic experts."[9] This gave mothers an important role in a society enamored of scientific fact, while it deepened their dependence on the experts to interpret the results. This home-laboratory approach reflected the values of industry in the belief that every operation (mothering not excluded) should be measured to evaluate its effectiveness. In essence, the child raised with a hypothetical grid superimposed over his development was being groomed for inclusion in the industrial world.

Child study, with its determination of norms, led naturally to the application of these norms. Early in the century the clear emphasis was on standardization. "Regular" habits were given top priority. Toilet training was to begin at two or three months, with the use of suppositories suggested if the results were not satisfactory.[10] Bad habits were to be blotted out. To discourage thumb sucking, one could attach splints to a sleeping child's elbow. The threat of masturbation called for more radical measures, like forcing the child to wear aluminum mittens and pinning down the child's nightgown sleeves and/or feet.

While some of the cruder paraphernalia had been abandoned by this time (most mothers, wisely, had given them up much earlier, relying on mere scoldings or the passage of time to remedy childhood "misbehavior"), the philosophy of child regulation reached an apogee with the Behaviorists in the 1920s. John Watson, the movement's chief proponent, describes the "sensible" way to bring up children in his 1928 guidebook, *Psychological Care of the Infant and Child:* "Let your behaviour always be objective and kindly firm. Never hug and kiss them. Never let them sit in your lap. If you must, kiss them once on the forehead when they say goodnight. Shake hands with them in the morning."[11] Maternal love was completely dismissed: it was regarded as unmeasurable, untrustworthy, a mere inconvenience. A standardized childhood was the basis for fitting into the system, with conformity emphasized over individual expression.

After the Second World War, childhood was again transformed. The new guru, Dr. Benjamin Spock, assured mothers that they could relax a bit. Mothering need not involve a constant war between instinct and propriety; mother and child could enjoy each other. The stress shifted from impulses denied to impulses indulged. Down with regulation; the call was now for permissiveness.

As Barbara Ehrenreich points out in *Fear of Falling,* this probably had as much to do with the nation's new affluence as with any enlightened philosophy. Whereas earlier child-care experts had been concerned with what the next generation would produce, the issue now became what the next generation would *consume.* Authoritarianism just didn't seem to fit in a period of abundance driven by a constant need for material goods. The emphasis on conformity eased; an interest in individuality soared. The childhood requirement to be well behaved gave way to the mandate to be happy. And childhood happiness, in the modern American sense, demanded all sorts of accessories, like swing sets or jungle gyms in the backyard and birthday parties with all the trimmings.

Despite the laxity that the word suggests, permissiveness took a great deal of effort—at least on mothers' part. Time-saving consumer items like premixed meals, vacuum cleaners, and easy-to-clean Formica counters were needed to lighten mothers' burden and free up time not for her own pursuits but to keep the children happy. The popularization of the theories of John Bowlby and Jean Piaget only confirmed mothers' suspicions that children needed their constant presence. Bowlby, a Briton who made "maternal bonding" a household term, studied the effect on infants of maternal deprivation, basing his research on children who had been hospitalized or orphaned during the war. Piaget, a Swiss psychologist, studied how children learned. As their work was interpreted by the popular press, mothers were led to believe that any lapse in attention would leave their children emotionally damaged or deprived of a key opportunity for development.

The approach to child rearing—and the language used to articulate it—has always paralleled the ideology of the era. In the early 1800s there was Romanticism, with an emphasis on the "purity" of the young and of childhood as a "paradise." In the early twentieth century we saw the industrial concern with the "proper management" of children and the establishment of "schedules." Midcentury child rearing was dominated by psychoanalytic theory (or a watered-down popular version of it), encouraging children to express—and not repress—their emotions. Today, the canon seems to be technology and science.

Play is not just play anymore. It involves the honing of "large motor skills," "communication skills," "hand-eye coordination," and the establishment of "developmentally appropriate behavior." One mother who started her daughter learning early with flash cards calls her one-year-old "a new computer in a world of typewriters."[12] Toys for young tots derive not from whimsy but from scientific research on infant development. Just as packaged foods must list their ingredients, today's toys spell out their "developmental value." The latest generation of learning videos not only teach children how to be smarter, more coordinated, better socialized children, they teach parents how to be better parents. Parents can choose videos that allow them to "model their behavior," or, for a consulting fee, they can be videotaped themselves so experts can evaluate how they interact with their children. In the age of "scientific motherhood," mothers became scientists observing their children, but in postmodern motherhood they, too, have become the object of study. The expert has now come into the home, as educator and as critic. At least when the experts came to us in book form, parents could take a break and put them down.

For the most part, mainstream child rearing has pretty much stayed within the permissive mode. Science is employed not to control and limit the child's behavior but to expand his potential. Discipline is discussed in terms of "negotiating" with the child; creative self-expression is encouraged over self-control. What's striking, however, is how the notion of the child as consumer, which began with the postwar baby-boom generation, has become even more marked with time.

In an essay in *Harper's,* Tom Engelhardt discusses how this bias has made its way into children's literature. Parents, many of whom have delayed childbearing and have money to spend, have been buying books like crazy, prompting a surge in the once-staid children's book industry. But what the current generation of books represents, suggests Engelhardt, is not necessarily an invitation to the imaginative realm. Rather, it serves as an introduction into the consumer culture. He describes books whose plots revolve around purchases at the mall; stories in which "character" is revealed through shopping habits. A children's book, instead of a window into a larger world, is a Product. Books are sold with poster, greeting card, and video tie-ins. Rather than launch young readers into more challenging and complex material, publishers are trying to get them hooked onto series, in essence building loyalty to the "brand."[13]

Many child-product companies are on similar brand-building missions. Gymboree, which franchises exercise classes for preschoolers, has expanded to sell clothing. According to *Working Woman,* the play classes serve as a "marketing platform"; the stores are set up like the classrooms, complete with tumbling mats, capitalizing on the class's appeal to kids.[14]

Richard Louv points out that "latchkey" children, those who are left on their own for much of the day, are described as the "advertisers' dream." While parents and child-care professionals are trying to determine the degree of autonomy that's good for children, the ". . . overwhelming commercial message being sent to parents and kids is, it's fine for children to assume adult responsibilities early—because it's good for business."[15] Marketers are actively courting "Skippies" (*s*chool *k*ids with *i*ncome and *p*urchasing *p*ower) who, they find, have a great influence on family buying decisions. In some cities, twelve-year-olds can obtain credit cards, Louv reports. The effect is that children begin to see themselves as more adult and that they associate maturity with buying things.

So now, not only is the child seen as a consumer, he or she is also regarded as a *commodity*—the genetically, scholastically, developmentally perfect child—for reasons described earlier in the chapter. With estimates of the cost of raising a child to adulthood according to today's standards running about $200,000,[16] it's easy to see how parents are at least encouraged to view their children as *investments*. Teaching values to our children has been replaced by building value into them. And we do this the only way we know how: by preparing them to compete and giving them what we think they need to do so. Parental anxiety and market needs feed off each other, continually raising the costs, raising the fears, raising the stakes. We're both indulging and denying our children—giving to them materially yet being stingy with our time; showering them with opportunities to succeed but discouraging opportunities to dream—reflecting our own ambivalences and instilling ambivalence in them.

Of course, few parents simply succumb passively to all these pressures; most find ways to navigate around the various stressors, finding balances where they're comfortable. "I feel confident that as long as we love this child and are emotionally available, he'll turn out okay," says Tina. "A friend said she's never taken her child to a planned play group because she doesn't want anyone telling her how to play with her baby. My reaction was, this could be a nice way to spend time with my baby. I'm not competitive. I'm not afraid to be alone with the child, but I'm not afraid to look outside for nice ways to spend time either."

Katherine, who has two boys, four and seven, says her family has avoided some of the commercial pressures by simply not having a television set. "I grew up without one, so I know it's perfectly okay and that they won't suffer any consequences," she says. "The truth is, my kids require less attention than most because they get so used to entertaining themselves. They play a lot of imaginary games and are starting to play chess. They're enthralled with it."

Donna says that many of her ideas about how she could influence her daughter have simply disappeared in the wake of the child's strong personality:

> *I'm surprised at how much of her nature is just there. She's a lot like my husband, confident and headstrong, ten times stronger than I ever was. That's just who she is. When your baby's born you think this is a clean canvas and you can develop this person how you see fit. But I think you just have to understand what the child's personality is and facilitate that, rather than trying to create her to match some vision of your own.*

But the anxieties new parents face are severe enough that it's important not only to explore them, but to understand their implications. It's a strange reflection on our society that as the gap between the well-off and the poor is widening, middle- and upper-middle-class parents are so beset with fears about their children's competitiveness. One often unspoken dread underlying the anxiety is the danger and deprivation the poor and underprivileged represent. With our best efforts at parenting, we're not only building futures, we're building barricades for our children to hide behind. Of course we want to give our best to our children. Perhaps the best way to brighten their futures is to work to better the lives of all children, to preclude the need for the barricades, the pressures, and the fears.

EPILOGUE

Spring 1992

We're not going to have perfect children, and we're not going to be perfect mothers either, regardless of the technology, will, or material resources we bring to the task. In a sense that's frightening—with the urge to monitor, assert control, and seek reassurances informing all our decisions—but in a certain way it's liberating: We don't have to be in perfect mastery at every stage of our lives. We don't even have to try. After two years of dwelling among the questions and concerns of modern mothering, I can see that the quest for control that leads us to grasp at the technological or material bait only takes us farther from ourselves. It can cause us to misdirect our anger away from a society that fails to address the needs of women and toward our bodies or circumstance; it can cause us to accept the guidelines of others, so that we may doubt the choices we feel are right for us.

In order to grow as women, we need to live our experience rather than try to regulate it (which ultimately we can never do). We need to trust ourselves at least as much as we trust doctors and machines. Achieving such trust involves coming to know how our own attitudes—toward our bodies, our confusions, our relationships—have been formed. We need to remember that anxiety often points less to what needs fixing than to what needs to be understood.

Which brings us back to the mirror, the mirror we began with where our fears and desires regarding motherhood reside. With some exploration behind me, I can shine up to the glass, flirt with it even, without being afraid of any images that might beam back. Such images, I can now appreciate, are part of a larger set of associations, linked together by connections I am only now beginning to make.

Yet the terror of the looking glass is even more vivid to me, a terror that derives from its two-way aspect. It's not just that I glimpse my mother (and all that she represents) in the mirror, but that her eyes are looking out at me (as I imagine) with disapproval. When we see ourselves we also see how we appear to others: we are both the observer and the observed. Society's models are ever fluttering in the mirror's background—ungraspable sparks of color and light hinting at an ideal—determining what we measure ourselves by, never allowing us to measure up. We may leave the mirror or turn our backs, but as we contemplate changes that would recast the reflection our eyes are again drawn to it; we want to check that we're in command, our identities intact, our bodies contained.

The dual aspect of pregnancy and motherhood goes beyond the language of the looking glass. For women, the unfolding of new life is also the unfolding of paradox. It is empowering (we are amazed at what our bodies can do) yet overpowering (we are amazed at what *happens* to us). It is at once intensely private and exceedingly social. The transition to motherhood both concentrates our energies inward—throws us back on our resources and resistances—and connects us with others and the future.

We live with the pressures around us; we live with the pressures that derive from our past. We're aware that motherhood presents possibility; we're aware of how it can overwhelm. We have a right to our ambivalence. It is the price of our complexity. Rather than interfering with our growth, it can help direct us. It puts us in touch with who we are, as opposed to who (we believe) we're supposed to be.

In the course of this book we've examined the meaning of motherhood in our lives, working to decipher the images that linger at the mirror. We've tried to diffuse the force of those images that disturb us, and develop those that suggest our potential. As certain pictures recede and others come to the fore, we will be able to create our own vision: one where we can see our choices, our strengths, and ourselves, with clarity.

NOTES

Chapter One

1. Landon Y. Jones, *Great Expectations* (New York: Ballantine Books, 1980), 41.
2. Elaine Tyler May, *Homeward Bound: American Families in the Cold War Era* (New York: Basic Books, Inc., 1988), 135.
3. Flora Davis, *Moving the Mountain: The Women's Movement Since 1960* (New York: Simon & Schuster, 1991), 287.
4. Jones, *Great Expectations*, 224.
5. Ellen Peck and Judith Senderowitz, *Pronatalism: The Myth of Mom and Apple Pie* (New York: Crowell, 1974), 270.
6. Barbara Ehrenreich and Deirdre English, *For Her Own Good: 150 Years of the Experts' Advice to Women* (New York: Anchor Books, 1979), 300.
7. Quoted in Sheila Kitzinger, *Women As Mothers* (New York: Random House, 1978), 173.
8. Linda Wolfe, "The Coming Baby Boom," *New York*, January 10, 1977, 38.
9. Peck and Senderowitz, *Pronatalism*, 272.
10. Nancy and Chip McGrath, "Why Have a Baby?" *The New York Times Magazine*, May 25, 1975, 10.
11. Wolfe, "Baby Boom," 38.
12. "Three's a Crowd," *Newsweek*, September 1, 1986, 70.
13. Claudia Wallis, "Onward, Women!" *Time*, December 4, 1989, 81.
14. Elaine Heffner, *Mothering: The Emotional Experience of Motherhood After Freud and Feminism* (New York: Doubleday & Co., 1978), 4.
15. Examples are Barbara Basler, "Putting a Career on Hold," *The New York Times Magazine*, December 7, 1986, 152; and Alex Taylor III, "Why Women Managers Are Bailing Out," *Fortune*, August 18, 1986, 16.
16. Taylor, "Women Managers," 18.
17. Susan Bolotin, "Voices from the Post-Feminist Generation," *The New York Times Magazine*, October 17, 1982, 29.
18. "The Feminist Mistake," *National Review*, March 23, 1984; and "The Awful Truth About Women's Liberation," *Vanity Fair*, April 1986.
19. *Time*, December 4, 1989, cover.
20. An example is a 1990 study by the Roper Organization that found that more than half of single women questioned considered themselves happier than their married friends.
21. Mona Charen, "The Feminist Mistake," *National Review*, March 23, 1984, 26.

22. Laurel Richardson, *The New Other Woman* (New York: The Free Press, 1985), 5.

23. Valerie Hartouni, "Containing Women: Reproductive Discourse in the 1980s" in *Technoculture*, edited by Constance Penley and Andrew Ross (Minneapolis: University of Minnesota Press, 1991), 44.

24. Linda Gordon, *Woman's Body, Woman's Right* (New York: Viking Penguin, 1990 edition), 468.

25. Ibid., 469.

26. Trisha Thompson, "Premature Menopause," *Self*, December 1991, 132.

27. Robin Young, "The Selling of Motherhood," *Newsweek*, October 1, 1990, 12.

28. May, *Homeward Bound*, 145.

29. Ibid., 63.

30. Meryl Gordon, "In the Bedroom with Melanie," *Redbook*, January 1992, 58.

31. Kathryn Casey, "The New Romance of Being a Mom," *Ladies' Home Journal*, March 1992, 100.

32. Ann Trebbe, "Two Stars and a Baby," *McCall's*, September 1991, 98.

33. May, *Homeward Bound*, 140.

34. "Hollywood's Late-Blooming Moms," *McCall's*, October 1988, 41.

35. Judy Mann, "A Celebration of Reality," *The Washington Post*, July 17, 1991, B3; and Ellen Goodman, "Fertile Imagery," *The Washington Post*, July 20, 1991.

36. Molly Haskell, "Hollywood Madonnas," *Ms.*, May 1988, 84.

37. Ellen Goodman, *Making Sense* (New York: Atlantic Monthly Press, 1989), 293.

38. Elaine Louie, "Hear Ye! Hear Ye! Our Baby Is Here!" *The New York Times*, August 9, 1990, C1.

39. Lawrence M. Fisher, "All About Baby Products," *The New York Times* Sunday Business Section, December 8, 1991, 10.

40. *New York Woman*, October 1991, 68.

41. Diana Tonnessen, "Baby Lust," *Health*, October 1988, 69.

42. Amy Russell, "Baby Craving," *Glamour*, October 1988, 266.

43. Ann Hood, "The Baby Blues," *The Washington Post*, February 5, 1989, D1.

44. Molly McKaughan, *The Biological Clock* (New York: Penguin Books, 1989), 9.

45. Linda Wolfe, "The New York Mother: Bringing Up Baby on the Run, Run, Run," *New York*, September 10, 1984, 32.

46. Jennifer Allen, "Love Babies," *Mademoiselle*, August, 1985, 207.

47. *Working Woman*, February 1986, 71.

48. *GQ*, February 1992, 212.

49. Alessandra Stanley, "Romance Novels Discover a Baby Boom," *The New York Times*, April 3, 1991, A1.

50. Caryn James, "A Baby Boom on TV as Biological Clocks Cruelly Tick Away," *The New York Times*, October 16, 1991, C15.

51. Jeff Silverman, "TV's Creators Face a New Caution," *The New York Times* Sunday Arts Section, December 8, 1991, 1.

52. Bernice Kanner, column in *New York*, September 2, 1985, 16.

53. Shirley Lord, "Scents—and the New Sensibility," *Vogue*, November, 1988, 382.

54. Susan Faludi, *Backlash: The Undeclared War Against American Women* (New York: Crown, 1991), 192.

55. Meryl Gordon, "Is This What Women Want?" *Working Woman*, September 1991, 74.

56. Ellen Hopkins, "The Media Murder of Karen Valenstein's Career," *Working Woman*, March 1991, 70.

57. Paula Kamen, *Feminist Fatale* (New York: Donald I. Fine, Inc., 1991), 178.

58. Betty Friedan, *The Feminine Mystique* (New York: Dell, 1963), 50.
59. Cited in Faludi, *Backlash*, 41.
60. Bernard Weinraub, "Say Hello to the Nanny from Hell," *The New York Times* Sunday Arts Section, January 5, 1992, 1.
61. "When the Bough Breaks," *People*, February 24, 1992, 60.
62. Sue Woodman, "Bye-Bye, Baby," *New York Woman*, October 1990, 37.

Chapter Two

1. Simone de Beauvoir, *The Second Sex* (New York: Bantam Books, 1961), xvi.
2. Richard W. Wertz and Dorothy C. Wertz, *Lying-In: A History of Childbirth in America* (New Haven: Yale University Press, 1989), 185.
3. Ehrenreich and English, *For Her Own Good*, 272.
4. Ferdinand Lundberg and Marynia F. Farnham, M.D., *Modern Woman: The Lost Sex* (New York: Harper & Brothers Publishers, 1947), 235.
5. Ehrenreich and English, *For Her Own Good*, 270.
6. Ibid., 273.
7. Quoted in Friedan, *Feminine Mystique*, 132.
8. Quoted in ibid., 134.
9. Lundberg and Farnham, *Modern Woman*, 319.
10. Elisabeth Badinter, *Motherlove: Myth and Reality* (New York: Macmillan Publishing Co., Inc., 1981), 151.
11. Ibid., 164.
12. Ibid., 183.
13. G. Stanley Hall, *Youth: Its Education, Regimen, and Hygiene* (New York: D. Appleton and Company, 1907), 306.
14. Ehrenreich and English, *For Her Own Good*, 190.
15. Ellen Key, *Century of the Child* (New York: G. P. Putnam's Sons, 1909), 84.
16. Ehrenreich and English, *For Her Own Good*, 135.
17. Gordon, *Woman's Body*, 130.
18. Kristen Luker, *Abortion and the Politics of Motherhood* (Berkeley: University of California Press, 1985), 194.
19. Janna Malamud Smith, "Mothers: Tired of Taking the Rap," *The New York Times Magazine*, June 10, 1990, 32.
20. Shulamith Firestone, *The Dialectic of Sex* (New York: William Morrow and Company, Inc., 1970), 72, 198.
21. Ann Snitow, "Motherhood—Reclaiming the Demon Texts," *Ms.*, May/June 1991, 34.
22. Adrienne Rich, *Of Woman Born* (New York: W. W. Norton & Company, 1986 edition), 286.
23. Nancy J. Chodorow, *Feminism and Psychoanalytic Theory* (New Haven: Yale University Press, 1989), 41.
24. Miriam M. Johnson, *Strong Mothers, Weak Wives* (Berkeley: University of California Press, 1988), 43.

Chapter Three

1. Stephani Cook, "The Childless Executive," *Working Woman*, November 1990, 126.
2. Susan L. Williams, Ph.D., "Reproductive Motivations and Contemporary Feminine Development" in *The Psychology of Today's Woman*, edited by Toni Bernay and Dorothy W. Cantor (Cambridge, Mass: Harvard University Press, 1989), 181.
3. Rich, *Of Woman Born*, 251.

Chapter Four

1. Nancy Friday, *My Mother/My Self* (New York: Dell Publishing Co., Inc., 1978), 19.
2. Judith Arcana, *Our Mothers' Daughters* (Berkeley: Shameless Hussy Press), xiii.
3. Rich, *Of Woman Born*, 224.
4. Ibid., 235.
5. Arcana, *Our Mothers' Daughters*, 36.
6. Rich, *Of Woman Born*, 244.
7. Judith Lewis Herman, M.D. and Helen Block Lewis, Ph.D., "Anger in the Mother-Daughter Relationship" in Bernay and Cantor, *Psychology of Today's Woman*, 140.
8. de Beauvoir, *Second Sex*, 488.
9. Kim Chernin, *The Hungry Self* (New York: Random House, 1985), 43.
10. Ibid., 42.
11. Ibid., 72.
12. Betty Friedan, *The Second Stage* (New York: Summit Books, 1981), 96.
13. Sara Ruddick, *Maternal Thinking: Toward a Politics of Peace* (Boston, Mass: Beacon Press, 1989), 38.
14. Christopher Lasch, *The Culture of Narcissism* (New York: Warner Books, 1979), 360.
15. Friday, *My Mother/My Self*, 446.
16. Victoria Secunda, *When You and Your Mother Can't Be Friends* (New York: Delacorte Press), 177.
17. Friday, *My Mother/My Self*, 459.
18. Judith Arcana, *Every Mother's Son* (Seattle: The Seal Press, 1986), 30.

Chapter Five

1. Dena Kleiman, "Many Young Women Now Say They'd Pick Family Over Career," in *The New York Times*, December 28, 1980, A1.
2. Young, "Selling of Motherhood," in *Newsweek*, October 1, 1990, 12.
3. Quoted in Friedan, *The Feminine Mystique*, 135.
4. Arlene Rossen Cardozo, *Sequencing: Having It All but Not All at Once* (New York: Atheneum, 1986), 43.
5. Quoted in Maxine L. Margolis, *Mothers and Such: Views of American Women and Why They Changed* (Berkeley: University of California Press, 1984), 11.
6. Ibid., 15.
7. Cynthia Eagle Russet, *Sexual Science: The Victorian Construction of Womanhood* (Cambridge, Mass.: Harvard University Press, 1989), 149.
8. Hall, *Youth*, 305.
9. Ellen Key, *The Century of the Child* (New York: G.P. Putnam's Sons, 1909), 84.
10. Wertz and Wertz, *Lying-In*, 188.
11. Carl N. Degler, *At Odds: Women and the Family in America from the Revolution to the Present* (New York: Oxford University Press, 1981), 373.
12. Ibid., 396.
13. Ibid., 422.
14. Ibid., 440.
15. Friedan, *The Feminine Mystique*, 121.
16. Keith Bradsher, "Young Men Pressed to Wed for Success," *The New York Times*, December 13, 1989, C1.
17. Barbara Ehrenreich, "Strategies of Corporate Women," *The New Republic*, January 27, 1986, 28.

Chapter Six

1. George Leonard, "The Physiology of Sex," *Esquire*, May 1989, 144.
2. Kristin Luker, *Taking Chances: Abortion and the Decision Not to Contracept* (Berkeley: University of California Press, 1975), 41.
3. Jacqueline Darroch Forrest, "Unwanted Pregnancy Among American Women," *Family Planning Perspectives*, Vol. 19, No. 2, March/April 1987, 76.
4. Luker, *Taking Chances*, 36.
5. Gail Sheehy, *Passages* (New York: Dutton, 1976), 238.
6. Thomas Laqueur, *Making Sex: Body and Gender from the Greeks to Freud* (Cambridge: Harvard University Press, 1990), 3.
7. Ibid., 3.
8. John D'Emilio and Estelle B. Freedman, *Intimate Matters: A History of Sexuality in America* (New York: Harper & Row, 1988), 70.
9. Mary Jacobus, Evelyn Fox Keller, and Sally Shuttleworth, eds., *Body/Politics: Women and the Discourses of Science* (New York: Routledge, Chapman and Hall, 1990), 63.
10. Gordon, *Woman's Body*, 154.
11. Lundberg and Farnham, *Modern Woman*, 265.
12. Friedan, *Feminine Mystique*, 247.
13. Barbara Ehrenreich, Elizabeth Hess, and Gloria Jacobs, *Re-Making Love: The Feminization of Sex* (Garden City, NY: Anchor Books, 1987), 11.
14. "Not Tonight, Dear," *Newsweek*, October 26, 1987, 64.
15. Quoted in Sheila Jeffreys, *Anticlimax: A Feminist Perspective on the Sexual Revolution* (London: The Women's Press, 1990), 119.
16. Ehrenreich, Hess, and Jacobs, *Re-Making Love*, 154.
17. Germaine Greer, *Sex and Destiny: The Politics of Human Fertility* (New York: Harper & Row, 1984), 257.
18. Ibid., 260.

Chapter Seven

1. Joan Jacobs Brumberg, *Fasting Girls: The History of Anorexia Nervosa* (New York: Plume, 1989), 231.
2. Naomi Wolf, *The Beauty Myth* (New York: William Morrow and Company, Inc., 1991), 10.
3. From interview with Ruth Striegel-Moore.
4. Susan R. Bordo, "The Body and the Reproduction of Femininity: A Feminist Appropriation of Foucault" in *Gender/Body/Knowledge*, edited by Alison M. Jaggar and Susan R. Bordo (New Brunswick, NJ: Rutgers University Press, 1989), 18.
5. Bordo, in *Gender/Body/Knowledge*, 23.
6. Susan Wooley, Ph.D., and O. Wayne Wooley, Ph.D., "Thinness Mania," *American Health*, October 1986, 68.
7. Rosalind Coward, *Female Desires* (New York: Grove Press, 1985), 24.
8. Susan R. Bordo, " 'Material Girl': The Effacements of Postmodern Culture" in *The Female Body* edited by Laurence Goldstein (Ann Arbor, MI: The University of Michigan Press, 1991), 106.
9. Elizabeth Stone, "Battle of the Bulge," *Savvy*, February 1988, 100.
10. Kim Wright Wiley, "Pregnancy 'Training,' " *Vogue*, October 1984, 532.
11. Lois W. Banner, *American Beauty* (New York: Knopf, 1983), 48.
12. Brumberg, *Fasting Girls*, 239.
13. Rita Freedman, *Beauty Bound* (Lexington, Mass.: Lexington Books, 1986), 149.

14. Susan Bordo, "Reading the Slender Body" in *Body/Politics, 90.*
15. Wolf, Beauty Myth, 98.

Chapter Eight

1. Jacques Gelis, *History of Childbirth* (Boston, Mass: Northeastern University Press, 1991), 27.
2. Nancy Caldwell Sorel, *Ever Since Eve: Personal Reflections on Childbirth* (New York: Oxford University Press, 1984), 165.
3. Paula Weideger, *History's Mistress* (Harmondsworth, Middlesex, England: Penguin Books, 1985), 165.
4. Irene Elia, *The Female Animal* (New York: Henry Holt and Co, 1988), 156.
5. Weideger, *History's Mistress,* 164.
6. Greer, *Sex and Destiny,* 61.
7. Rollo May, *Love and Will* (New York: Norton, 1969), 65–69.

Chapter Nine

1. Gina Kolata, "Menopause Is Found No Bar to Pregnancy," *The New York Times,* October 25, 1990, A1.
2. "Gifts for the Ovulating Woman," *New York Woman,* December 1991.
3. Laqueur, *Making Sex,* 49.
4. Firestone, *Dialectic of Sex,* 12.
5. Barbara Katz Rothman, "The Meanings of Choice in Reproductive Technology" in *Test-Tube Woman,* edited by Rita Arditti, Renate Duelli Klein, and Shelley Minden (London: Pandora Press, 1984), 24.
6. Ruth Hubbard, "Personal Courage Is Not Enough: Some Hazards of Childbearing in the 1980s" in *Test-Tube Woman,* 331–335.
7. Rothman in *Test-Tube Woman,* 30.
8. Jon Bowermaster, "The Babymaker," *Manhattan, Inc.,* November 1989, 84.
9. Sue Woodman, "Crazy for a Baby," *New York Woman,* November/December 1986, 140.
10. Arthur L. Greil, *Not Yet Pregnant* (New Brunswick: Rutgers University Press, 1991), 102.
11. Barbara Katz Rothman, *Recreating Motherhood* (New York: W.W. Norton & Company, 1989), 148.
12. Greil, *Not Yet Pregnant,* 35.
13. Quoted in ibid., 44.
14. Rothman, *Recreating Motherhood,* 148.
15. Alan H. DeCherney and Tammy C. Harris, "The Barren Woman Through History," in Alan H. DeCherney, *Reproductive Failure* (New York: Churchill Livingstone, 1986), 5.
16. Laqueur, *Making Sex,* 56.
17. Ibid., 51.
18. Ibid., 101.
19. Ibid., 102.
20. Sorel, *Ever Since Eve,* 44.
21. Laqueur, *Making Sex,* 100.
22. Greil, *Not Yet Pregnant,* 8.
23. Sarah Stage, *Female Complaints: Lydia Pinkham and the Business of Women's Medicine* (New York: Norton, 1979), 127.
24. Greil, *Not Yet Pregnant,* 41.
25. Ibid., 127.

26. Weideger, *History's Mistress,* 167.

27. H. W. Long, M.D., *Sane Sex Life and Sane Sex Living* (Boston: The Gorham Press, 1919), 146.

28. Barbara Katz Rothman, *In Labor: Women and Power in the Birthplace* (New York: W. W. Norton & Company, 1982), 127.

29. Rothman, *Recreating Motherhood,* 149.

30. Phyllis Chesler, *Sacred Bond: The Legacy of Baby M* (New York: Times Books, 1988), 12.

31. Ibid., 34.

32. Paula A. Treichler in Jacobus, et al., *Body/Politics,* 130.

Chapter Ten

1. Wertz and Wertz, *Lying-In,* 249.

2. Gina Kolata, "In Late Abortions, Decisions Are Painful and Options Few," *The New York Times,* January 5, 1992, A1.

3. Wertz and Wertz, *Lying-In,* 126.

4. Barbara Ehrenreich and Deirdre English, *Complaints and Disorders: The Sexual Politics of Sickness* (Old Westbury, NY: The Feminist Press, 1973), 24.

5. Sheryl Burt Ruzek, *The Women's Health Movement: Feminist Alternatives to Medical Control* (New York: Praeger, 1978).

6. Rich, *Of Woman Born,* 159.

7. Lundberg and Farnham, *Modern Woman,* 294.

8. Rich, *Of Woman Born,* 168.

9. Emily Martin, "The Ideology of Reproduction: The Reproduction of Ideology" in *Uncertain Terms,* edited by Faye Ginsburg and Anna Lowenhaupt Tsing (Boston: Beacon Press, 1990), 309.

10. Edward Shorter, *A History of Women's Bodies* (New York: Basic Books, Inc., 1982), 165.

11. Barbara Katz Rothman, quoted in Rosalind Pollack Petchesky, "Fetal Images: The Power of Visual Culture in the Politics of Reproduction," *Feminist Studies* 13, no. 2, (Summer 1987): 77.

12. Ibid., 265.

13. Susan Edmiston, "Here Come the Pregnancy Police," *Glamour,* August 1990, 202.

14. Rayna Rapp, "Constructing Amniocentesis: Maternal and Medical Discourses" in Ginsberg and Tsing, eds., *Uncertain Terms,* 31.

Chapter Eleven

1. In *Life,* April 28, 1972, 70.

2. Letty Cottin Pogrebin, "Fathers Must Earn Their 'Rights,' " *The New York Times,* June 17, 1990,

3. Melissa Goodman, "Men Demystified: 65 Simple Truths," *Glamour,* July 1990, 165.

4. Phyllis Chesler, *With Child: A Diary of Motherhood* (New York: Thomas Y. Crowell, 1979), 204.

5. Quoted from Michael J. Diamond, "Becoming a Father: A Psychoanalystic Perspective on the Forgotten Parent," *Psychoanalytic Review* 73, no. 4 (1976): 44.

6. Quoted in ibid., 44.

7. J. M. Ross, "The Roots of Fatherhood: Excursions into a Lost Literature" in S. H. Cath, M. R. Gurwitt, and J. M. Ross, eds. *Father and Child* (Boston: Little, Brown, 1982), 20.

8. Karen Horney, "The Flight from Womanhood" in *Psychoanalysis and Women,* edited by Jean Baker Miller, M.D. (New York: Penguin, 1973), 11.
9. *The New York Times,* December 20, 1984, VI 12.
10. Peter G. Filene, *Him/Her Self: Sex Roles in Modern America* (New York: Harcourt Brace Jovanovich, 1974), 173.
11. Ehrenreich and English, *For Her Own Good,* 241.
12. May, *Homeward Bound,* 147.
13. Filene, *Him/Her Self,* 172.
14. Anthony Astrachan, *How Men Feel: Their Responses to Women's Demands for Equality and Power* (New York: Anchor Press, 1988), 233.
15. Aimee Lee Ball, "The Daddy Track," *New York,* October 23, 1989, 52.
16. Joy Horowitz, "Poof! The Mommies Vanish in Sitcomland," *The New York Times,* Sunday Arts Section, May 26, 1991, 1.
17. *Time,* December 4, 1989, reports 90 percent of fathers attend births, but that seems high.
18. Barbara Ehrenreich, "A Feminist's View of the New Man," *The New York Times Magazine,* May 20, 1984.
19. Phyllis Chesler, "Mothers on Trial," *Ms.*, May/June 1991, 47.

Chapter Twelve

1. "The Gourmet Children," *People,* November 26, 1984, 43.
2. Petchesky, *Fetal Images,* 277.
3. *Ibid.*, 271.
4. Wertz and Wertz, *Lying-In,* 243.
5. Lauren Belfer, "What Child Is This?" *New York Woman,* August 1990, 96.
6. Stephanie Strom, "Creating the Well-Groomed Child," *The New York Times* Sunday Business Section, July 6, 1991, 1.
7. Annetta Miller, "Bundles of Joy, Bundles of Money," *Newsweek,* September 8, 1986, 44.
8. Holly Brubach, *The New Yorker,* November 5, 1990, 127.
9. Ehrenreich and English, *For Her Own Good,* 200.
10. Susan Strasser, *Never Done: A History of American Housework* (New York: Pantheon, 1982), 232.
11. Christina Hardyment, *Dream Babies: Three Centuries of Good Advice on Child Care* (New York: Harper & Row, 1983), 175.
12. *Newsweek,* March 28, 1983, 64.
13. Tom Engelhardt, "Reading May Be Harmful to Your Kids," *Harper's,* June 1991, 55.
14. Elie Winninghoff, "Grow, Baby, Grow!" *Working Woman,* September 1990, 101.
15. Richard Louv, *Childhood's Future* (Boston: Houghton-Mifflin, 1990), 90.
16. Ibid., 50.

BIBLIOGRAPHY

Ariès, Philippe. *Centuries of Childhood: A Social History of Family Life.* New York: Alfred A. Knopf, 1962.

Berger, Gary S., M.D., Goldstein, Marc, M.D., and Fuerst, Mark. *The Couple's Guide to Fertility.* New York: Doubleday, 1989.

Bernay, Toni and Cantor, Dorothy W., eds. *The Psychology of Today's Woman.* Cambridge, Mass.: Harvard University Press, 1989.

Bergum, Vangie. *Woman to Mother.* Granby, Mass.: Bergin & Garvey, 1989.

Bly, Robert. *Iron John.* Reading, Mass.: Addison-Wesley, 1990.

Brown, Helen Gurley. *Sex and the Single Girl.* New York: Bernard Geis Associates, 1972.

Brumberg, Joan Jacobs. *Fasting Girls: The History of Anorexia Nervosa.* New York: Plume, 1989.

Cahill, Susan, ed. *Motherhood: A Reader for Men and Women.* New York: Avon Books, 1982.

Chapple, Steve and Talbot, David. *Burning Desires: Sex in America—A Report from the Field.* New York: Doubleday, 1989.

Chernin, Kim. *The Hungry Self.* New York: Random House, 1985.

Chesler, Phyllis. *Women and Madness.* New York: Doubleday, 1972.

———. *With Child: A Diary of Motherhood.* New York: Thomas Crowell, 1979.

———. *Sacred Bond: The Legacy of Baby M.* New York: Times Books, 1988.

Chodorow, Nancy. *The Reproduction of Mothering: Psychoanalysis and the Sociology of Gender.* Berkeley: University of California Press, 1978.

Cohen, Nancy W. and Estner, Lois J. *Silent Knife: Cesarean Prevention and Vaginal Birth After Cesarean.* South Hadley, Mass: Bergin & Garvey, 1983.

Columbia University College of Physicians and Surgeons. *Complete Guide to Pregnancy.* New York: Crown, 1988.

Corea, Gena. *The Hidden Malpractice: How American Medicine Mistreats Women.* New York: Harper & Row, 1985.

Davis, Flora. *Moving the Mountain: The Women's Movement Since 1960.* New York: Simon & Schuster, 1991.

Degler, Carl. *At Odds: Women and the Family in America from the Revolution to the Present.* New York: Oxford University Press, 1981.

D'Emilio, John, and Freedman, Estelle, B. *Intimate Matters: A History of Sexuality in America.* New York: Harper & Row, 1988.

Ehrenreich, Barbara. *Fear of Falling: The Inner Life of the Middle Class.* New York: Pantheon Books, 1984.

———. *The Hearts of Men.* Garden City, NY: Anchor Books, 1983.

———. *The Worst Years of Our Lives: Irreverent Notes from a Decade of Greed.* New York: Pantheon, 1990.

———, Hess, Elizabeth, and Jacobs, Gloria. *Re-Making Love: The Feminization of Sex.* Garden City, NY: Anchor Doubleday, 1987.

——— and English, Deirdre. *For Her Own Good: 150 Years of the Experts' Advice to Women.* New York: Anchor Doubleday, 1979.

Eisenstein, Zillah. *The Female Body and the Law.* Berkeley: University of California Press, 1988.

Elkind, David. *The Hurried Child.* Reading, Mass: Addison-Wesley, 1981.

Faludi, Susan. *Backlash: The Undeclared War Against American Women.* New York: Crown, 1991.

Filene, Peter G. *Him/Her Self: Sex Roles in Modern America.* New York: Harcourt Brace Jovanovich, 1974.

Friday, Nancy. *My Mother/My Self.* New York: Dell, 1978.

Friedan, Betty. *The Feminine Mystique.* New York: Dell, 1963.

Gerson, Kathleen. *Hard Choices: How Women Decide About Work, Career, and Motherhood.* Berkeley: University of California Press, 1985.

Gordon, Linda. *Woman's Body, Woman's Right.* New York: Viking Penguin, 1990 edition.

Gornick, Vivian. *Fierce Attachments.* New York: Farrar Straus & Giroux, 1987.

——— and Moran, Barbara K., eds. *Women in Sexist Society: Studies in Power and Powerlessness.* New York: Basic Books, 1971.

Greer, Germaine. *Sex and Destiny: The Politics of Human Fertility.* New York: Harper & Row, 1984.

Hennig, Margaret and Jardim, Anne. *The Managerial Woman.* New York: Pocket Books, 1978.

Laqueur, Thomas. *Making Sex: Body and Gender from the Greeks to Freud.* Cambridge: Harvard University Press, 1990.

Lazarre, Jane. *The Mother Knot.* Boston: Beacon Press, 1976.

Louv, Richard. *Childhood's Future.* Boston: Houghton-Mifflin, 1990.

Luker, Kristen. *Abortion and the Politics of Motherhood.* Berkeley: University of California Press, 1985.

Mailer, Norman. *The Prisoner of Sex.* Boston: Little, Brown, 1971.

Margolis, Maxine. *Mothers and Such: Views of American Women and Why They Changed.* Berkeley: University of California Press, 1984.

Martin, Emily. *The Woman in the Body.* Boston: Beacon Press, 1987.

May, Elaine Tyler. *Homeward Bound: American Families in the Cold War Era.* New York: Basic Books, Inc. 1988.

Melpomene Institute for Women's Health Research. *The Bodywise Woman.* New York: Prentice-Hall Press, 1990.

Notman, Malkah T. and Nadelson, Carol C., eds. *The Woman Patient: Medical and Psychological Interfaces.* New York: Plenum, 1978.

O'Brien, Mary. *The Politics of Reproduction.* Boston: Routledge & Kegan Paul, 1981.

Paige, Karen E. and Paige, Jeffrey M. *The Politics of Reproductive Ritual.* Berkeley: University of California Press, 1981.

Payer, Lynn. *Medicine and Culture.* New York: Pantheon Books, 1988.

Postman, Neil. *The Disappearance of Childhood.* New York: Delacorte Press, 1982.

Rich, Adrienne. *Of Woman Born.* New York: W.W. Norton & Company, 1986 edition.

Rothman, Barbara Katz. *Recreating Motherhood.* New York: W.W. Norton & Company, 1989.

———. *The Tentative Pregnancy: Prenatal Diagnosis and the Future of Motherhood.* New York: Viking, 1986.

Ruddick, Sara. *Maternal Thinking: Toward a Politics of Peace*. Boston: Beacon Press, 1989.

Seid, Roberta Pollack. *Never Too Thin*. New York: Prentice Hall Press, 1989.

Shuttle, Penelope and Redgrove, Peter. *The Wise Wound: Myths, Realities, and Meanings of Menstruation*. New York: Grove Press, 1988.

Showalter, Elaine. *The Female Malady: Women, Madness, and Culture in England*. New York: Pantheon Books, 1985.

Skolnick, Arlene. *Embattled Paradise: The American Family in an Age of Uncertainty*. New York: Basic Books, 1991.

Strasser, Susan. *Never Done: A History of American Housework*. New York: Pantheon Books, 1982.

Thompson, D.S., M.D., consulting ed. *EveryWoman's Health: The Complete Guide to Body and Mind*. Garden City, NY: Doubleday, 1980.

Wajcman, Judy. *Feminism Confronts Technology*. University Park, Penn.: The Pennsylvania State University Press, 1991.

Wallerstein, Judith D. and Blakeslee, Sandra. *Second Chances: Men, Women and Children a Decade After Divorce*. New York: Ticknor and Fields, 1989.

Weideger, Paula. *History's Mistress*. Harmondsworth, England: Penguin, 1985.

Wertz, Richard W. and Wertz, Dorothy C. *Lying-In: A History of Childbirth in America*. New Haven: Yale University Press, 1989.

Weston, Carol. *From Here to Maternity: Confessions of a First-Time Mother*. Boston: Little, Brown, 1991.

Wolf, Naomi. *The Beauty Myth*. New York: William Morrow and Company, Inc., 1991.

Wymelenberg, Suzanne, for the Institute of Medicine. *Science and Babies: Private Decisions, Public Dilemmas*. Washington, DC: National Academy Press, 1990.

Zelizer, Viviana A. *Pricing the Priceless Child: The Changing Social Value of Children*. New York: Basic Books, 1985.

INDEX